Praise for
Girls Write Now On the Other Side of Everything: 2023 Anthology

"For too many centuries, girls' and women's voices have been silenced, ignored, demeaned. But no more! Thanks to organizations like Girls Write Now, the aspirations and accomplishments of girls and women are encouraged, freely expressed, and shared. The world is better for hearing our voices, for celebrating our resilience, confidence, good common sense, and faith in a better future for all."

> —**JACQUELINE ADAMS**, journalist and coauthor of *A Blessing: Women of Color Teaming Up to Lead, Empower and Thrive*

"The Girls Write Now anthology showcases just how much talent and wisdom young people have to offer if we truly listen and give them a platform from which to speak. These are the voices we should all be uplifting."

> —**ANDREA BEATRIZ ARANGO**, author of Newbery Honor–winner *Iveliz Explains It All*

"What beautiful, powerful voices, and how important to raise every one of them. Girls Write Now is doing the crucial work of making that happen. Brava!"

> —**ERICA BAUERMEISTER**, coauthor of *500 Great Books by Women*

"Finding your own true voice takes courage. Believing in yourself takes courage. And writing takes courage, especially for girls from diverse, underserved communities. After reading this anthology and learning about the extraordinary mission of Girls Write Now, I feel inspired by the ways these courageous girls have harnessed their power to transform the world—through writing."

> —**LAUREN BELFER**, author of *Ashton Hall* and *And After the Fire*

"As a mentor alum who came into the organization as a young woman in the year 2000, I'm grateful to say that the work Girls Write Now does to strengthen the voices of the girls in the program spills over to the women, boys, and men who stand with the mentees. The organization's thorough and tireless advocacy for these precious some has a residual benefit for all."

> —**NANA EKUA BREW-HAMMOND**, author of *Blue: A History of the Color as Deep as the Sea and as Wide as the Sky* and *Relations: An Anthology of African and Diaspora Voices*

D1320556

"By encouraging the generous process of mentorship to work its magic on the next generation of storytellers, Girls Write Now does the vital work of bringing women together and enabling girls to give voice to their stories."

    —**ADRIENNE BRODEUR**, author of *Wild Game: My Mother, Her Lover, and Me*

"I was really impressed by the stories and poems in this anthology. Totally beautiful reflections on a world out of balance by the next generation of our great literary minds."

    —**HALLE BUTLER**, author of *The New Me*

"By empowering young women to seize upon the life-changing, planet-quaking powers of writing—that is, entering into dialogue with the world—Girls Write Now provides us all with an early draft of our future."

    —**DELIA CAI**, author of *Central Places*

"Girls Write Now provides an unmatched platform for launching the next generation of women leaders who understand the importance of speaking out about their own experiences and speaking up for what constitutes an inclusive, emotionally intelligent, and polyphonic culture. There is nothing more important to building an equitable world than fostering and cultivating girls' voices."

    —**JENNA FISHER**, managing director at Russell Reynolds Associates and author of *To the Top: How Women in Corporate Leadership Are Rewriting the Rules for Success*

"Girls Write Now does incredible work supporting the growth and development of young women and gender-expansive youth. Its annual anthology is a testament to the power of young people's experiences."

    —**AMY FUSSELMAN**, author of *The Means*

"When a young girl is given the power to express herself through her art, she becomes brave and vulnerable at the same time. These are the foundations of a life lived with truth, passion, and color. Girls Write Now gives young, diverse, and underrepresented girls that gift."

    —**ANNA GOMEZ**, author of From Kona with Love series and *My Goodbye Girl*

"Girls Write Now reminds me daily that there is always light if only we are brave enough to see it, if only we are brave enough to be it."

    —**AMANDA GORMAN**, writer, poet, Girls Write Now honoree, and Estée Lauder Global Changemaker

"Writers hold the honored place of being the 'timekeepers' of our lived experiences. They find the words to express what most of us can only imagine. The Girls Write Now rising scribes—poets, essayists, novelists—can now add their names to the list of storytellers, walk in the footsteps of those who came before them, by using the power of their imaginations and the might of their pens to create and document new worlds to be explored."

—**DONNA HILL**, author of *I Am Ayah: The Way Home*

"All young people deserve a safe space for self-expression, a relationship with a trusted adult who celebrates their unique talents, and the freedom to imagine creative futures for themselves. Girls Write Now is indispensable."

—**CHANTAL V. JOHNSON**, author of *Post-Traumatic*

"Finding their voice can be a lifelong journey for many women, negatively impacting not only their confidence, but their contribution in making the world a better and more equitable place. This is why the mission of Girls Write Now is more important than ever, and a beautiful gift toward individual and collective flourishing."

—**HOMAIRA KABIR**, author of *Goodbye, Perfect*

"To improve our world, we need to empower the next generation. Get ready to see the future. The writers of Girls Write Now emerged from the pandemic with voices bold and unapologetic. Read this now and share it with someone you love."

—**LINDA KLEINBUB**, editor of Pink Trees Press, author of *Cover Charge*

"In a world that often encourages girls to listen rather than speak, Girls Write Now reminds us our power lies in boldly using our words and voices—as forces for change, to uplift one another, and to thoughtfully write and share the stories that matter most."

—**CRYSTAL MALDONADO**, *No Filter and Other Lies*

"I write fiction about resilient kids who learn the power of using their voices. So to witness this diverse group of young writers empowering themselves through their own words in Girls Write Now is both thrilling and inspiring."

—**JANAE MARKS**, *New York Times* bestselling author of *From the Desk of Zoe Washington* and *On Air with Zoe Washington*

"Young women writers are so often silenced, perhaps because those who silenced them knew the immense power their words hold. Girls Write Now is nothing short of a gift that allows these remarkable voices to be given the platform they rightly deserve. The world is so much better when we listen to what young women have to say."

> —**LANE MOORE**, author of *You Will Find Your People: How to Make Meaningful Friendships as an Adult*

"Writing is a path to freedom, and Girls Write Now points girls toward this path, empowering them to create bold, imaginative, original work. This collection is a powerful chorus of their voices."

> —**DEESHA PHILYAW**, author of *The Secret Lives of Church Ladies*, winner of the 2021 PEN/Faulkner Award for Fiction

"An anthology filled with passion and promise, and a blazing reminder of the importance of giving young writers a platform to let their voices be heard. Girls Write Now passes the mic to the next generation of writers and the beautiful stories they have to tell."

> —**ELLE GONZALEZ ROSE**, author of *Caught in a Bad Fauxmance*

"The writing in these pages burns bright with clarity and promise, and reminds us why we must nurture the vital voices of young writers. In fostering the creativity of young women and gender-nonconforming youth, Girls Write Now is doing the necessary work of making space for the stories that will save us."

> —**MARISA SIEGEL**, author of *Fixed Stars* and Girls Write Now mentor

"And girls will lead the way. Let us follow as they raise their voices in truth, sorrow, and joy, and create a just world just by imagining it."

> —**THELMA VIRATA DE CASTRO**, author of *The Fire in Me*

"Amplifying voices in literary expression even as they emerge and fledge, Girls Write Now is a gift of creative and collaborative female empowerment."

> —**MAMLE WOLO**, author of *The Kaya Girl*

"Girls Write Now is the heart, guts, and breath of the world that is coming. Thank oceans that emerging writers navigating the creative waves have this community to help each other swim. Brilliantly, and without fear."

> —**LIDIA YUKNAVITCH**, author of *Thrust* and *The Chronology of Water*

"A beautiful showcase, as always, of the talent and authenticity bursting from Girls Write Now. The clarity in these wonderful voices makes this anthology an inspiration and an honor to read."

> —**AMY ZHANG**, author of *The Cartographers*

GIRLS WRITE NOW

ON THE OTHER SIDE OF EVERYTHING:

2023 ANTHOLOGY

GIRLS WRITE NOW

ON THE OTHER SIDE OF EVERYTHING

2023 ANTHOLOGY

FOREWORD BY **CHRISSY KING**

Published 2023

Printed in the United States

Print ISBN: 978-0-9962772-7-3

E-ISBN: 9781558613324

Library of Congress Control Number: 2023902896
Copyright 2023 by Girls Write Now, Inc.

Cover design by: Dominique Jones

For information, write to:
Girls Write Now, 247 West 37 Street, Suite 1000
New York, NY 10018

info@girlswritenow.org
girlswritenow.org

GIRLS WRITE NOW

ON THE
OTHER SIDE
OF
EVERYTHING

2023 ANTHOLOGY

GIRLS WRITE NOW

ON THE
OTHER SIDE
OF
EVERYTHING

2023 ANTHOLOGY

Do you remember the tide pool where you found your first sea star, squeezed under a rock only you thought to pick up?

Or maybe you were the kid in a park playground who examined the profane and lovestruck graffiti scrawled on the slide, before it was painted over by the city.

Perhaps you were the one who found the old photos of your grandmother looking movie-star glamorous, tucked between her recipe books and medicine bottles, giving you a glimpse into an unknown past.

I ask only because I know from these, my own memories, that at some point in our lives, each of us came to know that the world was more than just its surface. That the sky was only gray below the cloud line, and the view outside our airplane window revealed a radiant blue. That our strict parents broke their curfews every night when they were our age. That the bursts of protests springing up across the country were not random sprouts, but the carefully sewn actions of young leaders growing in the shade of their elders.

In the past few years, it feels like the world has been turned upside down. Yet it is in the aftermath of a storm that new discoveries come to light: the structure of upended tree roots, the power lines that failed, who the politicians rush to blame, who gets left out in the cold, the generosity of neighbors with blankets to share, the stories that come out of it. The writing in this anthology speaks to and from the other side of things, inviting us to question what we know about our world and where we think we're going next. In the poems, short stories, scripts, essays, and musings of the young writers at Girls Write Now, we can experience the wonder (and discomfort) that comes from seeing things through the eyes of a new generation, one that dives headlong into the unknown and surfaces with treasure.

VAHNI KURRA is a multigenre writer from Brooklyn, New York, who has been published in *Peach Mag* and *Oyster River Pages*. She works as a community coordinator at Girls Write Now and served as a Co-Chair of Girls Write Now's 2023 Anthology Editorial Committee.

Anthology Editorial Committee

EDITOR

Molly MacDermot

COMMITTEE CO-CHAIRS

Rosie Black
Nana Ekua Brew-Hammond
Meg Cassidy
Mariah Dwyer
Amy Fusselman
Jenissa Graham
Becca James

Vahni Kurra
Soyolmaa Lkhagvadorj
Nadine Matthews
Carol Paik
Marisa Siegel
Kiki T.
Sophia Torres

COMMITTEE EDITORS

Michelle Baker
Nan Bauer-Maglin
Susanne Beck
Anne Caceres-Gonzalez
Shannon Carlin
Mary Darby
Morgan Leigh Davies
Katie Della Mora
Amy Flyntz
Gabriela Galvin

Catherine Greenman
Leigh Haber
Donna Hill
Lauren Kiel
Linda Kleinbub
Katie McGuire
Nikki Palumbo
Debra Register
Elle Gonzalez Rose
Patricia Rossi

Madeline Stone
Maryellen Tighe

Rebecca Lowry Warchut
Liza Wyles

PROMOTIONS CHAIR

Livia Nelson

EDITORIAL STAFF

Azia Armstead, Fellow
Sally Familia, Fellow
Vahni Kurra, Community Coordinator
Elmer Meza, Salesforce & Systems Manager
Maya Nussbaum, Founder & Executive Director

Lisbett Rodriguez, Senior Community Coordinator
Jeanine Marie Russaw, Community Coordinator
Erica Silberman, Director of Curriculum and Engagement
Annabel Young, Fellow

Contents

> **NOTE:** Stories that depict sensitive topics are necessary for many reasons. Facing the most difficult parts of the human experience can both help others feel less alone and inspire readers to work toward a better future. However, we recognize that certain topics may be distressing when they catch readers off guard. That is why we have included a Content Warning for some of the stories.

Foreword

Chrissy King

As a child, I spent all of my free time writing stories and going to the library to read books. I grew up in Wisconsin, born to high school–educated parents who did the best they could to give me and my three siblings a better future. My mom even homeschooled us until we reached the third grade. I dreamed about being a writer, but I didn't really have the examples or the mentorship to see that as a viable option for myself. As a first-generation college student, I was just focused on getting a degree and earning a living. I wanted stability, and I didn't think I could do that with writing. So it took me a long time to come back to my love of writing, but I'm so grateful that I found my way. That's why I think the work of Girls Write Now is so important. It's exactly what I needed when I was a teenager, and the mission of Girls Write Now is absolutely fostering the next generation of storytellers.

Our words matter, and our words and stories have the capacity to create change in a world that desperately needs change. Sometimes being a changemaker means facing discomfort. However, despite the discomfort, I am empowered to speak and write my truth, always remembering the words of Audre Lorde:

> I write for those who do not have a voice because they were so terrified, because we are taught to respect fear more than ourselves. We've been taught that silence will save us, but it won't.

Silence won't save us. Remaining complicit won't save us. While we may not be able to single-handedly create the change we wish to see in the world, our words will undoubtedly have an impact.

Much of the work I do focuses on liberation, such as my book *The Body Liberation Project*, and on the idea of setting ourselves free to be whomever we want to be in the world. When we set ourselves free from the confines of societal conditioning, we open the floodgates for others to do the same. Imagine the change we could create in the world if we started breaking more molds and living more liberated lives.

When I had the honor to be recognized as a Girls Write Now 2022 Agent of Change, one of my favorite parts of the evening was hearing the young writers perform. I witnessed individuals who are breaking the molds. There is so much going on in this world and so much reason for concern, but the Girls Write Now mentees give me hope for the leadership of our future. They are using their words and stories and with so much more poise and confidence than I had at their age.

My hope for everyone reading this is that you always remember that one of your greatest gifts to the world is being your true self unapologetically. We all have a specific magic to share in this lifetime. Someone is waiting to see you shine. Someone is waiting to be inspired by you. Someone is waiting for your story.

CHRISSY KING is a writer, speaker, former strength coach, and educator. Chrissy is a Girls Write Now honoree and the author of *The Body Liberation Project: How Understanding Racism and Diet Culture Helps Cultivate Joy and Build Collective Freedom.*

GIRLS WRITE NOW

ON THE
OTHER SIDE
OF
EVERYTHING

2023 ANTHOLOGY

MARSHAL ACQUAROLI

LIVES: Coral Springs, Florida

Marshal (they/them) is a queer nineteen-year-old writer living in Florida, striving to become an educator.

MENTEE'S ANECDOTE:

I have loved writing since I could pick up a pencil; I'd spend days and days throughout my life making stories and poems in my notebook. During my first year of high school, I joined the post-class creative writing club and was enamored with it. I went to every single meeting, and at the beginning of my senior year, I became president of the club and found my passion in guiding my peers through their own writing journeys.

SARAH MOORS

LIVES: Providence, Rhode Island

Sarah (she/her) is a journalist for Digital Health Insights, originally from Florida, who is working on her first novel.

MENTOR'S ANECDOTE:

Every session with Marshal is a meditation on bravery and expansion. Their poetry is limitless and it's inspiring to see work with such self-exploration and expression. Reading Marshal's work is like unlocking a cage you didn't know you were in—it's a reminder that there are no bounds to our creativity. Thanks to Marshal, I feel free to release my inner critic and be unafraid to step into new depths.

in sickness and in health

MARSHAL ACQUAROLI

A body in the woods finds meaning within the insects that find it.

when the news reports my disappearance my body will lie still in the
 earth beneath me, and i will be complete
when the search-and-rescue team finds me they will carry me out
 from the mud, place me on a stretcher, and take me to the nearest
 morgue
when the undertakers tear their scalpels through the flesh of my chest
 and find a hornet's nest embedded between my lungs
i will be nothing short of a spectacle

there is a thrumming beneath my skin
an infestation consuming me vein to vein
and i am in love
a hive pulsing within my heart
humming
echoing through my ears and mouth as i lie in the soil gazing at the sky
 above me
i am in love and they love me
and they need me
i am their sanctuary
warm flesh as food and shelter
tear me apart for i am yours

if the pain was a problem i'd tear them out myself
free myself from every sting, every bite, every burn
but pain is a part of love
and to love is to rot
i love you and you devour me

make me into something new
make me whole by taking away every last part of me
like i was born for this
like i died for this
so i can be complete

SANYA AFSAR

LIVES: Woodside, New York

Sanya Afsar writes poetry, prose, and memoir, exploring her words cathartically and dreaming for others to take refuge in them as well.

MENTEE'S ANECDOTE:

I cannot thank Girls Write Now enough for pairing me with Melanie. Every meeting we have is filled with laughter and excitement, and we've connected on so many different levels. I find myself looking forward to our weekly meetings no matter how exhausting it's been, and talking to her is a breath of fresh air amid a crazy week. We read and write together, and she's been a huge help in the insane college application process. We never run out of things to talk about. It's been a fantastic blessing to work with her, and I'm eternally grateful.

MELANIE HORTON

LIVES: Santa Clarita, California

Melanie Horton writes emotional poetry that dances between the abstract and the sensual and grapples with trauma, desire, and loss.

MENTOR'S ANECDOTE:

Working with Sanya this year has been such a pleasure! Each week I look forward to reading her amazing written work, sharing our mutual love for poetry and poetic prose, and getting to witness all of her amazing accomplishments, like completing her college application process! Easily the highlight of my week. I feel so lucky to have gotten paired with someone as wonderful as Sanya! She has such a distinct voice to her writing. I couldn't be more of a fan of the way she utilizes lowercase, repetition, and inventive wordplay to invert a reader's expectations in her work.

medallic weight

SANYA AFSAR

> a poem that reveals the hidden realities and an-
> guished cries of eye bags.

my eye bags
are trophies
i carry everywhere
a display to the world
look how hard i work
look how strong i've been
look how much better i am

but really
they weigh me down
pulling me underground
until only my arms can be seen
flailing for help
from the dirt of nature
and humankind

they are my poems
my troubles
my cares
my worries
their darkness and their depth
bearing the weight of the words
i just can't say aloud

these medals that hang from my eyes
are awards nonetheless
they don't grant me

the acceptance i desperately chase
but they grant me
a voice my throat can't produce

they scream for me
that look
this girl is doing something
is doing enough
is doing too much

my eye bags are my vocal chords
and it seems as though
the darker my burdens etch them
the louder i get to be

GRETA AHLEFELD

LIVES: Liberty, Maine

Greta Ahlefeld is a high school senior who hopes to go to college next year to study environmental science or biology, hopefully focusing on conservation.

MENTEE'S ANECDOTE:
Working with Lennox for the past few months has definitely been a fun, enjoyable, and learning-filled experience. We have worked together on my college essays, something that I have found super-helpful to have input on, and I have enjoyed getting feedback about how to improve my writing skills. This piece of writing was a big jump for me in terms of learning to write creatively, but with Lennox's input and suggestions I have learned to think more out of the box while writing and expand my skills. As a result, I have really enjoyed and appreciated this mentorship!

LENNOX McGRAIN

LIVES: New York, New York

Lennox McGrain is a social media marketer at Disney Streaming in New York. In her spare time, she loves traveling, writing, and cooking.

MENTOR'S ANECDOTE:
Working with Greta has been absolutely inspiring. Her writing demonstrates her vast range of creative abilities, incorporating vivid imagery from her personal experiences as well as refined research on topics that she is most passionate about. I am so impressed by her drive to learn and explore new themes and styles within her writing, and I can't wait to see her continue to use her talents!

Sea Glass

GRETA AHLEFELD

In this piece, I tried to incorporate memories from my childhood with some of today's environmental issues by comparing two alternate storylines—one of my memories growing up, and another displaying climate crises—over time.

I am nine years old, skipping along a pebbly beach, the ocean's waves gently lapping against my feet. There is a breeze, cool enough to wipe away the heat of the summer day, and the beach seems almost alive, with birds diving in and out of the water, crabs scuttling from rock to rock, and seaweed being carried in and out with each wave. I hop around the waves, making a game of seeing if they can catch me as I weave between them. As I make my way along the shore, I notice something that seems foreign among the grays of the rocks and green-brown of the seaweed. Bending down to pick up the glint of material, I see that it is a small piece of glass that has been worn by the ocean until its edges have dulled. I hold it up to the sun, observing how it seems to glow when lit up from behind, then run off to go show it to my nearest family member before moving on to explore a tidepool.

   2014: This January saw a major heat wave in Alaska, hosting record-breaking temperatures that reached up to 62°F (16.7°C). This has caused statewide cancellations of sled dog races due to lack of ice and melted snow; some have stated that it would be better to run marathons instead. Heat-waves and wildfires have also been prevalent throughout Australia, with players at the Australian Open being impacted by 109°F (43°C) temperatures in Melbourne. In the North American winter, temperatures dove significantly below average during what was dubbed the "Polar Vortex," and

California's drought continues to worsen. All of these add up to yet another year of climate crisis, which scientists say we can't afford many more of before irreparable damage is caused.

Now seventeen, I find myself walking along the same beach, marveling at how my life has changed since I stood here eight years ago. I look at the beach's pebbles in the hopes of finding a new piece of sea glass, and a new color quickly catches my eye. Mirroring my actions from years before, I stoop over and unearth the fragment. Instead of glass, though, I notice that this is part of an old plastic container. Looking closer, I realize that this is not the only plastic I see on the beach, and in what used to be a pristine environment I cannot stop noticing pieces of washed-up garbage. Haunted by the thought of all my favorite places in nature being swamped with waste, I collect all the plastic that my hands can hold and throw it into the nearest trash bin before returning home.

2022: With wildfires and drought raging throughout the western U.S. and climate catastrophes touching every region of the world, the past few years have been among the worst recorded for climate change. Hurricane Ida, the Texas freeze, and heat waves across North America and Australia have been only a few of these costly, and often deadly, problems. The latest report from the Intergovernmental Panel on Climate Change (IPCC) demonstrates that climate change's effects will continue worsening without drastic changes in emissions. It is already clear that climate change–related problems will increase in the short term, but unless immediate action is taken, it will continue escalating, disproportionately impacting the areas of the world that have fewer resources to deal with it.

Filled with a desire to rid the world of its plastic-covered beaches and resolve the problems caused by climate change, I decide to search for ways to make a difference. But after spending hours combing Google for articles about "Ways to Reduce Your Carbon Footprint" and "How to Produce Less Waste," looking at organizations to support, and finding activists to follow, I realize that my efforts seem futile compared to what is needed to achieve my goal. After all, I am just one person, and what can I do to stop a global crisis?

Today: A large study, covering ten countries around the world, has found strong evidence to suggest that climate change and its impacts often cause negative mental and emotional impacts on young people worldwide. Termed "eco-anxiety," this phenomenon has been shown to reduce the quality of life of teens worldwide, with those in countries that have been hardest hit by climate catastrophes reporting the most anxiety, anger, and fear over the issue. Combined with a general feeling of powerlessness, climate change is causing a new source for worldwide mental health issues.

Over time, I learn I am not the only one who feels such a tangled web of emotions about this issue. I realize that, though substantial change needs to be made, if I work with others we can slowly start to solve an issue that has been around since before we were born. By moving quickly and demanding changes from our leaders, we can try to mitigate climate change's effects. But unless immediate action is taken to solve these issues, the consequences of human impact are approaching quickly and will undoubtedly cause problems for us all.

ZAYNAB AHMED

LIVES: Blaine, Minnesota

Zaynab Ahmed is a biology student at the University of Minnesota pursuing public health and enjoys creative writing, especially poetry.

MENTEE'S ANECDOTE:

Mary has been so supportive of me exploring my creativity, enhancing my writing skills, and, most important, stepping outside my comfort zone. I have been able to accomplish so many of the goals we have set, as our one-on-one sessions provide me with resources, practice, and confidence. Mary is so passionate about mentorship and has encouraged me to strive for my goals. This has made my experience as her mentee so impactful.

MARY APESOS

LIVES: Brooklyn, New York

Mary Apesos is a digital marketer for food & travel brands in Brooklyn, New York. She has a B.A. in journalism and is originally from Boston.

MENTOR'S ANECDOTE:

Even though Zaynab and I come from different professional and academic worlds, we come together at Girls Write Now through creative writing and poetry. During our one-on-one sessions we start with a creative prompt that always results in something profoundly different than we ever imagined. Zaynab inspires me not only with the feeling and meaning she puts into her creative work, but with her advocacy work and passion to change the future.

Amazing Disgrace

ZAYNAB AHMED

This poem is a piece I wrote about the struggles of connecting with family overseas.

Today you called again.

Saturday morning as usual.

I didn't pick up like I should have.

Because I should have
spoken with you about every minuscule detail of my week so you can
    feel like you have me
close again for a moment.

So you can know me just like you should.
Because family should never be separated like this,
between papers and passports and evil ruling perpetrators,
between salted oceans and red seas,
between time zones and phone bills and censorship.

Shhhhhhhh
Pleaseee don't say that when you call.
Don't you know they listen through our phones?

So I keep quiet.
It's solely my being, our *being*, that bothers them.
Our Black African descent that labors their whole land so they can
    never send my uncle his paychecks.
So they can work my aunts till they are skin and bones.
My grandpa never saw retirement at 78

and when he . . .
you didn't deserve to shed a tear.

How do I tell you?

It's so hard to call sometimes,

to pick up sometimes.

Because now my nana straddles in that chair alone
and I'm never home.
Out at ungodly hours.
Doing things I shouldn't be.
In places where I shouldn't be.

I'm so sorry.

I didn't call for so long.

Just to talk more with a man, a boy who will never walk me down
    an aisle.

I didn't call for so long.

Because Saturdays are the worst.

I would just lie in my filth and guilt and heartbreak.

Little did I know that was nothing for a heartbreak.

Nothing like yours would if I ever told you.

What I do when I don't call.

ASMA AL-MASYABI

LIVES: Aurora, Colorado

Asma Al-Masyabi is a creative writing major, poet, and artist always plotting her next excursion to the bookstore.

MENTEE'S ANECDOTE:
When every other Tuesday evening rolls around, I sit ready at my laptop for a dose of inspiration and a promising writing prompt. From black-out poetry to interviews, Katie has not only helped me grow my writing skills, but also jump into new or intimidating projects without hesitation.

KATIE REILLY

LIVES: Brooklyn, New York

Katie Reilly is a reporter who has covered national news and education issues for *Time* magazine and Reuters.

MENTOR'S ANECDOTE:
With every pair meeting, I love the enthusiasm and creativity that Asma brings to every writing prompt we explore. Whether she's writing a sci-fi poem about the lone person left on a distant planet or crafting a clever hundred-word story about the search for a coffee mug, I always enjoy reading her words and exploring new writing styles together.

Punctures of Light in the Darkness

ASMA AL-MASYABI

A traveler finds herself stranded on a distant planet, alone.

heaven falls on the far side
of this field, lit by flames
too far and hot to touch. my footsteps
fall heavy, breaking
new grass, blue-tipped, earth bent, scurries
of little creatures screaming the names
of their home. this planet was not meant
for me. tilted axis swinging too quickly, moons
bent toward destruction, sun too red
to last. I am meant to float in darkness, to punctuate
the mystery with numbers of fleeing embers, pit stops
at dwindling galaxies, bareboned and
so often empty.
by the register, a note, sometimes,
stardust-coated words explaining
evacuation. radiation. the way the space
between Everything only grows, just as it
shrinks.
the last face I saw tucked
into the pocket of my suit, Your broken
smile slowly fading from the glow
of the universe. I tell myself this
too, that it will not be so bad to die
alone, a strange air sucking
itself into my lungs. when I reach

the end, I am not yet convinced,
landscape barren, emptiness stretching
into yellow tinted clouds, double orbs
mirroring a dying
light. I force my lungs
shallow,
oxygen tank blinking red, ticking
quietly. I touch broken earth
to my cheek, cover my eyes with limp
wrists, attempting a final rest.

they open
to silence, blurring sky falling   slowly
into punctures of light
in the darkness. my lungs heave
to call out their names, forgetting Yours.
instead, sparks swim
into mist,
kaleidoscope
as I sigh into sleep.

AYAH AL-MASYABI

LIVES: Aurora, Colorado

Ayah Al-Masyabi is a high school writer and artist who stresses over U.S. soccer, Liverpool FC, and Rapids matches; plays Minecraft; and listens to many podcasts.

MENTEE'S ANECDOTE:

When I first met Anne, I knew we were a perfect match. Being able to consult a more experienced writer and creative for help on any of my creative endeavors has helped me grow both personally and creatively. We love to talk about things we have read, our lives, and, more important, soccer. During the World Cup, Anne and I would often delay our meetings to watch the matches and then talk about them after. Using Anne's advice and prompts has helped me feel comfortable pushing the walls of what I used to think writing was supposed to be.

ANNE HELLMAN

LIVES: Brooklyn, New York

Anne Hellman is a Brooklyn-based writer and the founder of the Grandmother Project. Other than writing fiction, Anne published *Design Brooklyn* with Abrams in 2013.

MENTOR'S ANECDOTE:

I knew by the end of my first session with Ayah, when we seamlessly started talking about our mutual obsession with geography, that we were meant to work together. Ayah's intelligence is a gift that has inspired me in my own writing, and her inquisitive energy and original voice will take her to great heights in both fiction and nonfiction. After a World Cup game this past fall that was a little too close, Ayah and I met and first exalted in the excitement of the match, then we got down to work. I am truly a lucky mentor.

Shopping List

AYAH AL-MASYABI

The musty glass doors slid open and half-heartedly welcomed me into my local King Soopers...

The musty glass doors slid open and half-heartedly welcomed me into my local King Soopers. Hundreds of beeps and small conversations invaded my ears, making a brassy and lonely song. Perfect lines of cash registers, gloomy adults, crying children, and a few jolly families crowded the store. The place felt on the brink of explosion. The all-too-familiar mix of numerous smells canceling themselves out made its way into my nostrils. It was such a familiar smell that it almost felt like I was visiting an old friend's house. I realized I hadn't been there in a long time.

I didn't bother to get a cart, because I hated pushing them, so I grabbed a basket to hold instead. I felt like I was a ghost in a dream. I adjusted my black mask over my nose and pulled Mom's list out of my pocket. Her faultless handwriting covered the busy page, with the important writing in a thick red pen in the middle. Mom wrote down all her thoughts, often running out of paper to write on. When no pages were left, she tended to write over the used paper with different colored pens until new notebooks arrived from Amazon.

I strolled toward the bakery section, with the first item being bread. The smell of the baked goods led me to them; I barely needed to focus on any directions. Just as I reached the breads, I accidentally bumped into a gray-haired lady. She aggressively turned around, flinging her hands up. It seemed like she wanted to scold me, but since she had no visible face, she couldn't.

An older man, who saw the incident, tapped on my shoulder and proclaimed, "So you see that, too? She is so weird."

I was shocked and emphatically blurted, "She still has ears!"

The next item on the list was cheese, located far from the baked goods. I arrived in the meat section, where a deceased-fish aroma covered the area. The cheese was no more than fifty feet away. I suddenly stopped when my eye caught one of the clerks. He was stocking frozen fish and was tall, with a strikingly handsome face, but when I looked closer, there were small holes running down his neck to his chest that he brazenly showed off. My jaw fell to the ground and my eyes were glued to him. I was confused and doubted the image my eyes were giving me. Then I noticed the holes quivering every time he breathed. He must have gills, meaning he was some sort of fish-and-human hybrid. Shivers shot down my back and through my limbs. I didn't want to be mean, but, hell, he was terrifying! He must have felt my eyes on him, because he started to glare at me.

My heart rate accelerated, causing me to snatch my jaw off the floor and sprint to the cheese. My sneakers squeaked on the recently mopped floor as I hastily grabbed cheddar. I bumped into many people as I ran, but didn't bother to say sorry. I didn't care, I needed to get away from him before he could get to me and . . . and do what? I wasn't sure, but my mind demanded I run. After what felt like hours, all my energy was spent. My legs painfully stopped, and I kneeled over, gasping for air. His face was burned into my vision. Attempting to slow my breath, I started to repeatedly count from one to four.

In.

1

2

Out.

3

4

In.

1

2

Out.

3

4

My eyes opened. Not wanting to draw much attention, I lifted my basket and turned around. A beautiful stack of eggs in an open refrigerator beamed at me. My small smile grew as I remembered eggs were the next item on the list. I carefully removed a dozen eggs and deliberately placed them next to the loaves of bread.

As I walked to the cash registers, putting each foot in front of the other, I passed aisles where I spent my childhood. The toy aisle was much less pink than before, now having a brown theme. I remember trying to find the coolest toy car while Mom was in the next aisle looking at stationery. Instincts compelled me to walk into the snack aisle, where Mom would let me choose a small treat if I behaved well. A small chocolate bar was my favorite thing to get, but after a few years, they stopped selling them.

The cashier startled me when she abruptly shouted, "NEXT!"

I walked up and muttered, "Sorry, I'm here." When the time came to pay, I tried to swipe the card, but the cashier irritatedly explained that they don't swipe cards anymore, they now just tap them.

She bagged the items, passed them to me, then screamed, "NEXT!"

I headed to the exit. Once I made it outside, a small smile appeared on my face as I pulled down my mask and breathed in the fresh air.

JULIA ANDRESAKIS

LIVES: Brooklyn, New York

Julia is a writer, long-distance walker, and mockumentary enthusiast from Brooklyn, New York.

MENTEE'S ANECDOTE:

You can tell how remarkable Sarah is as a mentor by the number of times I've written and rewritten this paragraph. I can tell you that she's been a beacon of support through my professional and creative goals, but even that seems to undermine the sheer positive impact she has had on me. Her thoughtful edits on my writing, candid advice, and organization skills are only a few ways in which she's helped me as a young creative. Beyond that, she is also hilarious, kind, and a supremely talented writer. I am immeasurably grateful for her guidance.

SARAH ELIZABETH "ESSIE" BODE

LIVES: Wilmington, North Carolina

Sarah E. Bode works for Penguin Random House. You can find her work in various literary journals—*Palaver, Under the Gum Tree*, and *The Carolina Quarterly*.

MENTOR'S ANECDOTE:

Working with Julia has been such a delightful experience this year. Her vision and drive are truly an inspiration. I appreciate how clear she is with her goals and how focused she is in her work on those goals. I am in constant awe of her talent as a writer—each piece I read of hers is stronger and more unique than the last. She really shines with her character work as well as her thoughtful approach to the social commentary she layers in.

Thanksgiving

JULIA ANDRESAKIS

Content Warning: Death, Alcoholism

How does holiday tradition shapeshift with tragedy?

It always gave me a low-grade headache waking up those autumn mornings to clatter in the kitchen, voices of terse disagreement that tried and failed to whisper. Sometimes the smooth jazz station played on the TV before the parade, followed by the dog show, hours of unstimulating programming that were, so I was told, for the sake of tradition.

We held dinner at our house. Not because it was the biggest, the most convenient, or the nicest even, but because Mom never made an enemy out of anyone, so she was the even-tempered host. The crooked woodcut framed above our kitchen sink said, *Bless This House and All Who Enter It.* I remember hearing the hum of Aunt Joanie's SUV roll into the driveway and poking my head through the curtains, seeing Cleo and Benji bounding up the steps before their mother cut the engine. They were thirteen and fourteen to my six, and made a contest of knocking the hardest at the door. I tried to answer, but I couldn't work the lock. Inside, they laughed about people at their school two states away and internet videos I hadn't seen. I sat silently on the big chair while they stretched out on the couch and drank the soda I wasn't allowed to have before dinner.

As we grew older I tried harder to connect, but the two of them still had a shorthand I struggled to pick up, the tragedy of my development lagging too far behind theirs. Still, they were enthralling: I loved the easy way they cursed when the adults were out of earshot, the underground music they insisted I listen to, their stick-and-poke tattoos and piercings I could only imagine my mother crying about if I followed suit. Late into their teenage years, they became the family entertainers, cohosting the yearly game night, coordinating the anonymous gift exchange, charming us as amateur musicians. I adored them and knew I'd never catch up.

Then Benji got sick and it was sad; so sad I haven't found a way to deal with it quite yet. I see him hobbling up the steps with his cane that last holiday, Cleo a support beam latching to his arm. How he tried to speak but the words came out garbled and he often shook his head in frustration followed by sadness at our pity. "You're fine," said Aunt Joanie, smoothing the fabric of his button-up on his shoulder. "Take your time. We're listening."

With Benji gone we lost Cleo also. She moved coasts and conjured vague reasons for not attending family gatherings. Too much work. The cat has to go to the vet. My car doesn't have enough gas. For her there was no life without Benji, so she went out and created a new one that had nothing to do with any of us. Not that I could blame her—holidays were thenceforth somber affairs, tangibly filled more with absence than presence. I, too, avoided them when I could, spending the Thanksgivings of my collegiate years with the international students who stayed put.

The year Mom died, the remainder of us, including a rare Cleo, gathered at Aunt Joanie's third-floor walk-up, and she set two chairs out for the deceased: a picture of Mom on her wedding day on one, Benji's yearbook portrait on the other. While we waited for the food I reached for the television remote to offset the miserable silence. Aunt Joanie shook her head. "That good-for-nothing numbnuts landlord," she muttered. "Been broken for a month. The oven, three." Hours later, she brought out the turkey, its innards still partially frozen. She read fast and low from a small prayer book, pausing only a couple of times to wipe a tear and regain her composure. Afterward we said Amen and ate what we could. Cleo grabbed her coat before dessert.

Families bloomed from the friends I once had, until everyone I knew was traveling elsewhere, to in-laws, friends of friends, or their parents for Thanksgiving. I offered to host a couple of times, but it was too much for the elders to travel to the far south of the city, plus I hardly had room for myself there. Aunt Joanie grew too sick with grief to carry on the holiday. The handful of aunts and uncles I had left at that time were too broken in other ways to push for celebration. One was always in the middle of a messy divorce. Another booked a Darwinian cruise to the Galápagos Islands one year and never returned. And another drank himself to death and they found him in an alley next to a Waffle House. So on until it was just me.

I don't know what to make of this imperfect life. Most often, the easiest thing for me to do this time of year is watch the parade, even if I don't recognize the cartoon characters on the balloons anymore and the performing acts look so bright and young and unbruised.

It's a simple action, but it's one within my reach.

CHENYI ANDREW

LIVES: New York, New York

Chenyi Andrew is a current high school student in New York City who is passionate in exploring aspects of art, culture, writing, and science.

MENTEE'S ANECDOTE:

I lacked confidence in my writing, or perhaps in my language skills in general. Seven years ago, I was only able to say just one word, "hello," in English when I first came to America. I struggled to transform my vast fictional world into reality in the form of writing, but with the help of my mentor I didn't choose to give up. I received so many incredible suggestions that guided my way to the end. After this priceless experience, I am proud to announce I am now able to write with confidence.

VICTORIA MALLORGA HERNANDEZ

LIVES: Brooklyn, New York

Victoria Mallorga Hernandez is a queer Peruvian Taurus, poet, and literary associate. She is the author of *albión* (alastor editores) and *absolución* and loves cheesecake.

MENTOR'S ANECDOTE:

My favorite things about sessions with Chenyi have been her resilience and her constant willingness to try new things. She is so open to exploring different perspectives and ideas, and it was beautiful to see her grow into her own style, embracing her own particularities. As we both write mostly in our native languages, to embrace translation and rewriting as a natural part of expression was such a shared joy. Revising and editing together Ilos's story across language, preserving patterns, culture, and more, remains one of the most beautiful experiences I've ever had as a mentor or as an editor.

Temper of the Snow

CHENYI ANDREW

"Temper of the Snow" is an excerpt derived from the short story "That Boy I Named," which depicts Ling Xu's recount of one of his most precious memories in the winter seven years ago.

"Ling, what is that?" a boy with a foreign European appearance asked suddenly, while pointing to the snowflakes falling down from the sky.

"That's snow, Ilos," Ling Xu whispered to him. "It snows in the winter sometimes when it gets really cold."

This was the first snow in Yan Cha in many years. Ilos frowned as a snowflake hit his face. He had just turned seven years old, and he had never seen anything like it before.

Ling Xu turned around and laughed as he saw the snowflakes landing on Ilos's slightly flushed face.

"Snow is fascinating if you look at it closely." Ling Xu captured a few snowflakes, then held out his hand in front of Ilos. "Every snowflake has a different shape, and is unique, just like fingerprints." He pointed at one of the snowflakes. "Look, this is a hexagonal-shaped snowflake, and that one is in the shape of triangular crystal . . ." The last time Ling Xu saw snow had been when he was five years old. Ever since then, he had read many books about snow and the winter. Just like cherry blossoms in spring seasons, snow is a form of beautiful scenery in this world, from the moment of its arrival to its fond farewell in a swift transient blow.

Ilos blinked, half understanding while looking at the snowflakes in Ling Xu's hands. He had never thought about winter like that before. Winter to him had always been just cold, but now the snow was full of wonder.

As the snow melted and faded in Ling Xu's hands, he squatted down and dug two clumps of snow from the ground.

"If you gather many of these snowflakes together, you are able to create many different shapes from them. For example, you can create something like this," said Ling Xu, as he showed Ilos the star-shaped snowball rolled in his hands.

Ilos stared at the star in Ling Xu's hands for a good while, as if he was processing something very difficult, then finally laughed. He squatted down next to Ling Xu and started to dig and play with the snow.

"How is it? Do you like it?" Ling Xu asked.

"It's fun," Ilos responded quietly, then held up a smaller star-shaped snowball and showed it to Ling Xu. "I like snow, it's really pretty."

Ling Xu patted Ilos, who was brimming with satisfaction and joy, on the head.

The two of them played for hours. In the distance, snowflakes lightly fell on top of the orphanage, seeming to create a gentle white mink coat on the rooftop. The sky became dim with gentle touches of pink and orange as the sun slowly hid behind the western hills of Yan Cha, and the coldness intensified with the fading light.

"It's getting cold, let's go home," Ling Xu whispered, softly pulling Ilos's hand. His comforting scent of maple trees reached Ilos.

"It's not cold," Ilos replied.

"Don't lie to me, both of your hands are red." Ling Xu lifted Ilos from the ground and stuffed his hands into his own pockets. "It's warmer this way."

"I'm not!" Ilos laughed. "I am actually not cold."

"Well, it's getting dark, too," said Ling Xu, pressing his forehead against Ilos's. "Come on, let's go home. We can always play tomorrow."

Being two years older, Ling Xu was about a head taller than Ilos. In close distance, Ling Xu looked into Ilos's eyes. His pupils were like a pair of amber stones, full of childlike mischief. At that moment, Ling Xu felt an urge of protection, a desire to hide Ilos away from anyone besides himself.

Ilos giggled. The warmth of the maple, like the drifting dawn in the autumn, embraced him and shielded him away from the coldness.

"I want to play in the snow with you in all the upcoming winters."

Seven years later, another winter, another round of snow, but the wish that was once made seemed to be so unattainable now. He had waited, hoped, and dreamed, but he was still unable to find the boy from his memory. There were times where he stayed up all night, looking up at the stars, hoping they would one day guide him to find the boy that he had lost. Ling Xu looked down at the few snowflakes that landed in his palm, overwhelmed by an unexplainable emotion.

". . . Ling Xu?"

"Huh?" He was taken aback by the sudden interruption.

"Are you okay? I've been calling you for a long time," asked Hong with a concerned voice. "Is there something on your mind?"

Almost imperceptibly, Ling Xu froze, but immediately replied, "Sorry, I'm fine, Hong, just a bit cold."

"You look a little lost," Hong said as he patted Ling Xu on the shoulder. "Come on, shake it off. Let's go for some noodles."

"Yeah . . ." said Ling Xu. He gently pressed the lasting temper of the melted snowflakes into his palm.

"Let's go."

JAMILAH ARAF

LIVES: East Elmhurst, New York

Jamilah Araf (she/her) is a high school sophomore who aspires to write a character as good as Alex Karev from *Grey's Anatomy*.

MENTEE'S ANECDOTE:

Changing programs must not have been easy for Kate, but it only goes to show how amazing she really is. Selfless, passionate, kind: These are only a few of the words I would use to describe Kate. Meeting with her every week is a joy. She is constantly exposing me to new things, whether it's story dice or a book she really loved. I am so grateful to have gained such an amazing friend through this experience.

KATE RILEY

LIVES: Huntington, New York

Kate Riley (she/her) is the institutional giving manager at the Brooklyn Conservatory of Music.

MENTOR'S ANECDOTE:

I didn't fully understand Publishing 360 (the Girls Write Now program) when it was unveiled, yet when Jamilah (metaphorically) extended her hand and beckoned me to come along, how could I say no? Today, I'm so glad we're on this adventure together. Jamilah continues to inspire and impress me: Her writing conveys a depth of emotion, economy of phrasing, and clarity of viewpoint. Our one-on-ones are a balm and a kick in the pants. It's a treasure to scaffold on the connection and skills we developed last year, and to see her confidence and mastery grow.

How will they tell me you are dead?

JAMILAH ARAF

Content Warning: War, Violence

In a World War I foxhole, Felix, a German soldier, has survived brutal hand-to-hand combat with Nikolai, who carries letters and photos from his wife, Svetlana. What happens when Felix assumes Nikolai's identity ... and writes back?

Dear Nikolai,

How will they tell me you are dead?

Just answer me this: It seems like that is all you can do for me in those bloody trenches. Literally. Your shoes drenched in so much of your brother's blood that the worn-out leather has turned red.

How will they tell me you are dead?

Will they tell me you were a hero? Would they disrespect me in such a way as to lie to my face while breaking the news?

Will they talk to me like a visitor in a hospital's waiting room (at least, how they used to talk to visitors)? Will they tell me they did everything they could, try to dumb it down for me as if I don't hear the stories and screams from soldiers who have shot off their legs, just to return to nightmares?

Of course, the doctors no longer talk like this. With so many dying from the famine, it's more of a shock to hear that whoever you were waiting for, praying for, is alive.

Will they even tell me? Will I just have to search for your name in every newspaper's obituary, all the while my grief spreads, until it infects my entire heart and soul, eating me alive, a death more painful than you could ever imagine in those hellholes you call trenches?

There are no good outcomes here. Even surviving, and returning home on a train filled to the brim with carcasses and the demented, is a bad outcome. I have seen those who have returned. Those whose prayers made it to God through all the overlapping messages and static, overwhelming the channel to the point where he has abandoned his dumbest creation.

I know that if you returned, it wouldn't be you. Your skin, soft like snow, would be hard like the metal under which you hide the worthless brain that decided to leave me. And its white color would be a reddish brown, from the blood and dirt which would never come off, no matter how many times you'd try to scrub it off. Every time you would look in a mirror, you would see it, see them, and eventually, you'd find comfort in imagining ripping off your skin and forever shedding the past. Your shiny blue eyes will be dull and will be looking through people to the trenches you left in France, as you would watch your buddy die on replay,

over

and over

so many different times until you can't take it anymore! Until screams replace your friendly hellos and you are nicknamed mad!

So, I am asking you to die.

Peacefully and quickly, die without pain.

Do with that information as you will.

Just know that you ruined my life the second you walked out the door.

My dearest Svetlana,

I wish I could say I was grateful to receive your note. I am racked with grief, knowing I can't comfort you, tell you you're wrong. Because you aren't wrong: it's a sorry lot for both of us. I can't bear to think of you and my Leni starving, struggling to survive, not knowing how you will live to see another day. I can only imagine it's the hunger that drives you to such flights of fancy. My love, I will return to you, God willing—yes, I found him in a trench (what a cliché)—and we will begin a new life together, all of us, when I return.

Don't waste your precious energy looking for my name. You'll know where I am and what happened to me when I darken our threshold and speak your name. You and Leni are what I'm fighting for, so that we are safe to grow old together and dangle grandsons on our knees. We are apart now, sacrificing (almost) everything so our children and their children won't have to.

Promise me you will shake these terrible thoughts (at least when you write to me) and replace them with the memory of our day by the lake, when we sipped vodka and held each other close. Soon we will look in each other's blue eyes and remember what we saw there.

I refuse: I will not die.

YOURS ALWAYS,
NIKOLAI

IJEOMA ASONYE

LIVES: Bowie, Maryland

Ijeoma/E. Ozie is a multimedia artist, author, screenwriter, and entrepreneur making waves as the "human hummingbird."

MENTEE'S ANECDOTE:

I have loved having Viviana as a mentor. We bond so much on films and TV shows. I am happy that we can let ourselves loose when we meet and laugh for a long time together. I have become inspired by her background in acting and theater and I want to take acting classes now.

VIVIANA LEO

LIVES: New York, New York

Viviana Leo is a writer, director, and founder of a film production company focused on stories at the crossroads of comedy and social impact.

MENTOR'S ANECDOTE:

Ijeoma is an intelligent and hardworking girl on her way to doing amazing and impactful things. I am amazed that she was able to publish a book while still in college. I think the world should watch out for Ijeoma, because she is going to shock everyone with her talents and charisma.

What would you even call what you see outside the window.

IJEOMA ASONYE

> Someone once told me they saw me looking out a window and there was a lot going on inside. The floor was made of clouds and I was scared to jump.

The story I want to tell is how the world doesn't get me
And how I've made a fool of myself trying to save me.

And so the room gets quieter, the hole gets tinier and I can't control
myself.
What is your intention to save me now from my dreams.

I dreamt a dream, looking out a window
Clouds as cement, I became fearful
How could I fear something as sweet as snow on my feet.

Whether it's I'm a stranger to this world or someone that came from
the past,
These footsteps are afraid to jump out of the window.

Being kissed by the waves and the sand
I wanna go high but I don't know where to land.

Looking out the window trying to see right past,
The future of me that I want so bad
And focus on the present, which makes me sad
I think I know me but they don't know that.

I brush past these writings and understand why they don't get me
My life is written in riddles, my poetic rhythms all over the place
You would have to come into this hole to try and understand
That contrary to belief this hole isn't dark,
It has a window for a pretty fool to look out of,
trying to see right past,
The future of me that I want so bad.

SHAYLA ASTUDILLO

LIVES: Queens, New York

Shayla Astudillo is an eighteen-year-old college student who spends their time writing poetry about their life experiences and how it has impacted them.

MENTEE'S ANECDOTE:

Danielle has been there for me through various events in my life. This includes college applications, my first anthology, my medical leave, and my writing insecurities. She and I have been working together for three years now, and each year she demonstrates to me more and more how much she cares about me and my writing. She is someone I look up to, can count on, and am excited to work with again in the present and the future!

DANIELLE MAZZEO

LIVES: Brooklyn, New York

Danielle Mazzeo is a New York City native who currently works for the American Museum of Natural History. She loves poetry, storytelling, and watching movies.

MENTOR'S ANECDOTE:

Shayla is such a resourceful and honest writer, drawing from their own personal experiences to articulate universal truths. They earnestly care about their readers, offering works that are generous and vulnerable. They are curious, empathetic, and deeply creative. Now in our third year of Girls Write Now together, I am thrilled to see Shayla continue to grow as a writer and as a truly special human being.

My words were hiding from me. Oops.

SHAYLA ASTUDILLO

Writing is one of the most important aspects of my life. Yet my words hid from me. As a poet, where does that leave me?

A loss for words:

I've been a poet for a long period of time.

Sitting on the train, alone in my room, in the space of love.
These various words tend to float around my head until I write them
     on a page,
such vivid colors, shapes, and sizes they all are.
Anger, words, honesty, and frustration tend to come up most often.
So eager to be included in writing as they come from the inside looking
     for understanding.

Recently, however, they've locked themselves in my chest, refusing to
     come out.
All these words I surround myself with
shaking their head when I ask them where they went.

Oh please come out, I have experiences to cope with, I plead.
Silence on their end.

I'm borrowing words from previous works.
          It just doesn't work the same.
Write, write, write, write.

I just want to write.
And yet I can't seem to as these little annoying words don't want to
   come out anymore.

VALUE:

Where could this have started?
I couldn't have possibly woken up one day,
                                    and words just decided to revolt.

They are doing this for a reason, I just can't put my finger on why.
So I ponder, and ponder, and ponder, and ponder until my grammar
   becomes weak, and my head begins to lose its value.
I sit, take a breath, look around and see the words still inside.
Honesty begins scratching at the lock.
Importance sits in a corner refusing to look at me.

                  Importance sits in a corner!
                        That is it!

These words have been told over and over again they hold no value.
Needing to be used countless times to *hopefully* be taken seriously.
I repeat them and repeat them and nothing seems to change.
Why write if my words hold no significance?

Writing:
It is supposed to come easy to me.
And yet it doesn't anymore.

I repeat and repeat and nothing changes.

I repeat and repeat and nothing changes.

These words are tired and hopeless.
What am I supposed to do?

Understanding:

I write for myself.

Words help me put together the experiences I go through.

Why do I focus,
on others hearing me.
When I don't even know if
I am hearing myself?

I write for myself.
I state it again to reemphasize that my words are just that. Mine.
No one can take that from me.
I'm sorry to my words for making them feel like they exist for others.

. . .

The lock on the cage comes undone,
Importance floats to the front.
I smile,
they smile back.

JESSICA BAKAR

LIVES: Pleasanton, California

Jessica Bakar is a high school senior and writer from California.

MENTEE'S ANECDOTE:

I am so grateful to have Amy as a mentor. She has been such a positive influence in my writing experience, especially when the process is difficult. Through her encouragement and guidance, she has enabled me to find new value in my work. She has helped me refine old pieces and generate new ones to explore different parts of myself, and she's always ready to help me experiment with whatever new form I want to tackle. I've enjoyed working with Amy, and I look forward to continuing our writing journey together.

AMY SOUZA

LIVES: Portland, Oregon

Amy Souza is a freelance writer and editor based in Portland, Oregon. She's also the founder of Spark: a call-and-response project for artists, writers, and musicians.

MENTOR'S ANECDOTE:

I love working with Jessica! She tackles tough subjects in her writing with both thought and heart. She also impresses me by regularly trying out new forms and using life experiences not only as subject matter, but to shape her essays and poems—such as a story written like a family recipe or a list essay that incorporates her constitutional knowledge. She puts significant effort into creating new work and editing pieces to enhance their impact. I've enjoyed getting to know her these past few months and really look forward to watching her create more and more.

How Feminist Art Was Invented

JESSICA BAKAR

This poem is inspired largely by Artemisia Gentileschi's art and life, and my own experiences.

Artemisia,
you blessed blank
canvases with the green
serenity of landscapes, but
barricaded bedroom doors
by his spoiled
undried paintings.

Artemisia,
I asked you to
purify me as St. Catherine,
to paint me as
Judith. Judith knows
of vengeance. Vengeance
knows the taste of
blood. I know you
crave metallic affection.

Artemisia,
you Temptress. You
Thing. You
Threat. You
Woman in Tassi's
world, you asked for it

We asked for it
I ask for it.

Artemisia,
when I came to
You, bleary-eyed,
Teary-eyed, unable
To speak, you
Said, babe,
This is how feminist
art was invented.

So I ask you
to show me the beauty
of pain.

ANNAYA M. BAYNES

LIVES: Atlanta, Georgia

Annaya (she/they) is a graduating senior English and French double major at Spelman College who loves baking and table-top role-playing games.

MENTEE'S ANECDOTE:

Ann has really been my biggest cheerleader for my writing. Often, I can feel very protective over what I write, and she always makes me feel so safe and secure when we're discussing a piece. We talk about everything from poetic forms to politics to pronouns. She creates a really welcoming space where my opinions are valued. After we discuss the chapters of the novel I'm writing, she always tells me that she can't wait for the next installment and that she's on the edge of her seat. I leave our sessions with so much love in my heart.

ANN VAN BUREN

LIVES: Little Deer Isle, Maine

A graduate of Barnard College, Ann van Buren earned her M.A. in writing at NYU and MLIS from the Palmer School. More at annvanburen.com.

MENTOR'S ANECDOTE:

I love Annaya's ability to tell a story and am always surprised, intrigued, and left anticipating what will happen next in the writing we share on Zoom. Annaya's characters are other-worldly even as they are down-to-earth and describe universal experiences and feelings. I am moved by the tenderness in her work. It explores the rough edges of our imperfect world and imagines new ways of looking past appearances to get to the heart of human relationships. It is mind-opening to work with Annaya and to connect with a young person who is so focused, brilliant, creative, and gentle.

The Devouring

ANNAYA M. BAYNES

Content Warning: Cannibalism

> **Faced with systemic oppression, two lovers choose a ritual called "The Devouring" and a world made from love.**

My lover and I decided to consume each other. Despite how it sounds, this is a rational decision. Have you seen the world lately? Maybe you're one of those people who can choose the life of the veil, the life of willful ignorance, the life of joy at the expense of distant pain. Here, our eyelids stay peeled back to spot the constant barrage of threats before they reach us. So, many have chosen The Devouring.

No one knows for sure who was the first. Just that one day whispers started creeping under doors saying someone had devised a way to go somewhere completely and utterly safe. There were rules; otherwise, the whole ritual wouldn't work. You'd just be left with a mess of flesh and bone and blood.

1. You and your partner for The Devouring must love each other truly.

My lover holds my beating heart, and I have no fear because I know she would never hurt it or me. Her love for me has soaked into the marrow of my bones.

2. The two of you must both want this with no doubts in your body or mind.

Over our morning coffee, we discussed going through with the ritual. We giggled over which body parts we'd eat first. I always chose her hands because they hold an immense wealth of power. One finger trailing down the curve of my neck sends shivers down my spine to the tips of my toes. A carefully placed palm can stop the complaint racing out of my mouth dead in its tracks. The woes of the world disappear if I just close my eyes and focus on the warmth of her hand. She always chose my butt. Her reasoning was simpler: It looks like it'd taste the best.

3. You had to maintain eye contact for as long as possible.

That was no problem for us. Many an evening we spent lying in bed staring into each other's eyes and tracing blind constellations on the skin that we could reach. Those conditions met, we were ready.

So we decided to strip down bare. Naked of the defenses we learned to put up, the constructs we built to make an unacceptable world acceptable. I held her gaze in mine. We weren't scared. The true horrors were everything outside of our two bodies. Maybe you don't know that, but we did. And anyway, they say that once the ritual is complete, you'll join the rest of the Devoured and Devouring.

Wordlessly, she presented her right ring finger. It went down smoother than you'd think. We went back and forth, offering our body parts on the sacrificial altar of our love. I could feel the parts of me in her stomach. It was warm and wet and calm. It felt like a returning.

Love is giving someone the power to destroy you, and they never do. You can't help exercising any power in your grasp, huh? You maim and hurt and destroy people, animals, the planet. We cannot accept that, so those of us who can turn to The Devouring. Maybe we want to revert to the wombs that held and cared for us, nourished us, imprisoned and shielded us. Maybe this is a last-ditch effort to escape the pain that the world has tattooed into the skin of our destiny. Maybe we just wanted to be loved.

Instead of letting ourselves be destroyed by those who have never cared for us, we created a world of our own that accepted only those who know of love. Parents, children, lovers, and friends are all welcome here. You may believe that we chose escape, but you're more wrong than you've ever been. We chose a life full of richness and care. We chose a place where people can imagine beyond harm in the name of profit. We chose to love and be loved.

ALEX BERMAN

LIVES: New York, New York

Alex is a senior at the High School of American Studies at Lehman College who enjoys normal earth human behaviors like sleeping, breathing, and eating.

MENTEE'S ANECDOTE:
Jennifer and I have worked together for three years now, and each year is better than the last as we become closer. I love talking about the books we like and even more so the ones we don't. I always appreciate her sharp eye for commas and ever-relevant advice and critique. I have grown so much as a writer in these three years, and I'm looking forward to continuing to expand my horizons this semester.

JENNIFER L. BROWN

LIVES: New York, New York

Jennifer writes middle-grade novels. When not writing, you might catch her walking her dog, Freddy, or flirting with bankruptcy at a local bookstore.

MENTOR'S ANECDOTE:
This is my third year meeting with Alex. Our meetings are always a highlight of my week. It has been absolutely amazing watching them grow as a writer, artist, and person over our years together. They always bring such creative spirit to our sessions and an irrepressible desire to explore new genres, techniques, and more. I love our conversations about media, whether they want to gush about a current read (this year, *Moby-Dick* and Melville's letters to Hawthorne have featured prominently) or the latest show we both streamed. I'm excited for another semester of writing and learning together.

In the Tree House

ALEX BERMAN

Like most stories about friendship, this one does not involve whale bones.

As we got older (but looking back on it, we were so young), the conversation shifted to love. It was winter, and we were huddling even closer than necessary on the small bed for warmth. We had been laughing at something, and every time one of us looked at the other, the laughter would start again. And it went like that, off and on, for a few minutes until the fun had been used up.

"Do you ever think about what your life is gonna be like?" asked Caroline. "You know, when you're an adult?"

"Yeah," I said, because I had. Extensively.

"Let's talk about what it's gonna be like when we're grown up."

This was often how we started these midnight conversations: with a formal topic introduction.

"Okay," I said, because that's what I always said. "You go first."

"Okay." Caroline gesticulated toward the popcorn ceiling as she laid out her plans. "When I grow up, I'm gonna marry an Italian doctor. He is going to be very handsome and good at cooking. When he proposes to me, he's going to pick me up and sweep me off my feet and there will be a huge diamond ring, and it's going to be very romantic, like, what's it called when the planes? In the sky?"

"Skywriting?"

"Skywriting. He's gonna skywrite in the sky 'Will you marry me?' And I'll say yes, and we'll have a very classy wedding, and I'm gonna wear a dress with a train with lots of lace. And we're going to have three kids: a girl, a boy, and another girl. And they will be named Poppy, Jackson, and then either Silver or Willow, I haven't decided."

"I don't think you can choose whether your baby is a boy or a girl."

"No, you can." Caroline spoke in edicts. "My mom took a pill when she was pregnant with me because she wanted to have a girl."

I turned away so Caroline wouldn't see my face. On the floor below me, there were indents from Caroline's two front teeth, which got stuck there in first grade when she fell while we were trying to fly (she would jump off the bed over and over again, and each time she didn't fly she'd say "That wasn't it," and try again).

"What about you?" she asked.

I was grateful that she had gone first because I had assumed that we would live together when we grew up. We would stay best friends and live in a treehouse together in a dense forest, and it would have different levels for our bedrooms, the kitchen, the living room, a game room, and even a pool, and there would be a Rube Goldberg—esque series of ladders and slides and pneumatic tubes that would transport us and our belongings throughout the expansive treehouse. We would spend our days playing board games and making puzzles by a crackling fire. It would be eternally fall where we lived, and soft syrupy light would filter through the trees into our home. We would cook soup in a huge cauldron like witches and talk through every night. But obviously that wasn't what Caroline had in mind.

"I think . . ." I tried to trace my story in the air like Caroline had, but it looked stupid when I did it, so I just tucked my hands under the covers instead. "I will marry, um, a man. And . . . he will be a chef. A French chef. And we will eat chocolate all the time, the fancy kind, because he will be very good at making chocolate."

"And what about your kids?"

"I don't— I'm not sure."

Caroline wrinkled her nose. "What do you mean you're not sure?"

Some people might think Caroline's expression was one of disgust, but I knew she was genuinely confused. The issue was that up until a few minutes before this, I *had* been sure, so sure about our future in the tree-house in the woods, but obviously Caroline was sure too, of something totally different, and I wasn't sure what my life would look like without her at its center. But she could imagine what hers would look like without me.

"My mom says," Caroline began, filling the growing silence, "that some people don't want kids when they're younger, but when they reach a certain age, they go crazy, and it's like they need kids." Caroline's voice took on a reassuring tone. "So that's probably what'll happen to you."

"Probably." I forced a smile that in my head was so strained she would be sure to notice and ask what was wrong, and I would tell her, and she would find a way to fix it all, because she knew me well enough to tell when my face was frozen like I'd spent hours outside and smiling hurt like ice cracking on my cheeks.

But she just sighed and shifted in the bed. "We should probably go to sleep now."

"Okay," I said. "Good night, then."

"Good night."

JACQUELINE BERNABE

LIVES: Bronx, New York

Jacqueline Bernabe is a college student studying psychology and English. She enjoys reading, playing *The Sims*, and spending time with friends and family.

MENTEE'S ANECDOTE:

This past year working with Hannah has been a joyous experience filled with learning and creativity. Our shared interest in the women in *The Odyssey* and our introverted nature have allowed us to work and get to know each other. Our Zoom sessions are filled with mutual understanding and a variety of emotions, such as happiness and comfort. I have learned a lot from Hannah, with one of the key lessons being the importance of sharing my voice—no matter what.

HANNAH WEST

LIVES: Kill Devil Hills, North Carolina

Hannah Bunn West is a freelance writer, North Carolina native, and author of the book *Remarkable Women of the Outer Banks*.

MENTOR'S ANECDOTE:

Jacqueline is the bloom that reveals itself slowly, the still water that runs deep. Her writing is the gateway to those depths, revealing the ambitious, expressive, deeply feeling young woman that she is. Our pair sessions are comfortable and relaxed. We are "quiet people" with a lot to say. Each time we meet and work and write together, we allow another petal to unfold and I walk away inspired by what she has offered up to me.

Sun and Moon

JACQUELINE BERNABE

A short essay I wrote while staring at my sun and moon.

A sun and a moon live together on my dining room wall. They have stared at me for most of my life.

They first arrived in my home in the Bronx in 2010. My family had just returned from El Salvador. Our trip to my mother's hometown was almost extended as she made a last-minute decision to go to the nearby market. She's always eager to bring back an abundance of items that range from cultural foods to colorful beaded jewelry and, this time, an intricate wooden sun and moon piece.

They have rested on the wall ever since.

I was six when the sun and the moon entered my home. This year I'll turn nineteen. I am in my second semester of college. I have one fewer cat than I had back then. I have two more pairs of glasses. Everything in my life has either increased or decreased. I keep a count in the little journal in my head, which takes in all of the differences and indifferences, the losses and wins. Yet from what I can remember, my sun and moon have not changed. They sit day after day, without complaining.

The sun is carved so that it looks directly at you, and the moon is carved in a side profile but it can see everything through its peripheral vision. I was initially afraid of the duo. Perhaps it was my childlike delusion that the sun blinked at me once, or my ignorance of the solar system. Maybe it was the glares they gave me.

As I've gotten older, I see that my sun and moon don't glare at me anymore, just observe.

This could be attributed to simply growing up and leaving my

childish view of the world behind. But I think it's more about confront-
ing my fears. The fear of being in the spotlight, the fear of how I am perceived. I am not famous by any means, but the stage of the world terrifies
me. Having the sun and moon stare at me at home while going through
life stages could be terrifying. It took me a while to realize it was a gift.
We all share the sun and moon on this earth, but I have my own personal set.

If my sun and moon can remain unscathed through the gardens of
life, who says I can't do the same and grow my own flowers?

I fixate on the duo's constant presence and fixed point on my wall.
Even amid the chaos that my home emitted, the cracks of age that surround them, and the tunes of emotion that sang out daily, my sun and
moon continued to display values that I came to admire—balance,
steadiness, and the ability to view the world through different perspectives.

When I did not feel the warmth of the sun's rays or see the glow of the
moon in the sky a few years ago during the pandemic, I sought comfort
in the sun and moon situated just inches away from me, hanging for all
to enjoy on the small dining room wall.

As I trace the surface of my sun and moon, the pads of my fingers
worn out by years of paper cuts and pen markings, I feel the intricate
lines and crevices in the wood and a growing roughness. My sun and
moon too have aged. They have seen me finish trails and start down new
pathways. They have helped shape my values. I thank them for their silent watch over my life.

CAMILA BONILLA

LIVES: New York, New York

Camila is a high school senior in New York City. She likes to write short stories and is currently reading *Sister Outsider* by Audre Lorde.

MENTEE'S ANECDOTE:

Leslie is an amazing mentor. She gives great advice about navigating the world, not just as a growing person, but artistically! This is something I value greatly.

LESLIE HENDRICKSON

LIVES: New York, New York

Leslie Hendrickson is a writer and editor based in New York.

MENTOR'S ANECDOTE:

My first name was a secret from Camila for more than a year. But in the fall, I shared my link to a Zoom with her and she found out on the call that my first name is actually Victoria!

Yellow Lines

CAMILA BONILLA

The melting of ice in lemonade. The feeling of watching yourself from the outside as reality begins to unfold. The moments that occur after impatience.

I stayed outside that night. I imagined myself, over and over again, saying those words. My lips moved around the air, barely exhaling my desire in a hot wisp. I imagined myself. Walking down the porch and over to the red pickup. It was too dark to see the steps now. I might trip and fall. I got bored tonight. I bet my lips were pink now, instead of red, from all the fidgeting and imagining things. I did that a lot, when I got in my head.

The lot beyond me mostly consisted of dry, grassy plains that never rolled romantically like in the pictures. Just a vast space, where you could see exactly what is ahead of you at all times. Sometimes I got scared when the tufts rustled, and then excited because something would finally be coming for me. It was always a rabbit.

But when the sun came down, I wondered how anything even ever existed at all in that swallowing darkness. I could reach out and start to dissipate in the black. I imagined running straight into there and falling victim to the murk.

If I stood on the roof, I would be able to see small luminescence, dotting the large pastoral in the form of passing cars, and usually never homes. Cars never stopped, only kept moving and passing through. I resonated with this fact and did not blame them.

I was sitting for three hours. The glass jar next to me collected water from melted ice, traces of lemon seeds and thick pulp gathering at the bottom. Everything I had spent so long stringing together that morning unraveled. I felt too shameful to walk back inside, with my blue dress and smudged lipstick. Past the kitchen, and over to the buzzing fridge. I heard John Denver playing inside on the cassette player, and imagined my mom knocked out on the stained couch, television fluorescence moving on her face. I know for a fact that my parents used the same player, and rocking to the twang. I knew his face, from pictures, that scruffy beard tucked tightly into her shoulder as they swung around. You could almost believe it to be true love.

When did things go from dancing to shuffling around feet to sitting down to sleeping forever? Did people still go dancing?

I hated to sit down. A gust of wind picked up my hair. The current remained a gentle push on my skin, an encouragement. I stood up.

I did not fall down the porch steps when I walked down, in the dark. Anticlimactic nevertheless, but I still felt myself whispering the words as I made my way onto the road. All the way to the main highway. I sat down on the curb outlined by a thicker line of rocks. The air now whipped my cheeks with every passing vehicle. Maroon Toyota. Gray Land Rover. Silver Buick. They rolled right over the two yellow lines that lead to enigmatic darkness.

The red pickup was not coming for me. I realized this.

I put my thumb out. If I leaned forward just an inch, the wheels could tear a chunk of it. I kept my hand there, barely brushing the vehicles. I stayed a moment, maybe a couple of minutes before a yellow car, which I did not know the name of, only that it looked like a city cab from the pictures, slowed down and came to a stop where I sat. The right door popped, and slowly turned from its hinge.

I imagined myself from the outside; standing up, and my face becoming illuminated by the tiny lights inside. I imagined myself sliding inside the car—my hair becoming sifted into all the right places, once out of the wind's way. I imagined myself speaking—my smudged red lips, opening into a perfect circle and my front teeth barely showing in all the right places. I did all of these things and hoped that it was okay.

The man inside the car gave me no confirmation of any of those things, or whether they played out in reality the way they did in my head.

He only raised his eyebrow, sparse and patchy on his young face, then nodded toward the seat when I hesitated. Hesitation was not a part of my imagination.

The car jerked forward as soon as I closed the door. It ran fast. Over the thick, yellow lines, and with a slight surprise, I realized that now the lines ran under me, instead of me going outside to see them static on the black concrete. Then looking at all of the cars, leaving and passing and never stopping for me. My imagination has morphed into a blurry haze. When I looked at the man next to me, his hands almost looked like they were melting into the wheel. I was afraid he'd lose balance, but the car never shifted away from the lines. They continued unfaltering, electric and bright.

PALMARES BUSTAMANTE

LIVES: Brooklyn, New York

Palmares Bustamante is a high school sophomore living in New York City. She works in many mediums: sewing, writing, and painting.

MENTEE'S ANECDOTE:

Emma has helped me grow so much as a writer. It's so helpful to have an outside eye to show you all the possibilities for your work and push you to expand your horizons. We've taken writing all over New York, from Industry City to Levain's six-ounce cookie! I look forward to working together more throughout the year.

EMMA COURT

LIVES: Brooklyn, New York

Emma is an amazing journalist from New York, who is currently working on a poem a day.

MENTOR'S ANECDOTE:

Working on Palmares's pieces, I've gotten to learn a lot about her. Her writing is inspired by the world around her, so we've gotten to meet in some great places to discuss character building and world development. One of my favorite meetings was going to see architectural styles on the Upper West Side for setting inspiration. Working together was a great way to find inspiration in our city!

The Hill

PALMARES BUSTAMANTE

We all live in a world of constant turnover and change. All it takes is a moment to recognize that every change lives inside of us.

I live in a house perched on the ledge of a far-reaching peak
If you were to look up from the rocky bay it appears as daunting as it is
    bleak
Yet I never had a worry or fear until the day that I turned three
When I grew terrified of the darkness that rolled out of the room with
    no key
Then at six my greatest fear was the spiders that hid within the
    crumbling stones
At eight I was wary of the beams that sprouted like flesh from bones
At ten I had been petrified of the howling sound of the creaks in the floor
At thirteen I feared the splinters that shattered surrounding the
    handleless door

Until one stormy day never had I thought something so gripping
The sudden realization that a house on a hill might be in danger of
    tipping
Along with it every pot and pan and picture in a frame
Every yearbook, every journal, every poem with no name
But what cannot fall, the feeling of cold floors prickling my feet
What cannot fall, the sound of foghorns following the fleet
I still live in the house and one day the lesson will come clear
That a house is just a house and a fear is just a fear.

EMMY CAI

LIVES: Brooklyn, New York

Emmy is a high school senior who enjoys creating art. She has won an Honorary Mention for her painting from the Scholastic Art & Writing Awards.

MENTEE'S ANECDOTE:

Kym is supportive and encouraging and has just the right advice for me when needed. Her pursuit of photography and writing gives me hope that someday I can be just like her and have a career revolving around something I love, too. During my first year, Kym told me she had submitted her photography in a contest and won! Hearing this pushed me to submit my work to the Scholastic Art & Writing contest and share my writing with everyone. Thank you, Kym, for always inspiring me to hone my craft and rooting for me from the beginning.

KYM RICHARDSON

LIVES: Silver Spring, Maryland

Kym is a writer who received a MacDowell and New York Foundation for the Arts fellowship and is working on a YA novel.

MENTOR'S ANECDOTE:

Writing sessions with Emmy are about more than writing. Sure, we talk about storytelling and ways to craft her essays and short stories. But her interest in the visual arts creates a space for us to talk about her painting and sculpture projects, too. Once, Emmy shared what it means for her to be able to work on her art and how she feels like she's "in the moment" when she paints, letting herself go with the flow—and that experience became a short story! Thanks to Emmy, I'm always learning something new and staying inspired to keep writing!

The Rise of Fame, The Fall of Family

EMMY CAI

After spending the past year becoming a rising star, Daisy comes home, her name plastered on the front page of *The Times*. Her parents disapprove of Daisy's lifestyle, forcing her to choose between them and her fame.

"Late Friday night, Miss Sirene sported a backless Dior designed just for her. Yves Saint Laurent hinted that the rising socialite could be his latest muse for the new season." Mama slapped *The Times* next to Daisy's plate. "What do you have to say for yourself, Daisy? What's all this?"

"Mama, please, it was just an article," she said good-heartedly, poking at her waffles. "Y'know, they really loved the movie. Mr. Leonard said it could be nominated in three categories for the next round of Oscars," Daisy boasted, reaching for her mother's hand. "Yeah, he said he's never directed anything like it!" Mama swiped her hand away. She reached for her coffee, now cold, and shakily took a sip.

"Sweetheart," Father tried to reason from across the table. "It just is not the way we raised you. With Joleen grown and gone to New York, we were hoping you'd live close to home after you finished college. We just . . . Baby girl, the world is a dangerous place now and Ma's only looking out for you."

Mama sniffled and raked her fingers through her graying hair.

Maybe coming back home for Thanksgiving was a mistake. Daisy would've been fine staying in California alone for the holiday even though she hadn't been back to Georgia for almost a year.

"This is all I've worked for and you both know this!" Daisy began again. "What do you want me to do, then? I didn't take all those choir lessons to sing a lullaby for a husband. The traditional lifestyle you guys always talk about: staying home, raising children, living in a picket-fence-bordered house . . . It's not *me*. It's not what I want. I was working on something, something big like this!" Daisy stabbed at the newspaper with her finger right where there was a smiling picture of her entering the annual Chairman's Gala, her brown hair tossed in the wind and her green eyes vibrant. "I always wanted to be on the big screen!"

"Those choir lessons were to keep you close to God, Daisy!" Mama was beginning to cry. "Never in a million years did we expect this to come out of you," gesturing to the newspaper.

"Hon', let's finish this later." Father was growing impatient.

He had long awaited a peaceful Thanksgiving weekend, especially after Daisy and Joleen had moved out of the house this year, but it was evidently not going as planned.

"No!" Mama slapped her hand on the table. "I see the news, I see the films; all the violence on the streets, everything in the films these days is more graphic, more nude . . . More tramp-y!"

"Well, I am not a tramp, Ma!" Daisy shouted back with disbelief.

"You *are* if you're on a big screen half naked, musing around showing off the latest fashion line, and kissing any man that gives you a leg up. Cause that's what you're doing, Daisy!"

"I worked for everything I got! I made the front page by myself, not anyone else but me." Daisy put her hand to her chest, desperate to get Mama to realize how wrong she was. "I am the one who's making the numbers at the box office go up. I'm the one—"

"That's enough," Father said, deadly serious and at the end of his rope. "The solution is simple, we will eat this meal together, so help me God. Then, Daisy, you will wear that blue dress of yours upstairs after washing up and we will go to church. You will atone for your irrational behavior. It just isn't like you!"

Daisy's mouth gaped. It was like her words held no weight to them. She knew of so many people who would have clawed their way up to where she was right now, and here her parents were, trying to bring her down.

"I'd rather starve than sit here and listen to all this crap," Daisy replied with all the venom in her voice she could muster.

"If you'd rather starve, then do it on the street. If you aren't going to be a righteous child of God"—Father took in a heavy breath as if to create a dam for his tears—"you aren't a child of ours."

At this, Mama fully turned and left the table, but not before letting out a loud sob.

"Daddy," Daisy resolved sadly, almost pathetically. "You don't mean such a thing. How can you say that to me?"

Father couldn't look into her eyes. "Make a decision. I'll either be driving you to the airport or to church. The choice is yours, Daisy. But I'm really begging you to make the right one."

He left the table for the kitchen, taking his pancakes with him. As he walked out of Daisy's sight, tears cascaded freely down his face at the thought of practically losing a daughter. After everything the family had been through together and everything he and Margaret had given, it didn't make sense why their little girls chose to run away from the family they had built together.

TARANIS CASTELANT

LIVES: New York, New York

Taranis Castelant (he/it) is a high school sophomore who enjoys art and history.

MENTEE'S ANECDOTE:

Laura has been a kind and accommodating mentor, and over time I have come to consider her a friend. As it is my first time having a mentor, it was a bit of an adjustment having to consider outside perspectives on my work; I usually keep my writing to myself. We've been able to foster a comfortable environment where we can both share our work without judgment as we learn from and grow with each other. I've enjoyed the relaxed, laid-back atmosphere of our meetings without the suffocating constraints of "professionalism," where we can get to know each other outside of work.

LAURA MURPHY

LIVES: Brooklyn, New York

Laura is a publishing professional and freelance writer living in Brooklyn, New York.

MENTOR'S ANECDOTE:

Taranis's natural talent as a writer and enthusiasm for the craft has made working with him delightful and easy. One of my go-to activities for our meetings is to have us both write using the same prompt, and it is always interesting to see how different his take on the prompt was from mine, even when we're both writing in a dark fantasy vein. His feedback on my own writing has often been very helpful and spot-on. I'm looking forward to watching him continue to develop his style and voice as an artist.

The Life of a Teenage Superhero

TARANIS CASTELANT

An excerpt of a piece soon to be part of a larger novel.

1.

You were only fourteen when you ran away from home.

Living with your parents was absolute misery. They were the type of parents who were full of hate: They hated their jobs, hated their spouses, hated everything about themselves. You didn't really care why they did what they did, and you never will, but even if there was some sad sob story behind their abuse, it wouldn't matter. By the time they were stable enough to say they were sorry, you were long gone.

You grew up far too quickly—or perhaps too slowly for your home— and you have to leave behind the things that don't serve you. So you left.

You spent two years on your own, doing things you know you'd regret because you were a teenager and that's what teenagers do. You hurt people. You made friends. You partied, you fought, wasted your time. Then you woke up with superpowers.

You went to sleep, and the next morning, objects were floating around you.

2.

Two weeks after you woke up with powers, you met Annales. You've heard of her before. Everyone in New York has.

She was the director of the Order at the time, the premier superhero team based out of Manhattan. She was also a key player in bringing down the last director, Solar Flare, who was—for lack of better words—a murderer.

Solar Flare was boundless in physical power, but he was traumatized. Scarred. It was a shock to no one when a group of telepaths took advantage of his mental state and did their bidding through his hands. *He* did not murder anyone, but his body did. Nuance matters none to heroes, and so Annales killed him.

Regular people became even more paranoid, and rightfully so. It *could* happen again. The media imagined a person sick enough—not necessarily ill, but bitter, scorned, or traumatized—and pictured them winning the power lottery. Now imagine them winning again. Now they're a reality bender, a telepath, a healer, an elemental, or just plain invulnerable. People couldn't develop technology fast enough to combat it. What can you do against someone trying to kill you if they're bulletproof?

That's where the registry comes in, and that's what got you. Know your enemy. You intended to dodge it—as far as you knew, you wouldn't be using your powers—but she found you. There's no telling how she tracked you down. You had no address, and you hadn't used your legal name in years. Still, she found you. She found you and told you she was searching for others like you—recruiting the aimless, lost, and purposeless to make into heroes. You told her you were only sixteen. She said it did not matter, children can be heroes, too.

3.

After a few legal proceedings, you were officially a hero. They took your measurements, made you a suit, gave you housing, taught you how to fight. Annales taught you personally—taught you how to take the hurt, how to ignore your body's attempts at self-preservation, and how to walk on glass. She taught you how to be a hero, too—how to smile when you are missing teeth, how to handle the press, how to make your fame truly your own.

You fought a lot. You fought B-listers and cartoon villains ten years your senior. You personally tried not to kill, to instead help, but the people want rock: They want to see blood and carnage and guts, the shedding of skin. The cameras reflect well on gore for a reason, and that's what you're told to do and so you do it. They loved you for it.

4.

On the day before your birthday, you told yourself you'd bleed for better reasons. You turned seventeen at midnight on June 28, and that's exactly when you fought other heroes for the first time. You and a few others.

It was less hatred of them and more of an order; you don't even remember what you were fighting about. All that comes to mind is the standoff—the gritting of teeth, the clenching of fists, the tense air heavy with iron. It was the first time you felt intimidated.

You walked away with teeth dislodged and one less finger on your left hand. Still, you won. That's all that matters. The world was saved again.

5.

You are eighteen when the world ends.

It isn't the first time the world has ended, not for you. This time, you watch the world give way to nothingness as you stand on the station and look up at the coming void. It's spreading quickly. You aren't supposed to be here, but here you stand, in a full suit, as if nothing has truly changed. It hasn't. You are here to save the world.

You are the only one left who can.

VANETI CEUS

LIVES: Miami, Florida

Vaneti (she/her) is a high school junior who loves reading and binge-watching Netflix shows.

MENTEE'S ANECDOTE:

Isabella has helped me a lot with advice on my future goals, edited pieces for me, and helped me figure out what best steps to take for my career.

ISABELLA MARIE GARCIA

LIVES: Pembroke Pines, Florida

Isabella Marie Garcia (she/her/ella), or Isa, as she prefers to be called, is a writer and film photographer living in her native swampland of South Florida. For the past four years, Garcia has worked with local and national arts-based organizations such as Burnaway, Opa-locka Community Development Corporation, LnS Gallery, and UNTITLED, Art. Her writing has appeared in publications such as *The Art Newspaper, Burnaway, Miami New Times, FF2 Media,* and *So to Speak,* a feminist journal of language and art.

MENTOR'S ANECDOTE:

Over the past six months and as my first year participating with Girls Write Now, I've had the honor and pleasure of working with Vaneti in a Miami-based mentor/mentee partnership. Not only is Vaneti a talented and creative writer, she's stellar at communication and responds promptly to any messages or updates with our meetings. Most of all, Vaneti's professional drive is motivating as an individual myself in seeking our opportunities to connect and network within Miami, Florida, and beyond into other communities. I truly believe she can get anything she puts her heart—and pen!—into now and in the future.

Evolution of a Size

VANETI CEUS

Content Warning: Body Shaming, Fatphobia, Disordered Eating

This is the story of a teenager and how she navigates her life being plus-sized. It is a moving story about the way society's opinions about her body have influenced her life even in adulthood.

Welcome back, heroin chic. The taste of SlimFast burned deep into my brain as if the words "fat-free" would transport me from all the hatred I felt inside.

As if the low-calorie label and the complaints from strangers who have never noticed me before would have stopped me from dissecting and hating everything I see in the mirror.

As if watching a size-two supermodel walk down a runway and have people tell you "You know you could look like her one day" would stop the burning desire I had in me to just eat the cookie anyway.

You have to be skinny but not too skinny; people love thick women but not a fat stomach. If you fit into whatever box they put you in you will be beautiful, but if you even try to step outside of the box just a little, then you are worthless.

The first time someone hit on me and liked my body as it is, I nearly laughed in their face. I looked for lying behind their eyes, but there was only passion and desire. The type of desire that lit my first societal fire.

Now my first societal fire was similar to other people's. It first started with everyone's worst nightmare, particularly mine. I stand and look down at the flickering numbers on that scale telling me over and over again just how much I'm worth. Stomach too large, wishing that I could just button my jeans all the way. "Honey, suck it in more—you'll look skinny," my mother says to me as I struggle to button them up all the way. I eventually give up, I accept my defeat and let society and its ever-lasting love for a size chart win again. As we journey on through the mall, I scroll through my phone, looking at the endless array of models and influencers who have widened their hips surgically, purposely, embracing their size while I continue to slouch mine in shame. My mother and I come home from the mall feeling exhausted and a lot less proud of what some like to call our fupas.

My grandmother sits in the living room waiting for us, excited to see what we picked out. She encourages me to give her a fashion show of all the things I picked out, just so she can then proceed to pick apart every piece of clothing that doesn't look perfect on me. "What happened to the girls of your generation? I swear the women of my era looked much healthier." She says this as she smokes her cigarette and eats her handful of almonds as her lunch for the day.

From the wrinkles on my forehead, to the bridge of my nose, to the curved lines on my double chin, my body has turned into my prison. A prison that was built on the backbone of societies and my loved ones' malice.

My first attempt at stepping outside the box I was placed in was one that is still imprinted into my memory to this day. I went to the beach with my friends on a sunny Saturday already dreading the experience of having every watchful and lingering eye on me as I wore a two-piece bikini for the first time. My body continued to shiver with anxiety as we walked to the front of the beach. But then a state of epiphany washed over me as I noticed that no one cared as my belly jiggled when I ran across the beach playing volleyball. Or how the stretch marks cascaded down my arms. Everyone was too wrapped up in what was going on in their own lives to even notice.

That first feeling of societal freedom was so freeing that I never wanted to stop feeling it. I always remembered that feeling. It was the first time in my life that my body didn't feel like a prison destined for me, but instead a well-woven fortress. The first time I wore a crop top in public I remembered that feeling when I wore a bodycon dress for the first time. I allowed that feeling to engulf me like a warm hug. Years later, when I had my first child, I allowed that feeling to consume me even more than the stretch marks on my stomach did.

JOEY CHEN

LIVES: Brooklyn, New York

Joey graduated from Boston University with a B.A. in English in the spring of 2022. She's a climber, pie connoisseur, and reality TV (TLC) fan.

MENTEE'S ANECDOTE:

Djassi has already taught me so many important life lessons and has given me so much sound advice throughout the time we have been together. She has been so supportive of my law school journey and taught me how to manifest your dreams! Although it has been difficult to relinquish control, Djassi has shown me that there is beauty in the chaos and uncertainty of it all; I just have to lean in and trust the process.

DJASSI DaCOSTA JOHNSON

LIVES: Brooklyn, New York

Djassi DaCosta Johnson is a multihyphenate native New Yorker, dancer, choreographer, filmmaker, photographer, designer, mother, and writer with degrees from Barnard and NYU Tisch.

MENTOR'S ANECDOTE:

Joey is a very warm and intelligent young woman. Working with her since the fall has been mainly about supporting her and her endeavors with her applications for graduate school and studying for the LSATs. Although we've touched base about applications and creative writing projects, I very much enjoyed getting to know Joey through her interest in books, personal growth work, and shared intellectual and cultural pursuits. Joey's writing is strong and expressive. I have enjoyed working with her in helping her clarify her points within her creative mind for her greatest and highest artistic expression.

The Terror of Obesity

JOEY CHEN

Content Warning: Body Shaming, Fatphobia, Disordered Eating

Excerpted from a longer essay. Inspired by the hilarious Samantha Irby's "The Terror of Love."

Weight gain always begins with one or two pounds, then becomes ten, twenty, fifty—and before I know it I'll be bedbound. That's the thought that really terrifies me, being bedridden, because I don't want to wake up one day and realize I've reached that point in my life where my survival is no longer my own and is instead tethered to another person. Imagine needing someone else to bathe me, feed me, wheel me to the bathroom. Codependency as a result of my inability to govern myself. The concept of self-care rendered obsolete. Loss of my self-autonomy, identity, freedom. A regression so stark I revert back to infanthood. The shame I'll feel from willingly imprisoning myself! And how will others judge me? Will they think I'm a slob, a freak, a bum? I'd need to have my shades pulled down all the time because I don't want my neighbors staring into my window—or else they'll inevitably see that I can't get! my! fat! ass! up! and think I'm a moral failure.

On my worst days when I feel unmotivated and lazy and the only thing I can manage to do is watch trash reality TV in bed while polishing off two family-sized bags of From the Ground Up butternut squash pretzels, my inner-downward-spiraling mechanism kicks in loud and hard, screaming, "You got Fat Bitch Mentality!" I believe it: For salvaging the broken pieces and crumbs that have fallen into my cleavage and eating them off my chest, I offer no other justification for the slovenliness of my behavior than my FBM. I watch *1000-lb Sisters* on TLC and laugh, even though there is nothing intrinsically funny about a TV show following two morbidly obese sisters named Amy and Tammy on their weight-loss journeys. If they don't get help for their food addiction, they will soon literally eat themselves to death. I'll look through every sordid corner of YouTube to find free clips because watching *1000-lb Sisters* makes me feel good in a perverse way. Seeing Tammy's literal growth throughout the seasons reminds me of how far we can push the limits of the human body: Hidden somewhere inside of her is a skeleton the same size as mine, holding up all that weight. Quite an impressive biological feat, I daresay. I'll start to think about that Annie Dillard quote, "How we spend our days is, of course, how we spend our lives," and envision a future where I'm stuck in bed every day for the rest of my life. The momentary pleasure we get from indulging and then pitying ourselves is immense, so to hell with the consequences of bingeing. That's what tomorrow is for—dealing with the shame, guilt, and regrets of today.

A few weeks ago I was talking to my friend Gloria about her grandmother, Nana Bessie, who loved eating salami. I say loved, because Nana Bessie is no longer alive—she died at seventy-five of a salami addiction. The old woman got it bad with salami, and I mean bad like Usher "You know you got it bad, and if you miss a day without your friend, your whole life's off track" bad. Her doctor warned her of the dangers of salami overconsumption, saying she needed to keep her salami habits in check or else all that sodium intake would lead to heart failure or a heart attack sooner rather than later. Still, her faithfulness to those speckled salty sausage slices remained steadfast as long as she stayed alive. Salami in every meal with a side of death was preferable to the alternative of no salami at all, which she saw as just as bleak as death itself.

I want to believe I'm nothing like Nana Bessie and that I have enough self-discipline to change my bad habits when they become so evidently self-destructive. However, in the time it takes other people to decide whether moving across the country is a good idea, I've already bought my plane ticket for next month's departure, packed my bags, picked out which restaurants I want to dine in for Sunday brunch, and browsed home listings on Zillow because it's never too early to start manifesting my real-estate dreams. Given my track record of impulsivity, I'd be lying to myself.

MICHELLE CHEN

LIVES: Whitestone, New York

Michelle Chen embraces creative expression, paper mail, warm zephyrs, and fried noodles, as well as Inspiring Girls* Expeditions, Juniper Young Writers Workshop, and the Iowa Young Writers' Studio.

MENTEE'S ANECDOTE:

At our first Girls Write Now pair session on a perfectly warm fall afternoon, I saw Kathryn sitting at the very front table in Spongies' open-air cafe waiting for me. Getting a pandan coconut spongie for $1.00 and a cold moon lemonade for $3.50 has never been more magical; Kathryn was so welcoming and chill, with fantastic style. As we swapped anecdotes about our shared high school alma mater and cross-country adventures in the humanities, she started to feel like the older sister I never had. We shared the same creativity and determination, and I look forward to bonding even more!

KAT JAGAI

LIVES: Brooklyn, New York

K. A. Jagai is a queer, multiracial writer and artist pursuing the light that can be seen only when one is forced into the dark.

MENTOR'S ANECDOTE:

Michelle is a wonderful writer with a lot of experience and passion, and I enjoy hearing her speak on everything from heritage and history to creative writing. My favorite outing with Michelle was definitely the time we met up at Urban Hawker in Midtown. Michelle told me a little bit about her family and culture, and I tried lots of different foods I've never had before. It's been delightful to see how different our traditions are despite ostensibly coming from the same ethnic background. I hope we can keep encouraging each other to be our best creative selves.

Fire and Powder Make the Sweetest Honey

MICHELLE CHEN

A tragicomic reimagining of *Romeo and Juliet* drenched in 1950s Americana, centered on two merchant families enduring racial strife who compete to dominate their small town's economy with mild sci-fi powers specific to each family.

EXT. FAIR 1950s VERONA, OREGON. LATE AFTERNOON.

A bustling state fair with multicolored attractions, including a loud wooden roller coaster, a cattle show, and several stands selling cotton candy, corn dogs, and various merchandise. Elvis Presley music plays. Ground muddy and wet because of the drizzle that has since stopped.

CUT TO: Newsboy selling papers, a pig dozing off behind him. The headline reads MUDDIED BLOOD: CALIFORNIA DECLARES MISCEGENATION LAWS UNCONSTITUTIONAL.

CRANE SHOT: An antique but shining Bentley car slowly drives through the crowd on the main dirt concourse between the stands, which are set up on both sides.

CUT TO DEEP FOCUS: The Rotting drives by slowly, to the left, slightly bouncing as it goes through a mud puddle. In background are a group of Capulet women in pastel dresses who move away from the car as it passes. Some brace themselves against the stand behind them—it is portable yet enormous and lavish. The stand resembles a permanent wooden building that's simply had two walls removed, complete with wooden floor, windows, a corner counter, and wooden stools. Foxtails and animal pelts hang from the ceiling and adorn the walls. The large metal sign in front reads CAPULET FURS AND CO.

CUT TO DEEP FOCUS: The Rotting car continues to slowly weave toward the right between fairgoers who duck out of the way as it splashes mud around. Directly across from the Capulet stand is a similarly large wooden stand with shelves of delicate honey jars of all sizes as well as a bee-based apothecary with various tin containers of lotions and potions. In front is the hexagonal crest of MIYAGAWA BEE FARMS. Two MIYAGAWAS sit behind the two counters and one sits next to the large beehive box in front.

The Elvis Presley music dissolves into the sound of wood clashing, which dominates.

CUT TO: A Skee-Ball target, which a ball crashes into and knocks off a few splinters before falling into a forty-point hole—whistling and cheering.

CUT TO: Loud wooden roller coaster with many passengers, shot from the front as they thunder down a slope.

ESTABLISHING SHOT: A little boy passes a bunch of mini colorful foil balloons on sticks as his mother follows, hand a few inches from his back. Wood sounds end,

no soundtrack apart from the bustle and
conversation of carnival-goers.

HIGH ANGLE SHOT: Back of Romeo's head as
he pushes his fedora forward to hide his
Asian American eyes and face. His black
hair peeks out the back.

EXTREME ZOOM OUT: Through one of the top
rungs of a Ferris Wheel, with a loud
startling metallic squeal. On the lower
right of the shot are TYBALT, CAPULET,
and a SERVINGMAN in a Ferris Wheel cart,
shot from above as they move back down
to earth. The squealing sounds are
quieter and are discovered to be from
the cart rocking back and forth.

INT. FAIR—FERRIS WHEEL. LATE AFTERNOON.

TIGHT ON: Capulet, Tybalt, and
Servingman's faces, upper bodies, and a
portion of the Ferris Wheel cart.
Capulet and Tybalt are wearing wrinkled
open blazers with casual trousers and
shoes. Servingman is wearing overalls.
All three have face paint on—aware of
their status as adults, they have opted
not for the full animal face paint, but
small details such as colorful tiger
stripes and fox muzzles. All are
slightly drunk. Camera naturally follows
the cart's subtle rocking motion as it
descends. Tybalt sits in the middle,
staring intensely at the lower left of
the frame.

                    TYBALT

This, by his dirty hair, should be a
Miyagawa.

PEGGY CHEN

LIVES: Cary, North Carolina

Peggy (she/her) is a fifteen-year-old writer from North Carolina. She loves traveling and river rafting and wants to share her love of licorice with the world.

MENTEE'S ANECDOTE:

Kylie has been an incredible mentor during our time at Girls Write Now—aside from doing tons of writing, we've spent pair sessions bonding over our love of screenplays, overanalyzing sitcoms, and debriefing highlights from my psychology class. Kylie's mentorship has definitely introduced me to more than just writing—we're currently planning a podcast together and I've gained much more perspective in terms of my future plans. My time with her has been so special, and I've learned so much from her about structuring a well-defined plot, establishing character through smaller moments, and correcting my chronic comma usage!

KYLIE HOLLOWAY

LIVES: Brooklyn, New York

Kylie (she/her) is a writer and producer at Ethic TV. Outside of her work, she enjoys comedy writing, traveling, and watching sitcoms.

MENTOR'S ANECDOTE:

I've loved getting to know Peggy better—from our first meeting, we've been able to connect over so much. We've spent countless meetings brainstorming story ideas, fleshing out character profiles, planning out plotlines, and learning more about each other. Although we haven't been able to meet in person, our Zoom meetings have always been a pick-me-up in the day. She's been able to develop a ten-page script for her podcast, learn the basics of audio editing, and expand her horizons to new forms of media—I can't wait to see what she will do next!

From the Ancient Diary of an Unwilling Globetrotter

PEGGY CHEN

> **SHANGQIU, CHINA, 1294: a year of new promises and renewed ambition, but life is far from perfect for Zhao. What happens when her worst dream comes true: traveling across the infamous Silk Road?**

The vendor pinched off rolls of greasy flour and dropped them, one by one, into the sizzling vat of sunflower oil. I watched the little rounds of dough bob up to the surface before being strained through a webbed spatula and dusted with powdered sugar.

I had just one dinar, and Monkey would probably end up eating more than half of my purchases. What would be something that could last? A plate of sweet, chewy *qatayef* wouldn't last long enough, and *zainab* fingers would smear my blouse with honey and powdered sugar; not worth the risk of a scolding.

Standing in front of what felt like an expansive sea of pastries, I was unable to choose what to buy with the shiny dinar in my quivering hand.

"Well, what do you want?" the vendor asked me, irritatedly. I had been blocking the entrance of his stand for five minutes, puzzling over the great dessert debacle that I faced.

I had never known how familiar the city felt. If I closed my eyes, I could almost hear the shouts and yells of my old school friends, skipping rope and chasing birds. I could feel the light breeze that promised a winter that was yet to come. I could smell the soothing, slightly salty aroma of baked bread that I had known since I was a child.

By now, my parents were long gone. Mom had no interest in childish ponderings of dessert choices, and Father must have run into an old friend, of sorts. In a bustling market of at least a thousand, I had not a single friend to lean on.

I must have uttered some sort of apology, but my unfamiliar dialect was understood by the vendor as an order. He scooped a flat disk of dough into a paper, before stretching out his fat hand for my dinar.

I did not want to give him my dinar for the small paper package, which was now blotted with oil. The stains on the brown butcher paper seemed to mock me, as if they knew. I unwillingly handed him the shiny coin, before grabbing the cake and darting into my parents' line of sight.

Once Father had finished greeting the "old friend" that he probably knew no better than the snack vendor, we prepared to leave the city once more.

The sun had long vanished behind the mountains, the air still warm, buzzing with the excitement of a day's worth of shopping. Mom told the stories behind the sales she had struck and deals she had bargained for, as if they were magnificent pirate adventures on the sea. I couldn't help but smile, as her eyes lit up at the ratty, discolored carpet square that she called "antique."

I sat alone in the back of the wagon, after Monkey had refused my company because I hadn't brought him his qatayef. For once, the night was silent, as I looked beyond the mountains that came ahead.

Why had they forced me to go on this trip? I hated the place. It wasn't like home—not the language, not the clothing, not even Monkey wanted anything to do with them.

Leaning back against the canvas walls, I heard a crackle of paper. It was the sad little oil-blotted package of the treat.

I bit into the sweet, made from hand-spun phyllo—a luxury. Inside, the soft, clotted cream was all melted, dripping down my wrist as I desperately licked at it.

It tasted disgusting.

But familiar. A little stinky, but also pungent. Just like the durian from home. I smiled as I took a bite, thinking of the vendor and his fat hands, the bickering shopkeepers.

It wasn't all that different from the weekend market at home. Yes, I could barely understand their dialect, and their shoes weren't the same material. But they had the same tired, haggard look in their eyes, as if this day in the market were one of thousands of memories they had yet to tell.

I took another bite, and by now Monkey had smelled the cake. He scampered over, and I felt obliged to provide him with a piece. We sat, side by side, staring into the unshapely mountains that reminded me of the bald poets I read about in school.

On nights like these, I chose to think of the vendors, and the shop-keepers, and the tired old women who occupied the market stalls along this road. I thought of their families, and their stories.

Did they feel the same way I did, as I looked into the distance? Did they also dread the long journey that lay before them, or did they revert to scrubbing the mud off their nightgowns?

The moon seemed to mock my questions, and I gave it a hard, jutting glare. I sighed, before heading back to our camp to wash the dirt off the soles of my hands and feet, for the third time that night.

ANNE CHRISTELLE CHERY

LIVES: Brooklyn, New York

Anne Chery is a student at Brooklyn College studying psychology. She loves music, speaks multiple languages, and is learning to love writing.

MENTEE'S ANECDOTE:

I grew up enjoying other people's writing, but I was scared of writing myself. However, since starting college and Girls Write Now, I've been encouraged to write and I found a like for writing. I've been enjoying working with my mentor this year. Our sessions have been great, as I have been challenging myself to improve my writing and discover new genres.

SAMANTHA MAX

LIVES: New York, New York

Samantha Max is a journalist who loves telling stories and finding the perfect words.

MENTOR'S ANECDOTE:

Anne and I have really enjoyed working together this year. We start each session with some free-writing, so that Anne has time to get her writing brain worked up. Then we workshop! It's been so exciting to see Anne experiment with her writing and lean in to her voice.

Check

ANNE CHRISTELLE CHERY

This poem is about my complicated love-hate relationship with worry.

I swing my legs over my bed
I have to get ready for the day.
I set out my bowl,
it's dirty.
I clean it.
Instant oatmeal isn't instant enough.
I look in the fridge, I think I'll just have yogurt today.
I wash my bowl again.
I contemplate but it'll just take too long to make,
1:20 on the microwave feels like an eternity
when you're late.
Instead
I eat a bowl of worry,
the edges of the w's and the pointy ends of the y's are sharp,
they are hard to chew and they upset my stomach.
The o's with their round shape should be easier to go down but they are
    stuck,
they don't want to move.
The r's rebel,
the curvy parts lodge in my throat and they threaten to climb back up.
Before I leave the house, I'll pack my umbrella in case it rains.
I have to wash up.
I tried to wash yesterday away, but it stained my skin. I can only try to
    hide it.
I do my hair,
and I can't help it but I put my worry on my face.

I put some light worry on my eyelids, and I carefully paint the worry
    on my lips,
I tie it all up by brushing some worry on the apples of my cheeks.
I get dressed in my worry and I wear worry on my feet.
Before I head out the door I check my list for my worry. Have I got my
    worry, check. Have I got my worry for the train, check. Have I got
    my worry for the store.
Surely, I need my worry before I head out the door.
Where's my worry for school . . . When I get to school I'm ill prepared.
    It was a sunny day.
How do I better prepare for this . . .
I know. I'll worry some more.

ROGERLINE CHRISTOPHER

LIVES: Brooklyn, New York

Rogerline (they/them) is a junior at John Jay College of Criminal Justice studying to become a therapist. They love collecting Squishmallows and torturing their stomach with spicy food.

MENTEE'S ANECDOTE:
India is a friend, editor, and mentor all wrapped up in one. I'm actually very shy and secretive with my work, but I doubt that was the impression India got from our first meeting. Opening up to her about my work comes easy. I'm always looking forward to every Zoom meeting because I'm certain I'll leave a better writer.

INDIA CHOQUETTE

LIVES: New York, New York

India Choquette (she/her) is an adjunct professor at City College of New York, where she teaches English composition. Her fiction has been published in journals such as *Foglifter*.

MENTOR'S ANECDOTE:
From our first meeting, I could tell that Lilura loves to write. In our Zoom boxes, we beam at each other from across boroughs because while I love to read their work, they love to create and share it. And it's not just about the pages (and they have pages and pages and pages)—it's about their endless fountain of ideas, their vivid and natural turns of phrase, and their excitement for the craft of writing. From the undead, to mother/daughter relationships, to luscious descriptions of food, to morphing portraits, their work is filled with imagination, soul, and hypnotic storytelling.

Prologue

ROGERLINE CHRISTOPHER

This is part of my prologue from my novel *Faust and the Bleeding Hearts*. It follows Faust trying to get back her mortality from Death themselves.

I'm a freed woman. That's what I thought in the carriage that was bringing me to my new home. A free woman stuck in a stuffy box that feels like it's going across the country when I'm moving one state over.

I remember being desperate for a bath. I spent a long time in that carriage gagging at my own scent. Of course I was looking forward to cuddling up against my lover, but not as much as I was looking forward to a bath. After that I'll have all the time in the world to count the scars along their face. When the carriage came to a stop I wanted to kick down the door and suck in a lungful of air. That's not what It likes. They want a docile and delicate woman.

I've never been free or a woman before, but I was off to a good start and I won't ruin it. Off my plantation and free from the shackles of slavery, I won't dare do anything to set me back.

I think I arrived a few moments before sunset. The manor looked like it didn't belong here, like it erupted from the earth rather than being built. It wasn't made out of wood like many manors and plantation houses were. It was a big house, with high walls made of stucco. The setting sun turned the white walls from a rich golden yellow to amber. Heavy came the night, and it dominated any of the remaining light.

At night the stucco walls are bone white. They look like they're glowing against the darkness. The manor looks like a beast who comes alive under moonlight. I sometimes still feel the wind cutting against my skin like that night; how it came out of nowhere and was icy cold; the lightning that struck the earth despite there being no clouds in the sky. There wasn't a storm brewing because it was already here. Beside me in the form of a person. Or what I thought was a person.

It took my hand and led me toward the beast I called Anthropophagus.

"Death and the Maiden." That was the painting that hung above the dual staircase in our home. It's the first thing I saw. It's a renaissance painting of a partially naked woman being held by a cloak of darkness in the shape of a person. They're in a field of flowers. The maiden appears to be aroused in death's hands. One of her breasts spills out of her dress. She's completely smitten by It.

The painting, much like the house, is alive. It changes when you blink, possibly melts off the walls while you look away. It changed each time I looked at it. It showed me both men and women as the maiden and sometimes a person who looked like they were neither gender.

I remember walking through the manor thinking of every way I'd decorate each empty room It showed me. How good it felt to be clean and in an *Emma* Victorian evening gown like I had always imagined. It's a lavish gown with off-the-shoulder bell sleeves and a lace-trimmed bodice. I was in a manor, I owned it, and now I look the part. I felt more powerful with each step, so powerful the house didn't dare creak or groan as I walked it. The power of now owning such a large house vanished upon looking at the painting again.

The painting this time was featuring my love, It. The painting captured all of my favorite details about them. Their massive hands and the acne scars on their face. There was a scar in the painting that I've never seen on their face before. One that traveled up the outline of their jaw to their ear. I never recognized the clothes they had on, but based on all the layered pieces of a white dress and the headdress made of flowers, it must have been a wedding dress of some sort.

That was them without a doubt, but who was standing over them? A tall man or woman with a face that almost seemed purposefully scribbled out with paint. Whoever they were, they had a hand on It's shoulder. It looked like a painful grip.

The more I stared at the painting the more I felt the fear in each brushstroke. The strokes cried out for help in the parts that were thick with texture. The feeling dropped off the canvas and coated the walls of my home. The horror on their face is embedded in my memory. Pupils turned to dots, tears glazing over in their eyes. And although they tried to smile, fear was plastered on their face.

MAYA COLLINS

LIVES: Glen Mills, Pennsylvania

Maya is a passionate writer and artist. She enjoys travel, bubble tea, and time with family.

MENTEE'S ANECDOTE:

During our first Pair Session, my mentor, Aekta, led me in an introductory exercise. She asked me to write down my greatest fear on a piece of paper. Then she told me to tear up the piece of paper and throw it away. She said with a smile that our fears are not what define us. Every time we meet, I am forced to set aside my fears and meet my authentic self. Aekta continually inspires me with her passion for her craft as we seek to understand the good, the bad, and all the beauty in between.

AEKTA KHUBCHANDANI

LIVES: New York, New York

Aekta is the founder of Poetry Plant Project, conducting month-long generative workshops. She graduated with an M.F.A. in creative writing from the New School.

MENTOR'S ANECDOTE:

Maya is a force of nature. She's courageous and kind. Her fierce energy comes through in her writing. She has a knack for expressing her feelings in both prose and poetry. I have witnessed a turn in her writing—she's more conscious of the craft of storytelling. She's learning new ways of weaving words together. She's mindful of the length of sentences, punctuation, and verb choices, and the story she's submitted here has a strong transition in its narrative arc. I'm proud of her journey, and grateful to be a part of it.

Bitter Berries

MAYA COLLINS

Content Warning: Suicide, Suicidal Ideation, Mental Illness, Self-Harm

This piece explores the impact of grief and disenchantment on the experience of growing up.

My dad liked to joke that just like him, I ate nothing but fruit as a kid. The tartness of lemon made me scrunch up my face with a smile. I was delighted by the tiny blueberries that lined the streets near my cousin's home in Southampton, convinced that the fairies had bejeweled the English countryside when they'd heard that I was visiting.

On family trips to Dad's childhood home in England, he and I were always on the lookout for berries lining the sidewalks. We are a family of five, but my mom, sister, and brother don't share our love for fruit. After long hikes or small wanders, Dad and I often returned with pockets full of berries and scratches on our hands, pricked by brambles and thorns. We knew it was all worth it to pop those delicious jewels into our mouths.

Simple and sweet-tasting days came and went. In the years before our move from California to Pennsylvania, I began to sense that my family was not as happy as we'd once seemed. I spent many nights lying awake in bed, listening carefully to hushed conversations in the next room. Muffled words didn't make much sense to me, but my sister's sobs were hard to forget. I knew what it was to cry one's eyes out and I hated to sit and listen.

A secret was being kept from me, something everyone else knew. It made me feel stupid; it made me feel cut off from my family. My mom shared scraps of the story. She told us about a history of mental illness.

She told us that my dad's sister had killed herself. She told us about uncles and aunts living with depression or anxiety.

But it wasn't enough. Never quite understanding where my grief came from and why, it left a permanent stain on my heart. I indulged myself in tears. They tasted like those berries—the ones that made me bleed.

It wasn't until my sister sat me down to talk one night that I began to understand. She'd been waiting until I was older. She revealed that she had something called bipolar disorder. It meant that at times she would be extremely happy, happier than normal people could be. Other times she would become quite sad. It was a chemical imbalance in her brain; she didn't have much control over her emotions. She had frequent nightmares and scarier hallucinations but was seeing a therapist and a psychiatrist to get better. She asked if I had any questions. I didn't. I already knew she was bipolar. That was a lie, but it made me feel a semblance of control—less stupid.

From then on, certain lived experiences began to make more sense. That time I'd sat reading in our living room and was disrupted by the sound of bloodcurdling screams—I now understood that my sister had an episode. I refrained from asking her any questions because doing so would've made me feel small; it was better to pretend I understood things.

———

Snow covers our new home in Pennsylvania. I'm the only child still living at home. I breathe in the stale air, watching the moon glow outside my bedroom window. I creep inside my bathroom, close the door, and turn out the lights. My head is filled with a sour, sickening blackness.

I am shaky and hollow as the memory of my sister screaming stings my eyes. I still feel like my ten-year-old self—that little girl who wondered how to comfort her raging sister. I wonder now if everything was somehow my fault. Could I have been kinder to my sister? Might she have resisted the urge to overdose?

I look through the bathroom cabinet for my razor. Striking its edge against my skin, crimson red slips out. It reminds me of raspberries. I am still searching for jewels left by fairies, only now I find them hidden just beneath my skin. What looks pretty to my awe-filled eyes is complicated. It leaves scars.

What is this bitter and nauseating sweetness? It feels like a force apart from me—like a sad poem or a sweet song. Its echo holds a power to inhabit me. This is the bitter taste of lemon, the dark stain of pomegranate. Sitting beneath the sink with a bloody razor beside me, I recall the times I stuffed myself with too many berries. When those succulent jewels consumed me. When too many brambles made my small arms bleed. The gusting winds over barren English moors and vacant skies—how small they made me feel. How small I still feel. I can almost feel the prick of the brambles. I can nearly hear my sister's screams from the other side of the door. I can almost taste my tears.

LILIANA COLON

LIVES: Brooklyn, New York

Liliana Colon is a musician, writer, and artist. She attends Clark University in Massachusetts. She was a finalist for the My Simple Realization essay contest.

MENTEE'S ANECDOTE:

Vera is one of the kindest, warmest, and most inspiring people I have met. I am so beyond thankful to have had the opportunity to work with her these past two years. When I first joined Girls Write Now I was in need of guidance, and Vera has provided me with the best advice and encouragement that I could have ever asked for. She is constantly sending me creative opportunities to publish my work, and she has given me so much confidence to put my work out into the world. I could not be more happy for the work we have done together!

VERA SIROTA

LIVES: Hoboken, New Jersey

Vera Sirota is a poet. She is a 2022 Martha Award finalist. She is a cofounder of the West of Willow poetry and music collective.

MENTOR'S ANECDOTE:

Liliana carries a swallow's tune inside her soul. She has pursued performance opportunities on campus and enrolled in a poetry course. We've delved into Girls Write Now workshops and designed her website. Liliana's melody grows stronger each day. She inspires us both to keep soaring toward our creative dreams. We cannot imagine life without such daily inspiration. I am thankful to be on this journey with her!

The Patient Daughter

LILIANA COLON

We all carry many pieces of our identity with us
every day. This piece examines a core part of myself
and the role that I have been given in this life.

To be a patient daughter is to listen
with intention,
To say less and to hear more.
To take a deep breath . . .
Inhale
when the fear of time gets too overwhelming
Exhale.
Patient daughters feel anxious about unknown
futures,
An anxiety that rises and cannot be tamed by reassuring phrases.
To be a patient daughter is to love flavorful food,
To feel your stomach growl and hear it reverberate around the room,
To take the time to breathe in the rich smell of garlic and onion mixed
    together.
Patient daughters relish in the taste of the flavors of every piece of food
    they eat,
letting the unique taste melt on their tongue.
See the patient daughter, as she dances with her mother,
Loud music blaring through the apartment.
Hear the drum her father plays,
whose steady beat guides her feet,
Whose patient rhythm shapes her life.
Watch the patient daughter as a young child
Her face molded in concentration
As she reads with eager eyes
And anxiously skips to the end of her book,

Unable to leave anything to mystery.
See the patient daughter as she looks with patient eyes
At the world around her,
But has no patience for herself,
No grace for herself,
No place for herself,
No space for herself.

RENISHA CONNER

LIVES: Arverne, New York

Renisha is an undergraduate at Brooklyn College pursuing a B.F.A. in creative writing. She enjoys volunteering, dancing, and expressing herself through poetry and fiction.

MENTEE'S ANECDOTE:

Stacie has been nothing short of amazing to work with! I'm so grateful to have a mentor like her because, from the moment we met, she made me feel welcome and comfortable. Since she's an O.G. in the writing game, I appreciate her input and correction when it comes to my writing. She's always eager to help and is super-supportive. I always look forward to our meetings because we always have a great time working on pieces and bouncing ideas off of each other. I've learned so much from her and I'm so grateful we met.

STACIE ROSE

LIVES: Rutherford, New Jersey

Stacie Rose is a singer/songwriter, mother, TV producer, health coach, speaker, and published writer. She cultivates content about wellness, family, fitness, mindfulness, and intentional living.

MENTOR'S ANECDOTE:

Renisha is a smart, sweet, creative writer with the warmest smile. When we met, she said she wanted to take more chances with her writing and to self-edit less and let things flow. I thought this might imply a timidness or lack of confidence. I've come to find that she's a force of nature with her own wonderfully witty ideas. She searches for the perfect words, never content until a piece feels just right. She voices her ideas beautifully and is a joy to collaborate with. I feel I have seen her work bloom in the short time we've known each other.

To Be a Princess

RENISHA CONNER

I never realized that my dream of becoming a princess was fulfilled long before I was born.

Every little girl has a dream of becoming a princess.
Out of the 12 of them, I've experienced being 6.

I used to be Snow White.
Cuz in Genesis, through Eve, I was tricked into eating that
poison fruit and became a slave to my flesh.
Living a life of destruction, but my true love came to kiss me with
    salvation
Raising me from the dead into freedom
Seating me right beside Him.

Before my Prince Charming, I was Ariel
Wishing I could be a part of a world that actually had nothing
    for me
nothing I needed.
I wanted to be part of something that accepted me, valued me, and
    gave me worth.
Until I realized that searching for wholeness in a broken world would
    leave me empty,
So I ran to the One who was already pursuing me.
The One who accepted me, valued me, and revealed my worth.

I no longer want to be Cinderella.
Mistreated by the evil stepmother of sin,
tormented by the stepsisters of condemnation and shame.
I want to go to the ball, where I dance the night away

with my King
and rather than leaving my heart on those steps when that clock
    strikes 12,
I want to reveal to Him,
The rags that are hidden within

Oh wait, let me be real,
I may or may not have actually ran away.
The magic of that cover-up made my vision blurry and
Left me in delusion
Like "Yeah everything's cool, everything's fine"
Leaving me stuck with a false conclusion.

I was scared
Scared to show the rags of what was truly beneath
The gold that did not glitter.
But He knew where to find me.
He picked up my heart and replaced it with a better one.

When I showed Him my rags, He gave me riches.
When I showed Him my brokenness, He gave me
    wholeness.
When I questioned my existence, He comforted me,
When Jeremiah 1–5 with 29 and 11 sang hymns to me.

He didn't leave me the way He found me.
And even in this journey He never does.
'Cause I'm on a road to perfection
He gave me redirection
Not yet my final destination
But I am His beautiful creation
Here to proclaim to the nations
The goodness of who He is

Now I'm like Tiana, who's almost there in transforming
into the woman my Father and King has called me to be.
Trying to open the restaurant of my heart to feast on
the Truth so I can serve the people around me
in love.

He called me by name.
He took my heart made of ice when I channeled my
inner Elsa because the cold never bothered me
as I got used to having a wall up anyway.
And yet, only my King was able to defrost the layers of my heart with
    His Love.

I resisted it at some point in time.
But I can't deny, I want to be Merida.
Brave enough to stand up for what I know is right.
Fierce enough to completely step into my calling.
Rebel enough to be different in a world that tries its best to conform
    me. I won't do it.

Who would have thought I would have been married before 21?
Divorced from the enemy, I am bound no longer.
Married to Jesus, I will only get stronger.
'Cause Greater is He that lives in me
I am no longer subject to who I used to be.
He is Holy and Righteous and His blood made a way
For His grace and mercy to enter
And it's here to stay.

So yes, I was made a princess.
By the *precious* blood of the Lamb.
He came down from on High
It was His great plan.
To save me from my sins.
To wipe my slate clean,

To give me a new name
I am married to the King.

That dream of becoming a princess as a little girl?
I'm so glad that I know it's true.
'Cause now I'm the daughter of the Almighty King
No longer satisfied with a world I outgrew

Thank you, Jesus

MAYA CRUZ

LIVES: New York, New York

Maya Cruz is a New York City–born-and-raised daughter, sister, and student. She loves any and all art!

MENTEE'S ANECDOTE:
I believe there's nothing more valuable than interacting with someone that makes you feel like you wield a unique power. Meredith is one of those people in my life. She helps me plant seeds of ideas, and she helps me tend to them. More than anything, she helps me have confidence; I'm so lucky to be encouraged and supported by her for a second year at Girls Write Now. The impact of her help will last for as long as I write!

MEREDITH WESTGATE

LIVES: Brooklyn, New York

Meredith is the author of the novel *The Shimmering State*. She is originally from Lancaster, Pennsylvania. She loves dogs, sea otters, and pistachio ice cream.

MENTOR'S ANECDOTE:
Working with Maya over the past two years, I've watched her already-brilliant writing grow even stronger. It has been thrilling to see her editorial eye sharpen, too. It will never cease to amaze and inspire me how fully Maya dives into our freewrites and then emerges with something tender, human, and brimming with beautiful language. As someone who frequently gets stuck on works-in-progress, I've learned so much from Maya. I am trying to channel some of her energy myself!

The House

MAYA CRUZ

Spaces have personality; spaces can be unkind.

January 3, 1983

I finally understood. I was held just so; I struggled to breathe in the grip of the walls. Soft hands turned to fists: Something beat down on me, corralled, and gave it to me all in a single blow. The house's various voices crept closer; before I could feel them in the room, I was being deafened by some choir of chants. It eclipsed the crickets and the clock, the mumble of the tele, the dripping of the water in the sink—everything was drowned out except for this one grotesque understanding. They sang it to me over and over, layered in dissonance and harmony; nothing intelligible, yet all-consuming.

I wasn't built for this. Weakness overcame me and I was pulled in. I never wanted to be touched again, and there I was, throwing myself at the floor; I felt betrayed by gravity, but more so, by my own body. I've found the most disgusting line of symmetry. I'm always giving what is asked. Here I am. Pierce me with splinters and touch me all over with your wooden skin that had to be killed to be created. Fuck you, *and yet, there I was.*

Weighed down or pulled in, what difference does it make? It asked me to fall and I did because there was nothing else I could have done. I couldn't get up.

Silence. The guttural choir choked and for a moment, I was truly alone.

This is one of those moments where I wished I could float away, and I kind of did.

Body on the rug, eyes unset, I was taken elsewhere.

The van careened into the driveway out front, the once-distant struc-ture appearing monstrously large. Ivy coated the exterior, dense at the bottom perimeter, trickling up as if fighting gravity to just barely kiss the roof. Sun ricocheted from the glass, the bell, the cross.

"Why are we at church?" Yvette asked, her little hand softly jabbing into her mother's shoulder, voice tinged with disappointment.

"Don't let the house fool you," her mother said. "It might look like a church, but inside, it has rooms with beds and a kitchen." She turned to Yvette to poke her back.

"No Mass?" Yvette said through giggles.

"I promise, no Mass. Never in the house, at least," her mother re-plied, still smiling.

━━━━━━

The church house was described by previous inhabitants as breathtak-ing, alluring, and tempting. Being that these were previous inhabitants, it can safely be said that they'd all given in; they'd worded it in a strange manner, comparable to the way some men describe beautiful women, as if the estate begged to be lived on as an inch of skin called to be touched. The white paint, despite being many tens of years old, was still pristine. The stained glass was beautifully intricate, nearly lurid, as it was sur-rounded by a forest of ashy birch trees. In fact, the surroundings seemed nearly colorless. The church had a garish intensity to it, drawing one's eye from all else to its arched door. One would find that when the tar-nished knob was grabbed and twisted, they'd be rewarded by a wooden interior, aglow with warmth; this would soon ignite the Crane family through a comfort they didn't know they'd lost in the cold, crisp white of their previous house.

Caesar, after opening the car doors to let the kids out, turned to his wife.

"Do not ask again," she said, sharpened by intent and softened with disappointment. When he asked her questions she didn't like, her inhales became slow stabs: sharp in and softly out, paining him more each time she sighed.

"No, I think I will," he said as his eyes found hers, locking. She broke away and pulled her key from the van's ignition. "Are you ready." He paused. "Or are you sure you can do this? As far as I know, you could be, like, crumbling inside right now, and it's never too late to find a way out of—"

"Can you stop, please? Be a husband. Be a dad." In response, he tilted his head, mouth opened slightly in a way that said *You're joking*. She continued, "Don't give me that. It's not the church I grew up with. Apparently the inside is unrecognizable. Looks like a house," she said, the zipper of her coat speaking over her momentarily. Caesar killed the engine. She stopped her rustling, and, for a moment, the van went silent. "We know there's nothing else we can do. This is what we have. We have to work with what we have. I'm okay," she said, looking back at him. She then stepped over the threshold that stood between the van door and the grayness outside.

"Lord, protect my Bella," he muttered to himself. He rubbed his weary eyes as her tracks in the snow moved farther away from him.

JILLIAN DANESHWAR

LIVES: Bellerose, New York

Jillian is a junior in high school who has a passion and dedication to writing and robotics. She has accumulated numerous awards in both fields.

MENTEE'S ANECDOTE:

My writing was a block of marble. I sculpted until it formed a figure, yet I stopped as the fear of ruining it lingered. My writing would be just fine alone, but with Marisa's assistance, it shone. I was encouraged to polish my pieces and show the world. Soon, I was no longer fearful to be heard.

MARISA SIEGEL

LIVES: Evanston, Illinois

Marisa Siegel is the author of *Fixed Stars* (Burrow Press, 2022). She lives in Evanston, Illinois, and you'll find her online at marisasiegel.com.

MENTOR'S ANECDOTE:

This is my second year working with Jillian, and it remains a privilege to spend time with her each week. Regardless of the specific assignment, Jillian brings her poetic sensibilities to her writing and packs her prose with inspired sonic resonances that help push her stories forward. I'm always excited to see how she'll interpret a prompt and where she'll take it.

Kill Them with Laughter, Kill Me with Peanuts

JILLIAN DANESHWAR

Allergies make you vulnerable. In my case, more mentally than physically, despite the physical severity a peanut poses. The piece below takes the reader inside my mind as I fear for my life.

He told me before the show, "Beware of where you sit, you might get exposed."

He told me before the show, "If the slightest thing feels off, let me know."

He told me before the show, "Don't touch your eyes, ears, mouth, or nose."

As the words wafted into my mind, I followed suit behind. Each presentiment my father spoke inscribed itself over the bone that entombs my brain. Autopilot kept my expression engaged. It was indeterminable from my face that I was not in the same plane. The circus tent and austere lights faded into a stasis state of twilight.

Abruptly, awfully, a peanut could end my life. A trace, a crumb, a flake, could replace my lungs with blades to cut the circulation to my fragile frame. My metal train refused to refrain. What place had more of a risk of contact than a circus, where the nut is the most iconic snack? I felt a weight on my back. If my spine did not, my mind would crack. It might have fractured. My eyes were backward. I forced them to face front.

Oh look, there's an elephant.

I fought to stay present. The clown got soaked in rain, and I wondered if they were in pain behind their painted face. I wondered if that made me a clown. I suppose I was funny every now and then. People certainly thought so when they found out a nut could be my end, joking it'd be fun to use an EpiPen. Not to me, but I laughed anyway. I put on my red nose and big shoes and entertained.

Oh look, there's me onstage.

Reality was cloaked in an imaginative haze that was impenetrable by the strength of my partial-present gaze. Transfixed by trepidation, I watched my distant figure dance. It touched what it shouldn't have. My brown hand began to fringe with blue. The clown was trying to perform through, but ultimately asphyxiated. Anxiety marked my time of death, yet I survived.

This isn't real. This isn't real.

I fought to reattach to reality. My ears strained to comprehend the cacophony of voices and vibrations. My eyes struggled to regain focus, or anything acutely adjacent. If life was a party, I was in the bathroom. Completely consumed, yet distant. Hidden away, too afraid to risk it. Staying safe and alive only desensitized the threat to die.

A tap tore me out of my mind. The show was over, I realized. My father asked me how I was. I claimed I was "fine." However, the side of my right thumb revealed my lie, as newly raw skin made contact with oxygen. Under the other was a little packet of wet wipes that was absent-mindedly folded in on itself multiple times. Compactified, comparable with my corpse. Muscles tensed, with a crushing inward force.

The lights rose and crowds crammed the doors. I lifted my baggage and stood from my seat. Although I made it out alive, I hung my head in defeat.

DOM DAWES

LIVES: St.Albans, New York

Dom Dawes is a nineteen-year-old sophomore at Hunter College. He has been writing fiction, poetry, and nonfiction since 2015. He is also a cat enthusiast.

MENTEE'S ANECDOTE:

Forsyth has encouraged me to write without intention—to write freely and see what happens. I further explored this in my creative writing class, where I mentioned Girls Write Now. My professor was impressed I was a member!

FORSYTH HARMON

LIVES: Accord, New York

Forsyth Harmon is the author and illustrator of *Justine*. She is also the illustrator of *Girlhood* by Melissa Febos.

MENTOR'S ANECDOTE:

Meeting and writing with Dom has been a highlight for me over these past almost two years. I'm so impressed with his ability as a writer, and also his attitude. I feel like he is so much more sophisticated than I was at his age. He is so talented, and I look forward to reading more of his work.

Adult Adolescent in Limbo

DOM DAWES

Shortly after their admittance to the NYU Langone hospital for what began as unexplained dizziness, Dom turns eighteen, and they are confronted by reality cloaked in black fur.

A knock woke me from sleep. Sitting up in bed, I let out a tired "Come in."

In walked a lady wearing purple scrubs, the uniform for NYU Langone nurses. From the sound of the wailing baby down the hall, this was the pediatric floor. As much as I loved to tell people I'd be eighteen in a few days, it didn't change the fact that I was still in an adolescent body.

"Hello," she said. "I'm here to take your blood." She felt familiar, but, paired with the stress of classes and graduation, I couldn't differentiate faces and voices with masks. This hospital stay would either make me miss graduation in two weeks or massively mess up my incomplete salutatorian speech.

Rather than focus on hypotheticals, I asked a "reasonable" question. "How many times a day will you all be drawing my blood?" At the previous hospital, they drew blood before sending me here under the assumption I was having a stroke. At this hospital, they did the same this morning, and now they wanted more.

Though recent doctors' visits had erased my fear of needles, they had not erased my iron deficiency. I didn't want fainting from it to extend my visit. "We'll be drawing it twice a day to track your blood count, iron levels, and your reaction to steroids." I nodded as my thoughts drifted.

Did I mention on Saturday they placed me on steroids? No? Well, steroids are a part of my treatment for the chronic disease attacking my nerve cells called multiple sclerosis. I've had it since freshman year, and it went undiagnosed.

What I needed to ask was the crucial question I'd been dying to have answered since entering the ambulance four days before, yet I kept forgetting. "Can my cat be brought here?"

Her cheeks plumped under her mask in a smile as she closed a vial of my dark red blood. I knew it was silly, but my fluffy friend was probably starving at home. He usually ate three times a day. Papas kept me from being lonely with his cute snores and adorable ears. I got him following a psychiatric visit for what I now know is depression because COVID-19 prevented in-person interactions with human friends.

"No, there are patients with allergies, and there's the issue of your cat using the bathroom." I . . . hadn't thought that far ahead.

I hummed in understanding. I raised my head as a lightbulb illuminated. "So, he can't stay in here with pee pads? I'll change them twice a day. He's also too scared of others to leave the room, so you don't have to worry about him roaming the halls."

She laughed as she shook her head. "The morning nurse assigned to you is allergic—" How allergic? "Severely allergic," she added.

"Sorry, that was a silly question." She shook her head as she removed the needle from my forearm. "No. You've been to a few hospitals this week, so I understand you're missing him." Her empathy alleviated my anxiety, so my usual humor returned. "It would've been funny to see him spooked by the doctors and nurses walking in. He'd hide." She chuckled.

We began discussing my diagnosis, because I was confused after having gone down a rabbit hole of articles related to my symptoms, ultimately leading to my hypothesis: I have relapsing-remitting multiple sclerosis—possibly.

My first flare-up lasted for weeks and went untreated, then eventually, three years later, it flared up again. However, the main difference was this more recent flare-up was visible to doctors, so they couldn't pin my physical illness on mental illness. My hypothesis was valid, considering I fit a few of the symptom criteria. So far, the symptoms I noticed were numbness, problems with balance and coordination, and vision problems.

The issue with my hypothesis was it usually started in those twenty or older, but my first flare-up happened when I was fifteen. "Do I have relapsing-remitting MS?"

"You do. Dr. Krupp told you yesterday. You must've forgotten." Oh. Memory loss was another symptom.

She left, and I fell asleep.

I awoke to the sound of munching. My mother caved and returned to the hospital after I pleaded to stay alone once diagnosed because I'm almost an adult.

"I brought you food. It's on the table beside you." I nodded as I reached over and grabbed the paper bag. Inside was a salad and a pastry, perfect for a vegetarian.

Almost—adults need help, too.

YARALEE DE LA CRUZ

LIVES: Bronx, New York

Yaralee is an eighteen-year-old senior in high school majoring in art. She's going to college to become a screenwriter, director, and producer.

MENTEE'S ANECDOTE:

I was partnered with Lisa last year and I think this year we were stronger than ever. Last year we focused on improving my writing skills, but this year we focused more on improving myself as a person. I had a lot on my plate this time around because of all my college applications and schoolwork, which caused a lot of stress and a loss of passion in the things I love. Lisa taught me how to focus more on bettering my mental health and how to use writing as a stress reliever. Without Lisa I would have gone crazy.

LISA Y. GARIBAY

LIVES: Los Angeles, California

Lisa is a public relations/communications manager at the Division of Physical Sciences.

MENTOR'S ANECDOTE:

Given her passion for film, writing, and exploring new ways of sharing her voice, being paired with Yaralee has been like looking into a mirror—that is, if eighteen-year-old me were as confident, expressive, and bold as Yaralee is. When I learned of her passion for screenwriting, I felt like the luckiest mentor in the world to help lead her on her journey toward bringing out her passion more, more, more! Her imagination, voice, and stories are rich and real. The big screen sorely needs them.

Summer of 1977

YARALEE DE LA CRUZ

Summer is usually a time of glee and adventure, but the summer of 1977 in New York was a time of chaos and despair.

In July of 1977, the Bronx became a ghost town. The building that once felt tall fell to its misery. The streets were covered in rubble and orange sandlike dust. It was like the Great Migration all over again, but this time there was less hope and more despair in the people's eyes.

Back in June there was *esperanza* for better tomorrows. The schools and libraries, sanctuaries for the young blood, were boarded up and knocked down 'cause the Man from the street with walls of green and greed thought his desires were above the future. Spirits were high. People were liaising with community and music. The borough was buzzing with merengue and the birth of hip-hop. Bodegas, churches, and clubs were untouched and that's all that mattered.

Come July, the people lost their way. A black hole consumed the entire city. From the island called Manhattan all the way to the Boogie Down Bronx the evil era *tan fuerte* it killed. The city was pitch black! Our eyes played tricks on us. Couldn't tell what was shadow or a brotha tryna get home to his wife and kids. Couldn't tell what was road, what was street. *Clang Clang* The cars went crashing against one another like cymbals. Animosity filled the air. *Bang Bang* Hands sounded like congas as they went flying left and right, often missing as they are not nocturnal.

The light went back on on the island 'cause the Man got backups and importance. The light went back on in the Bronx too. It was hot, sizzling, and filled with power. The children went wild and the people were desperate. They lost hope. They lost their rhyme. Landlords lit flames to their property for the luxury of insurance money.

Cling Boom The youngins destroyed everything in sight. They banged up cars, broke into stores, busted open fire hydrants, you name it! Those cheeky slimy bastards fell prey to the evil and went along laughing as they did its bidding. *The scraping sound a *güira* makes* The people were consumed with greed. They had this rage in their eyes that was *tan feo*. They became monsters of the night. They ransacked the stores that glued the community together. Looted houses too. They were unrecognizable.

Clang Bang Cling Boom The chaos and horror that painted the streets with ruckus and blood. The chaos made a symphony of jazz and old-school ragtime that murdered the joy that came with salsa and tortured our ears. The evil turned us into the savages the Man told us we ought to be. *Ha Ha Ha* He goes as he finds entertainment in our suffering like we're a zoo for exotic life. We became lost, abandoned, and hopeless.

In June we had *esperanza*. She guided us out of the black hole we ran to when we discovered hardships. She was our savior and we needed her the most. That summer your *tíos* Don and Leo got jobs working at Clara's old man's barber shop that's now a McDonald's, sweeping and counting dollars. The Perez's oldest daughter, Isaura, was the first to get married rich since Abby Castillo back in the fifties. Our friend Ricky, who had passed that July, got caught up with the Black Spades, who spent most of their time creating hip-hop and rapping to the fine young thangs. And your mama, Mari, and I got stuck babysitting the neighborhood kids that didn't fall to gang pressure after the Man shut down their schools.

After the invasion of that evil, the Bronx, our home, felt stranger to us. The community fell apart. Many had no homes from the fire. Others lost their businesses after the lootings and riots. The immigrants that brought life to the borough lost everything that gave them purpose and an ounce of the American dream. We lost faith in one another. There was no trust, just streets flooded in disgust, guilt, and *vergüenza*. In August, we packed what survived and fled south to Florida. The Bronx had gone to shit. We were devastated to leave the only home we knew, but our hands were tied. *Esperanza* saw that we were dead and revived us. She guided us to a new beginning, better tomorrows, and gave us new blessings.

We grew old in Florida, but longed for the Bronx. Every summer we go back to replay all the memories we made. Pointing at all the places where we laughed, cried, danced. Places all long gone and replaced with highways and drive-throughs. Yet, the memories still stand. We remember the good, the bad, and the ugly things that made us strong and prepared for the future, as it's always unpredictable. At the time, I hated the Bronx for letting us down and forcing us to leave it behind. Now that I'm near eighty, I forgive it for the heartbreaks and take pride in its love. I will never forget the New York blackout of 1977.

PAOLA DOMINGUEZ

LIVES: New York, New York

Paola Dominguez is a junior from New York City who spends time playing the electric guitar and imitating the sounds of her favorite bands.

MENTEE'S ANECDOTE:

Throughout the process of writing this piece, I received a lot of good feedback from my mentor. Together, we take turns reading through the poem multiple times aloud and search for places to improve. I would ask for their opinion on certain things and loved having a different point of view. From there, I was able to decide what was best for the poem as a whole. I felt supported all throughout the process and enjoyed everything about working with my mentor.

KY LOHRENZ

LIVES: Brooklyn, New York

Ky Lohrenz is a marketing assistant at the Academy of American Poets. Their poetry has appeared in *Peach Mag* and *Ghost City Review*, among other publications.

MENTOR'S ANECDOTE:

Paola is an incredibly smart and ambitious writer who sees the world with such an insightful, individual perspective that inspires me to see things with fresh eyes. From the beginning, Paola has brought joy and ambition to every project we work on, and her genuine passion for writing and craft is evident. On top of her writing talent, she has incredible taste in music and I'm always excited to hear what new songs and albums she's been listening to that week. I look forward to seeing what great things Paola has in store for the future!

Wake Up for Me

PAOLA DOMINGUEZ

Sometimes we as people become so consumed in the mundane tasks of life that we forget to notice the small, beautiful things that constantly surround us.

Wake up
Raindrops hit the floor
Now again
Wake up
The slam of the door
Get up
Now look at you follow through

Get up
Without knowing for who
Get up
No choice but to

Repeat
Repeat until you forget
Forget you're alive
Forget you exist
Repeat

Get up!

You are so much more
Wake up
Tell me you're listening
Did you hear?
The creak of the wooden boards?

The flapping of the birds?
The drip of the faucet?

Wake up
There is so much more
Listen to me
Hear my words
Wake up

Do you feel the warmth of the sun
As I do?
Feel the whisper of cold into this dark night?
Do you hope to whisper back?
Tell me you feel it too

Wake up
Please can't you see
The stillness
Between you and me
Stay
Stay with me
Wake up!

FREDA DONG

LIVES: Brooklyn, New York

Freda Dong (she/her) is a high school junior who loves astronomy, playing puzzle games, and writing poetry.

MENTEE'S ANECDOTE:

This is Jen and my second year as a mentor/mentee pair, and I've been thoroughly enjoying it! Jen helps me improve a lot as a writer. She encourages me when I have writer's block and is really understanding when I'm busy. She also gives me lots of life advice outside of writing! There was one session when we went out for coffee and then browsed a bookstore, and I feel like I really got to learn more about Jen as a person. Thank you, Jen, for all your support!

JEN STRAUS

LIVES: Brooklyn, New York

Jen Straus lives in Brooklyn and is at work on her first novel. Her current writing focuses on disability, ableism, and identity.

MENTOR'S ANECDOTE:

This is my fourth year with Girls Write Now but my first time working with a mentee for multiple years, and it's been wonderful to see our relationship deepen from the foundation we established in our first year together. Without a doubt, the highlight so far has been meeting Freda in person for the first time since we began working together virtually in the fall of 2021. I'm proud and honored to watch her grow as a writer and person!

Swinging into Cycles at Sunset Park

FREDA DONG

Inspired by my experiences in a park I've been going to since childhood.

Orange flames in a sky of hot pink dawn,
The fiery sun sets at the time of dusk.
Try to convince yourself you can see stars
In the light-filled dark of Sunset Park.

The fiery sun sets at the time of dusk,
But you can still hear the children and elders
In the light-filled dark of Sunset Park,
Playing and dancing to Chinese songs.

You can still hear the children and elders
Enjoy their time together under the moon,
Playing and dancing to Chinese songs,
While you sit on the swing, contemplating.

Enjoy your time alone under the moon,
Living the same loop every day.
While you sit on the swing, contemplating,
Convincing Earth to reveal the answers.

Living the same loop every day,
Lying to yourself that you can see stars.
Earth refuses to reveal the answers as
Orange flames dance in the hot pink dusk.

ILANA DRAKE

LIVES: New York, New York

Ilana Drake is a sophomore at Vanderbilt University, and she is a student activist and writer (https://ilanadrake.wixsite.com /mysite/projects).

MENTEE'S ANECDOTE:
When I met Annie a few months ago over Zoom, I knew she was destined to be in my life. Over virtual meetings, we have talked about philosophy, grandparents, and the best poems we have read. I love writing with Annie and hearing her words, which are written so elegantly in just a few minutes. Annie inspires me every day, and I greatly admire her curiosity, kindness, and resilience.

ANNIE PROCTOR

LIVES: New York, New York

Annie Proctor is a chronically ill baker, songwriter, and public relations copywriter at DeVries Global. She is constantly looking for new ways to make art.

MENTOR'S ANECDOTE:
I was absolutely thrilled to be paired with Ilana last year and have loved being her mentor. Ilana is a thoughtful, reflective, and compassionate writer who always looks to make others feel better about themselves and the world we live in. A talented writer, her work always leaves her audience with something to think about. In our sessions together, we use our life experiences to fuel poetry and discuss how writing can help us inspire, process, and inform.

from here, my mountain lakes, changed

ILANA DRAKE

This poem focuses on my relationship to my grandparents' hometown, Mountain Lakes, New Jersey.
Throughout the poem, there is a theme of my grandparents aging and how this impacts my relationship
to their town.

five days against the
breeze of cars rushing down
the small tunnel, the only
tunnel which exists in
this small town, a
dot only a few know
shaded in by the green leaves

woods that continue for
miles, woods my grandmother
and i have walked through,
branches on the ground due
to the rushed winter because
of the changing climate,
buds that come because
of the five a.m. sun, the
sun that stays alive throughout
the summer

i learned what it was
like to be present as

i watched lacrosse games
and saw the lifeguards come
to island beach for the start
of the two months i craved

i learned what it was
like to be present,
to be at a home that
was not your "home,"
a town held by invisible
gates and white fences
which signaled codes
to outsiders

this is the town that
watched me grow up as
i ran miles to the top of
the boulevard when
my best friend attended
prom with her boyfriend
and i decided not to go

on that run, i saw the
egrets perched above the
brick walls guarding
the lake below like it
was their castle and they
were soldiers ready to march,
ready to fight for what they had

my best friend took
the train into the
nearest station and
i greeted her from the
back seat of the convertible,
us together after months
of worrying about the
virus, a virus which started
in our city

that night my grandparents
took us to dinner and i
recorded some of their words
about relationships, about time,
about this new adulthood we were
growing into

this was a time when my grandfather
could stand and when his words came
out as eloquently as the opera singers he
loved to hear at lincoln center when he was
younger, when age was just a number,
when he would push me on the swings
on island beach

a year and a half later, i ran
to the swings on this beach,
hoping my legs could
get my body higher up
to touch the trees which
have lost their color

the view has changed as
my world becomes less
like a canvas filled with
neon orange, ocean blue
, and bubbly pink
because my world is
less of this beach where
there are no waves
save those created by the
boats on the dock when
they are taken out
but my world is an ocean
which does not reach
land.

SALMA ELHANDAOUI

LIVES: Brooklyn, New York

Salma is a senior in high school and is a creative writer, photographer, and contemporary literature analyst with a significant interest in human behavior.

MENTEE'S ANECDOTE:

It's no surprise that Ashley and I can talk forever if given the chance. Every meeting is layered with intriguing topics, allowing us to expand our points of view. Throughout the year, we have shared our film recommendations and discussed many films and songs. I would call this "The Incredible Never-Ending Journey" because of how much we have learned from each other through our fun chats. One day we could be reading lyrics to "See You Again," while another we might talk about music bands we enjoy listening to. Every meeting is unpredictable and a true joy to attend.

ASHLEY ALBERT

LIVES: Brooklyn, New York

Ashley Albert holds an M.F.A. in fiction writing from Hunter College and has worked in trade book publishing for more than eight years.

MENTOR'S ANECDOTE:

When Salma has TV and movie recommendations, I know she is onto something powerful. Pun intended! Our discussions about Korean thrillers and TV dramas this year have been a natural tangent from our obsession last year with the Stanford Prison Experiment and Salma's piece about an intergalactic war and a fascist AI regime. We love to find connections across history, psychology, and art, especially those related to inequity, injustice, and crime.

Power Hungry

SALMA ELHANDAOUI

Imbalances of power drive various interpersonal interactions and can lead to extreme consequences, which are often explored in television. Social inequality is an example of how power disparities can have drastic effects on whole communities.

PERSPECTIVE #1

Brutal Reflection: Unhealed Scars

(Inspired by the television drama The Glory*)*

The sky is darkened with rebellious veins,
But I'm as fragile as a shattered drop of rain,
For I'm nothing but a mere glass of pouring pain.
My heart is drowning in yearning that makes me insane,
Yet I'm stranded alone in an ocean of eternal blame.

Walking into a school of high ethical standards and prestige,
I thought the students knew what fairness and equality meant with grace,
But I was shocked by their fervent ignorance and repulsive craze,
As they strangled my neck and cooked my pale skin with their
    burning gaze,
Because I'm impoverished inside and out with no person asking about
    my daily state.

My face has been struck with metallic rage;
My legs are painted with a scarry cage;

And my scorched arms are concealed with outrage,
But my heart was shot with hurtful insults from wealthy students with
no morals,
And I'm still imprisoned in a lonely ocean with no escape.

Even when I told the principal and teachers about my continuous
suffering, they simply ignored my pleas for help because I'm not
from an elite family, while obligating me to drop out of school with
my parentless history of shame, but what can I do except to accept
this abuse, bullying, and unfairness from children of this elite world?

A small hurt girl sits in my burning heart.
I want to see those who invaded my personal space and weak body beg
for forgiveness, and to know that the netherworld is awaiting their
filthy souls to arrive within God's realm, so their body and mind
shine with regret and repentance for their unpunished crimes, and
to water my burning heart with golden lights of hope.

PERSPECTIVE #2

Irresistible Lies

(Inspired by the television drama Anna*)*

It all started with a lie,
A lie that annihilated my soul from existence,
A lie that absorbed my filthy blood,
A lie that killed my dear father,
A lie that locked me in prison,
A lie that destroyed my entire worthless life,
A lie I will truly never forget,
A lie that framed my identity completely and took my body away.

Maybe it was my wrong conscience,
Or maybe it was my horrible perceptions,
Or maybe it was my impoverished circumstances,
Or maybe it was my terrible personality,
But I know for a fact that this lie turned me into a monster,

A monster that craves immense wealth and power,
A monster that deceives my close ones with unthinkable consequences,
A monster with a poker face and no emotions,
A monster that escalated its power all the way to the top.

Coming from an extremely poor family
That only owns a small grocery store
With my mother in a coma,
And my father approaching his death,
I had no choice but to lie.
But to lie to their face and tell them I got accepted into Hanyang
    Women's University,
That I'm a cosmetology major with a full scholarship,
That I'm living happily and healthily as ever,
That I'm going to travel to Paris to learn French,
But they were all lies.
Nothing that came out of my mouth was the truth.

Not only did I work for a chaebol family to earn filthy money,
I also slept in a nearby park because I didn't have a home.
I followed the young daughter's orders while she looked down on me,
And I cooked, cleaned the rooms, and constantly kneeled on my feet,
But I couldn't live like this anymore.
I couldn't live with the aristocracy controlling my mind, body, and
    actions,
I couldn't live as a poor girl who needed pity and small coins,
So I chose to follow a master plan I've been working on for the past five
    years,
And stole all the money I found in the "Grand Money" box owned by
    this ridiculously rich family.
I stole all of the money I could find in the corners of their home and the
    spoiled daughter's passport and resume,
And had plastic surgery to borrow her lavish face.
I stole her identity to change my life in reverse.

My greedy self became hungry for power and attention,
So I changed my name to Alice as she was named since birth to
    become a clone of her.

With my high social status and flawless credentials,
I ended up marrying a billionaire who owns a top tech company,
I ended up tricking all the people around me with my cheap yet
    profound deceptions,
I ended up eating golden food to match my petite body,
And I ended up in a bloody mess as I killed my supposed husband and
    his parents.

It all started with a lie,
A lie that drowned me in an endless loop of regret,
A lie that I will never forget,
A lie that will haunt me forever,
A lie that will send me to the netherworld,
And punish me for my horrible sins.

I shall never be forgiven.

ALLISON ELLIOTT

LIVES: Brooklyn, New York

Allison Elliott is an eighteen-year-old currently studying political science. Always looking to uplift diversity wherever she goes, her work reflects those goals.

MENTEE'S ANECDOTE:

Molly has been a lifeline that I didn't know I needed. She is able to walk the fine line of pushing me out of my comfort zones without pressuring me to make decisions I'm unsure about. Since working and writing with her, I have been able to truly hone my creativity and put my mind to work in ways I never did before. Meeting her was a blessing and I look forward to all of the future work we may do together. She's funny, smart, and really good at finding all the silly mistakes I've missed!

MOLLY SCHWARTZ

LIVES: Brooklyn, New York

Molly Schwartz is a journalist and radio producer at WNYC. She's usually listening to a podcast and dreaming about dumplings.

MENTOR'S ANECDOTE:

Allison is always drawing inspiration from the world around her. She'll peruse TikTok and make Pinterest boards into the wee hours of the morning, gathering ideas for her stories and immersing herself in the lives of the characters she creates. One night she sent a text excitedly proclaiming she'd found a building on Google Maps that will be the setting for a café in her novel. She loves to adventure with friends and rewatch *Bullet Train* (partly to draw inspiration from the fight scenes). When she's telling a particularly good anecdote, sometimes she'll slip into her delightful Jamaican accent.

Its Carnival

ALLISON ELLIOTT

The colors, sights, and sounds of Carnival have long been a favorite of Samantha's. West Indians take over Brooklyn for the Labor Day weekend, and make their presence known.

When her alarm sounded, the sun had yet to break the darkness of night. Samantha dragged herself out of bed and became aware of the soca music already blasting through her house. Despite its recurrence every year, her heart always awaited the arrival of Carnival. Today was Labor Day and she was finally going to play Mas again. Her walls were adorned with past headpieces from both the main and kiddie carnival.

A few hours later, Samantha and her family members were fully decked out. They all had on their costumes for their band. The theme this year was "Jewels of the Islands," having each section in rich jewel tones and plenty of bedazzling. Samantha had on a two-piece composed of sparkly turquoise material that had gems strategically placed throughout. Her mother helped decorate her box braids with various charms the night before and her makeup had been done to match her costume. She looked over at herself in the mirror; the headpiece and backpack were too large to wear indoors, but she could already imagine the completed look.

As they traveled to Eastern Parkway, the location of the West Indian Day Parade, it became clearer and clearer that everyone in the city intended to go. Samantha could not contain her smile. All around her, colors danced and the music boomed through her chest. She eyed different flags representing the entire Caribbean bobbing in the crowds and colorful costumes dancing alongside them. Her eyes caught an oversized Jamaican flag waving above the crowd.

After registering with their band, Samantha and her family members joined everyone else and completed their costumes. She did a few spins with her full costume on; the headpiece and backpack increased her wingspan as the feathers gently caught the wind. The parkway was nothing less than packed as their band joined the procession at the beginning. Ahead of them, they could see the remnants of J'ouvert celebrators, who had been going since the night before. They danced along the road covered in brightly colored paint or oil with their signature horns and chains. Her eyes continued to scan the processions, spotting a few heads that towered far above the crowds sporting Trinidadian flags.

Her heart was filled with nothing but joy as she danced alongside her band; Machel Montano's voice sounded out through the speakers over the crowds. Her costume jumped in the air with each movement she did, the sunlight reflecting off the gems on her outfit. The other masqueraders continued to play and dance in her midst; together they formed an amazing color-filled spectacle. Despite their attempts to remain "on duty," she spied many of the cops who accompanied them with bright smiles on their faces, dancing alongside them and having their own flags tied onto their uniforms.

Samantha finally pulled out her phone while dancing, capturing a short video of herself singing along to Beenie Man while also showing the rest of the parade. Flags and feathers bobbed all around her and she could only assume what the background sounded like as the soca already beat into her heart. Light on her feet, she continued to dance as she posted it to her social media and returned to the moment.

Farther down the parkway, Samantha almost missed their calls. Eventually, the fervent waving of a group of people caught her attention. When she looked their way, her smile widened. It was her friends. Each one of them had their own outfits on, making clear which countries they hailed from. She eyed Grenada, Barbados, and Haiti. Unable to stop for long, she did another grand spin as they recorded and cheered her on, the feathers bouncing around her.

Over the next few hours, Samantha continued to dance her way down the parkway. She watched as other people danced with each other. No parade-goer, including Samantha, could resist the powerful hold of the music, and the joy around them was nothing but infectious. She had also spied a few Caribbean performers atop trucks, singing their most popular hits and enjoying the parade.

When they finally reached the end of the parade route, Samantha's body began to realize how much exercise she had been doing. After capturing a few photos of her costume, she retrieved a large Jamaican flag from her father's bag, tying it around her shoulders. She handed off her headpiece and backpack to her aunt, then sought out her friends.

"Sam!" Samantha turned to the origin of the sound. Her friends waved her over and they exchanged hugs. She could hear the playing of steel pans, knowing a group must have passed earlier. Together, they danced down Flatbush Avenue, picking up food and goods from the vendors who lined the streets. She found herself losing track of time once again as they all enjoyed themselves. Samantha only realized it had become night when the blinding NYPD lights switched on at every corner. Soon they reached the end of the procession, and she rejoined her family members. Carnival was over for this year.

Samantha couldn't wait for next year.

JANA ELSAYED

LIVES: Brooklyn, New York

Jana (she/her) is a freshman at Baruch College majoring in international business. She is also double minoring in marketing and French.

MENTEE'S ANECDOTE:

My second year with Danielle as my mentor has been amazing! She has been supportive and helpful with everything I do, whether it's small accomplishments or life-changing decisions, and I know I always have her in my corner. I have learned so much from her. Her guidance and devotion, no matter what, make me have immense admiration and fondness for her! She has become someone in my life that I know I can go to for anything, even if I just need her to lend an ear!

DANIELLE SCHLANGER

LIVES: Brooklyn, New York

Danielle is a communications consultant and speechwriter who lives in Brooklyn, New York. She has been a Girls Write Now mentor for four years.

MENTOR'S ANECDOTE:

Working with Jana for the past two years has been an absolute pleasure. She is diligent in her schoolwork, dedicated to her many clubs and activities, and determined to make society better for others. I learn from Jana in every session; her thought-provoking questions challenge me, and her thoughtful insights help me reconsider what I thought I knew.

I am very proud of Jana's success during her first year of college, making balancing school, work, service projects, and Girls Write Now look easy. Jana's future is incredibly bright and I feel privileged to continue to watch her take on the world!

Love's Sacrifice

JANA ELSAYED

Most people know their boundaries when it comes to love. I'm still trying to figure out mine.

What would you do for love? That seems to be a loaded question. I've always been the type that would do anything for love. Or so I liked to think I would, but in reality, maybe I never had the chance to do so. Maybe I have never actually been in love, even though it might have felt like it at the moment. Maybe it was some semblance of *puppy love*, even though that term seems to belittle my own feelings I've had in previous relationships. Or maybe it was all just hormones—the intense feeling of oxytocin that rushed into my body—whenever I was around this specific person.

But now that question stares me in the face. As I am completely enveloped in the rush of oxytocin, *puppy love*, or whatever this thing may be, I have to question what I would do to hold on to this. Or, rather, what do normal *healthy* people do in a situation like this? So, what would you do for love? Would you kill for love? Would you be the devil's mistress? Would you be with someone who has proven to you multiple times they have the potential to hurt you? Would you stand on the edge for love? Would you cheat for love? Would you say "screw you" to your morals for love? To be with the person you wanted before they showed you how bad they can get.

I don't know what I'd do for love when I find the person that I believe I'm supposed to be with in this world. When I find someone that matches me so well, whose company I can never get enough of. Someone that makes me feel good and understands me. When I find someone I can't get enough of and I can't let go. Would I neglect all those promises I made to my young self years ago? Never betray yourself for someone else. Never hurt others for your happiness. Never lose a piece of yourself for anyone.

How bad can this love be if it makes me feel so good? Would you sell your soul for love? Would you bury another body for love? What love is worth all the pain when there can be another to come? But what if this is the great love that everyone talks about? What if it's finally come for me and I'll never find anything like it again?

What would *I* do for love?

NAOMI EYRE

LIVES: New York, New York

Naomi Eyre (she/her) is a college senior with a love of poetry, film, photography, psychology, mochi, book shopping, ice cream, bubble tea, and fashion!

MENTEE'S ANECDOTE:

Despite Tracy having years' worth of knowledge in writing and editing, she approaches our meetings with generous amounts of humility, professionalism, and thoughtfulness. She always puts effort into planning the curriculum, from the exercises we do to sending me motivational articles that encourage me to write, and her willingness to learn more about the fields of writing that I enjoy is remarkable. It's special to know that our values and writing goals align. This enables us to feed off each other and have authentic conversations that are not limited to the topic of writing but the scope of life. Tracy has been amazing!

TRACY MORIN

LIVES: Oxford, Mississippi

Tracy Morin is an award-winning writer and editor with twenty years of experience working in magazines. Her creative work encompasses personal essays and memoir, fiction, and photography.

MENTOR'S ANECDOTE:

From our first meeting, I was struck by Naomi's incredible work ethic, sensitivity to the world around her, maturity, and willingness to learn. She is wise beyond her years and demonstrates a level of perseverance and dedication that wows me. She's also multitalented, with a range of passions both within and outside of writing, from screenwriting and poetry to photography and psychology. I always come away from our meetings feeling rejuvenated and inspired. Plus, she's really fun to talk to! I know she is going to make an indelible mark on the world as her life path unfolds.

Uncoordinated Silhouettes

NAOMI EYRE

Sometimes individuals wish to be blinded by reflection, distraught by a truth from their childhood. This poem explores the duality of recollection and humanizes each perspective.

I am
jealous
of the energy
thatallowsyoutojuggleyourproblems
upon the brink of an iceberg.

How is it so
that you turn black ice into
ice rinks?
Skating upon the icy hearts of people until they

crack

Yet, you never fell through.

I stare at a photo of you. Oh, how
ANNOYING
those *glasses* look
   slipping
      off your nose
anduncoordinatedcolorsplasteredonyourclothes.
Arms decorated with bruises from the
concrete you fell on.
You were always the
clumsy one.

But you wiped the dust off your arms,
letting the bruise
blister and bleed.
Never felt the sting until playtime ended.
But you never had *regrets*
and didn't mind the burns of rubbing alcohol
for every bruise a bad memory inscribed
in your skin.

So,
you painted butterflies on your face for every good
memory
to remind yourself that it's a balance—
because you couldn't keep time upon your tiny
shoulders.

Too *large* for a keepsake.

So, you gallantly smile at the camera
as chicken bits snuck in between the gaps.
"Myteetharegrowing,"
you manage to say without choking on another tooth.
"A Happy Meal and a visit from the tooth fairy."
Your parents admire your *simplistic joy.*

Wait—
how do you possess the ability to savor the conversations,
    withoutlettingAIRslipbetweenyourtongue—a fickle one—engulfed
    in the sweet and sour
sauce you dipped your chicken nuggets in, that
savory ginger.
Carefree mind, but the eyes are never empty.
Merrily exploring the soul of the person in front of you,
the cat that
meows
incessantly for your attention,
and the *emotionless toys*
always receive the luxury of sleeping in your bed unlike

the *tarnishing coins* that gathered dust in an
abandoned corner of your
pillow.

Yet, somehow you slowly became disinterested in our dates—in US.
When your shadow escaped my *silhouette*
it was a relief for you.

It frightened me.

You became the host of someone else
and ended my life chapter
when our truths didn't align.

You gnash your teeth when I greedily obsess over liquid greens.
How righteous are you for not forgetting the kindness of natural
    greens
yet you're the little prick
who's selfish with your eye contact
because you're afraid I might steal a piece of your soul.
So
CURSED are your eyes that cannot see—

Bitter melon images
a past full of regrets
too many failed scrimmages
and pathetic stubborn happiness that blinds
you from the future, our fate.

A void that lived
Saudade, *"the love that remains."*
Until nostalgia is appealing
because I won't tell you that I am lonely.
Too big of an ego to admit that I hate
how you enjoy being alone—
Because your imagination was never the missing link.
The frisky mind that never allowed you to be bored.
For you couldn't even focus on a single thought.

So, how could sadness be the
concentrated one?

I guess you'll never understand the sense of l'appel du vide,
how it latches on to you
like an unnecessary pouch of
STINK
that'll engulf you till you're mad.

So, sitting here beside this photograph
made me realize that we don't reflect each other.

I'm still trying to reclaim the spark
that already glistens in your eyes
while mine blisters.

FELECIA B. FACEY

LIVES: New York, New York

Felecia is a high school senior pursuing both her high school diploma and associate's degree at Bard High School Early College Queens.

MENTEE'S ANECDOTE:
Working with Caroline has been a great experience. She has been one of my biggest cheerleaders. Applying to college was intimidating, and one of my biggest obstacles was the personal essay. She provided lots of support to help me reach the finish line with my applications. We also do fun prompts that lead to short narratives that I'm proud of. Her feedback and mentorship allowed me to improve as a student and writer. She often gushes over me, but I am in awe of her and her way with words.

CAROLINE SHIFKE

LIVES: New York, New York

Caroline Shifke is a writer and M.F.A. candidate in fiction at The New School. She writes essays about chronic illness and stories for young adults.

MENTOR'S ANECDOTE:
What a joy it has been to work with Felecia this year! Felecia is such a bright, thoughtful, kind young woman, and it has been a true pleasure to watch her grow into her beautiful and unique voice. Her talents are too many to count! From poetry, to prose, to exquisite drawings and paintings, Felecia has an incredible way of bringing her perspective to life. And she keeps me laughing throughout! I am so excited to see what next year has in store for her—I know she's going to take the world by storm!

Two Shores

FELECIA B. FACEY

Being an immigrant can feel like you're abandoning your roots. When you're younger, the new environment makes you feel like a sponge, impressionable. I'm learning to branch out and find home in my loved ones.

There's a song, "I Am I Said" by Jamaican Reggae artist Mikey Spice, that goes:

I'm a Jamaican boy, born and raised.
Nowadays, I am lost between two shores
L.A.'s fine, but it ain't home
New York is home,
but it ain't mine no more

When I was younger, reggae songs were something groovy to rock to at family gatherings, with a plate of rice and peas with oxtail not far out of reach, something to be annoyed at when my mother would play the stereo on a Saturday or Sunday morning signaling a cleaning day. I pay more attention to these lyrics now as they resonate with my feelings about being a young immigrant.

My complicated relationship with Jamaica has been bittersweet. Sweet like the mangoes on my aunty Marlene's tree. Bitter like the aloe vera she would use to make green tea. In the process of adapting to my new environment, losing the ties to what made Jamaica feel like home is not the fear; it's the goal. I once had a thick Jamaican accent that made me feel proud of my culture until it became something that invoked embarrassment. In elementary school, I would stop and restart my sentences to ensure that my accent wasn't on display. The very thing I tried to hide became the thing I regretted losing, a tangible reminder of my roots. Hibiscus flowers rooted in my grandparents' front yard, hot summer days spent by the river with corned beef sandwiches and a homemade suck-suck (bag juice), Bible studies in Sunday school and morning devotion in the red dirt schoolyard, moonshine that lights up the entire night sky have all become a distant faded memory.

My mom, Marine, works from 8 a.m. to 6 p.m. as a nanny, then goes on the night shift as a baby nurse from 8 p.m. to 6 a.m. If she remembers nothing else, she will remember her work schedule and the babies she has worked with over the years. The way she hustles embodies the spirit of the women in Jamaica's marketplaces, who are always on the move. She made life possible for me in America while keeping her Jamaican roots alive, whether in the music she listens to, the good-tasting food she cooks, or how she carries the hard-learned life lessons with her. Having people belittle her and take advantage of her naivety as an immigrant led her to internalize the belief that nothing good and worthwhile comes easy. I hope she will not only see her dreams become a reality, but also enjoy that reality for as long as she has worked to make it real.

Aunty Marlene and I have a funny sense of humor with each other. My mom often says "Mi nuh biznizz wid uno," meaning she doesn't care about how we go at each other's throats because she knows we will be laughing and joking together in the next few moments. I always look forward to the "back in the day" stories she tells of all sorts of mischief and shenanigans. With sayings like "Wa sweet nanny goat a go run dem belly," which means that what seems fine now can have consequences later on. Or "One, one coco full basket," which means things will happen slowly but surely; success doesn't come overnight. The impact lies in her hilarious delivery. These funny stories and sayings capture the essence of what it means to be Jamaican. I hope to grow and remain as bold and colorful as her and that she continues to live life the same way despite the setbacks that make life seem gray.

Before I had a U.S. passport, my aunty Shelly preached about education like it was the passport to a bright future. When I used to go to school in Jamaica, she never hesitated to get involved in my schooling. She would suddenly give spelling bees at home when I misbehaved or seemed to be having too much fun. When she went as far as sitting in the back of the classroom, I would stand at attention like a soldier. The school system and curriculum structure may have changed, but she laid the foundation for why I'm dedicated to my studies. She helped me realize that no matter where I was going, having my head on my shoulders would help me survive in the violent streets of Jamaica . . . and now far beyond those streets. May her passion for education continue to spread like a wildflower through the community.

If I hopped in the booth for an "I Am I Said" remix, my lyrics would go:

New York is fine, but it ain't home
Jamaica is home, but it ain't mine no more

These women, who have prayed for me, cried for me, and laughed with me, inspire me daily. One minute we're reminiscing over fading memories, and the next we are creating new ones, choosing laughter over tears. I've learned to keep on keeping on, love my culture, and take on life by enjoying the "one, one coco" that will one day fill my basket.

SUZETTE FALCON

LIVES: New York, New York

Suzette (she/her) is a high school senior with a passion for cross-country and all things coffee-related.

MENTEE'S ANECDOTE:

Jennifer Liu has been the greatest mentor and a compassionate friend when it comes to reading and writing. We have worked together in the Girls Write Now program through the school year and have gotten to know each other well. I enjoy spending time with Jennifer, sharing book recommendations, and analyzing characters from all sorts of media. In addition, I love her passion for all things fantasy-related!

JENNIFER LIU

LIVES: Flushing, New York

Jennifer (she/her) is a writer and dog-lover with a deep love for the fantasy genre.

MENTOR'S ANECDOTE:

Suzette is a creative mentee and eager learner with ambitious goals to create more works of writing in the future. Through the Girls Write Now program, we have been able to get to know each other and discuss fantasy-themed worlds of all kinds. I've enjoyed being able to get to know each other and share our deep experiences together.

Empowering

SUZETTE FALCON

Content Warning: Self-Harm, Violence, Depression, Suicidal Ideation

These six poems show that although we internalize our own experiences, we deserve to have our emotions and experiences acknowledged and become empowered by them.

Tunnel Vision

Being only able to focus on one particular object or to limit yourself to a single objective/goal hinders your point of view.

No exit in sight and trapped in a box of your own demise.

The need to survive and thrive yet holding back because everything else is covered in pitch black. Limiting yourself to past experiences because getting hurt is almost too much to bear and no longer a risk you are willing to take.

Almost ending it all and seeking self-destruction because you can't handle that big wave of raw emotion threatening to drown you in doom. Having to fight against the current despite no beacon of light because your story cannot end here. Having to float because swimming is a foreign concept and you've been in survival mode for too long.

Crying yourself to sleep and every waking moment wishing you could sleep forever. Feeling like you've wasted your youth on nothingness and feeling inadequate to live with the peers around you.

Admitting you feel there is no way out, and having to distinguish faint
    whispers of encouragement from the yelling voices of self-criticism
    and hate.

Ultimately, being stuck in a tunnel of faint light.

Steel Armor

Swords and weapons are forged from fire
The strongest swords have survived the hottest fires
You built stable armor that others can't get in a lifetime
Each wound is a story of survival and grace
You learn to take risks, not to fear falling or failing

The looks of proudness are what make everything worth it
Knowing that nothing is stable, you realize it might hurt to rebuild
    again
But you have experienced building
Wood and *hammer* are no foreign concept
They are woven into you like the blessing of a soul

Humans are not genetically made to be satisfied
So maybe your obstacles have stopped you from searching for
    something you would never be able to get
Whatever it is, you can say you've walked the hottest fires and live to
    tell the tale

Hidden

The native tongues of my language get muddied
Echoes of car engines, flashing of lights, a flapping singular flag
I twist and turn my tongue trying to conform to the normal
Distinct words make their way toward me at rapid-fire pace
None of which I may understand
I badger on to the people hoping for a clue
Till I find my way

Of What Was Once Mine

I prance around wearing a mask
I tie the silk ribbon firmly in place
Each mask has been delicately crafted
My favorite of which contains precious minerals
The song of my people and land
Each curve and dip has been made to suit
The face of which once was mine

Ready to Unite

We stare into the glass of what once was
shards of insecurity and disciplinary etching themselves into bone-
    deep aches
Because it will never be enough for one to frolic in the rise of dawn or
    allow oneself peace of war
Because one must always be war-ready as they strap their boots on,
    ready for incoming fire
Even when standing in the presence of serene nature we are always
    ready, a finger barely above the trigger waiting for the command

We all remember the stories of our brothers and sisters
Of flesh and blood morphing into spirit as we live but never forget
As we try to carry on a part of us and them
We wave our flags trying to show we exist
Despite the constant fire they are sent up into
Precious cloth set ablaze

So I weave the fabric of time
For one day I can hope
For one day I can show
For one day I can fly and see the world with new eyes

Hiding

We ought to be seen
We ought to be heard

Yet I have ignored
I have tried to bury myself alive
The dirt covering my hand-sewn clothes
Air being squeezed from the soft of flesh

No longer can I ignore the cries or whistles
I live my truth and walk my journey
I unveil the inner me and show the world
I won't be molded to its ideals

STARASIA FOSTER

LIVES: Bronx, New York

Starasia Foster is eighteen years old. She loves learning new things, writing, picnics, Coney Island, doing hair, and music. She lives in the Bronx.

MENTEE'S ANECDOTE:

Samantha is really kind. She listens. She gives great advice. Samantha is like a bee, helping pollinate the flowers. She helps them bloom. She is very patient and understanding. There were times I was supposed to submit drafts of my essay but didn't meet the deadline, and Samantha was always very nice about it.

SAMANTHA STOREY

LIVES: Brooklyn, New York

Samantha Storey was born in New York City and raised in London. Now she lives in Brooklyn. She loves reading, writing, cooking, and running.

MENTOR'S ANECDOTE:

I love working with Starasia because she inspires me. She works hard and has interesting ideas about the world and unique ways to describe it. She has a great voice in her writing and I can't wait to read more of her work.

Did You Find Out Something New Today?

STARASIA FOSTER

Content Warning: Graphic Depictions of Slavery, Incest, Violence

Discovering some truths about history that are not in our history books.

Imagine being captive, everything you have ever known ripped away from you. Everything is stolen: you, your family, your name, your culture. EVERYTHING.

Imagine being shipped on a boat, like animals. Being treated like nothing. Imagine having to smell dead flesh because you are packed under a boat like a can of sardines, and of course they don't bother to remove the deceased. Imagine being forced to have incestuous relations with your sister and brother, cousins, and more. Imagine hearing your loved ones scream—in fear, in pain—for help but you can't do anything about it because you might be harmed even worse, or killed.

Imagine being on a boat naked, chained up, sitting in your and other people's feces, urine, and vomit. Imagine the mental state of these people. Imagine working day in and day out only to make nothing. Imagine that after giving birth to your child, instead of resting and healing you will have to go right back into the field and work. Imagine the boat you are on stops at a port and some of your friends, your family, are sold far away from where you will be sold. Imagine feeling like your only escape is jumping in the water and drowning yourself.

Just imagine. Crazy, right?

But it's true. This is the history of African American people. I wasn't taught any of this in school, and I want people to know it—to be educated about this history, because it shouldn't be pushed under the rug. There is so much information hidden from us. There is so much we don't know. Every day more comes out about what happened, and each new piece of information learned is more shocking than the last. More hurtful. If I can teach even one person about this history, it will make my heart smile. It will set this history free.

Do you know who Sarah Baartman is? It's okay if you don't; I'll tell you. Sarah was a woman from Camdeboo, South Africa. Of course, her real name was not Sarah. Unfortunately, her real name is unknown. Sarah was a Khoekhoe woman born in 1789. She lost both of her parents at a young age. When her husband was killed, Sarah was sold into slavery to a trader named Pieter Willem Cesars. She was exhibited as a freak show in nineteenth-century Europe because of her large buttocks. Sarah became the object of sexual intrigue and desire by many men in Europe. Allegedly, Sarah signed a contract to participate in these shows. But Sarah didn't speak English, or know how to read or write. Could she really have given consent to what was done to her? Sarah died on December 29, 1815.

"Fun" fact: Sarah's deceased body was put on display in Paris for more than one hundred years. It was finally returned to her home country of South Africa in 2002. "Fun" fact: people brought their children to see Sarah in the freak show. Disgusting.

Did you know that slaves called New Year's Day "Heartbreak Day"? For them, the day was marked by separation. During the winter months, enslavers needed more money, and so it was common for them to rent or even sell slaves at the start of the new year. Many slave families waited, scared and anxious, on New Year's Eve, fearing that they or their family member would be sold and taken from them. Many times, they wouldn't see them again for years, or even a lifetime.

Do you know who Mary Turner is? Mary Turner was a Black woman in her early twenties who had two children, was eight months pregnant with her third, and was married to her husband, a man named Hazel Sadly, Hazel was hanged by a lynch mob in the South. They let his body rot and hang off the trees for days, for everyone to see. Mary wanted to know who did this to her husband. She said that if she knew who did it, she'd warn everyone about who was involved. When the mob found out about what she said, they became furious. They put a bounty on her head. Unfortunately, they were able to catch Mary, and dragged her to a tree. They tied her ankles together and hung her upside down from a tree branch. Then, the men ran to their cars to get gasoline, and roasted her alive. When they saw her naked, eight-months-pregnant stomach, one man took a knife and sliced open her stomach so that the baby fell out of the womb and gave two cries. Someone from the mob stepped forward and smashed the child's head into the red Georgia dirt with the heel of his boot.

Too many Black people.

You've at least once seen braids? But do your history. Many enslaved women and girls would create braid patterns on slaves' heads to help them escape. These braids were really detailed and done neatly. They would also weave grains of rice into the braids so that the slave would have something to eat while on the run.

Speaking of hair, for some reason, slave owners would use slave hair as cotton, which I don't understand because they had the luxury of *real* cotton. Instead, they cut off the beautiful hair of enslaved women and girls and stuffed it into their chairs.

Their lives, their identity, their husbands, their children, even their hair—everything pulled from the root, taken away from them and smashed to pieces. Everything was taken away from them, nothing returned. I think of Sarah and Mary. I think of braided hair, and hair stuffed in chairs, and I feel angry that no one taught us about this. I am angry that my ancestors weren't given a voice. The only way we can find out their stories is through the words of their masters. It's frustrating. We know certain things were hidden, and we know the way it was told was altered, made to be less terrible, when in reality it was so much worse. How many stories are untold? How many more Sarahs and Marys existed?

Did you learn something new today?

ALYSSA FOWLER

LIVES: New York, New York

Alyssa (she/her) is a high school senior who has a profound love for writing. At Girls Write Now, she is learning how to harness it.

MENTEE'S ANECDOTE:
Working with Nora has been a delight. She is my missing half, finishing my sentences. Together, we have tackled towering college applications and have explored creative writing. Nora has taught me how to communicate my thoughts on paper. I look forward to what we will continue to do together.

NORA WALLS

LIVES: Brooklyn, New York

Nora Walls is a Brooklyn-based writer. She studied creative writing at the University of Virginia and is pursuing a master's in professional writing at NYU.

MENTOR'S ANECDOTE:
It has been so much fun getting to work with Alyssa on this piece. She is great at conjuring up vivid images and crafting her pieces carefully to convey them to her readers (in this case, she started with the image of the man with the wings and built the entire piece from there). We both love thinking about details, down to each and every word, so we spent time reading this piece line by line together, making a lot of small edits that come together to create a powerful set of poems.

Idol

ALYSSA FOWLER

Content Warning: Suicide

Breaking News! A well-known member of the community, Gabriel, has been involved in a fatality. Reports say that he died by his own hand.

Anecdotal 1

Your presence was a melody
That us mere mortals doted on
Soaring above the skies
Higher than we could hope to reach
Your face and blessed name
Held in the greatest glory
Yet you never gained an ego
Your pride, the size of a pea
And you continued to fly with those stainless white wings
Sacrificed doves upon your body

Anecdotal 2

It was as if the feathers gravitated toward him and shaped themselves
    into wings
The tip stuck out with prominence while the lower half tucked in
If you ever saw him flying
It was always his color that could be seen
Because among the dismal gray clouds, his pearly white gleamed

Gleaming in the sky, he was the image of hope
Alone in this world with nowhere to go
He ran to heaven's gates and pled his sorrowful case
To be blessed
As he was
Clean heart
I seek

Gabriel's Truth

*We are all mere mortals, beings born to live in pain. We search for an
unobtainable joy and run ourselves ragged, trying to be the exception.
But in the end, there is only . . .*

Death is on my mind as I close my eyes and
Dream of the doors I will be able to cross
Without the weight of the world on my back

Some would say they are my better half
With the color of pearls
Awe followed me close
But their hopeful stares loitered

How does a heart as weak as my own
Hold up their hopeful expectations
How do I soar to great heights
Knowing little, innocent eyes, watch me

Their votes of confidence have manifested into chains
Each day they rust
Under the glaring light

Chains

They tugged at me
The scathing imprint on my back

Chains

Are what killed me

Now my wings lay in a velvet box
I watch them from the corner of my eyes as I lay on the other side,
Withering away

I was never fit to hold up God's gift
I should have stayed on the land
Instead of running up to the skies

I cried
A thousand more tears by soaring

ISABELLA GEORGE

LIVES: Leland, Illinois

Isabella (she/her) is a high school junior with a love of writing and reading who hopes to publish a novel someday.

MENTEE'S ANECDOTE:

Christine is always there with her feedback and support. If I'm worried about a particular creative liberty or direction I took with a piece, she is quick to assure me and give me feedback about the quality of that piece. When we meet, I have a fun time going through pieces and writing processes with her. She's amazing and truly an inspiration to me. She inspires me to write more consistently, and I've become a better writer because of it. Christine is the loveliest mentor I could ever ask for, and I'm grateful that I'm able to work with her.

CHRISTINE MOORE

LIVES: Hoboken, New Jersey

Christine (she/her) works in marketing for an online professional community and spends her free time reading, writing, and with friends and family.

MENTOR'S ANECDOTE:

Reading Isabella's work is a true joy for me. I get so excited when she shares a new piece, and even have a (somewhat strange) habit of "saving" them to read at the end of a long workday or week as a treat and an escape from the corporate world. I love hearing about her process for writing pieces and what has inspired her, and her plans for future writing. I feel transported when I read her stories and poems, and I'm constantly amazed at both the wisdom in her words and the beauty of what she shares.

rewind

ISABELLA GEORGE

Content Warning: Self-Harm

**In memoriam: a friend and all the lovely people who
sadly aren't here. This is a piece about the grief and
healing that comes with loss.**

00:01 mezzo piano
little songbird, little songbird,
contrite, they still say there was nothing i could have done,
nails pinpricking flesh, a presto tempo darting through my veins,
words upon my lips slamming into a crescendo,
tasting the symbols of what-ifs across my tongue, yet the world is too
    oblivious. i'm frozen

in the late night, 1 a.m. again, "just hold on, and talk to me, i'm here
    for you," i say,
don't you remember that promise? halfway across the world, on
    different screens, we found our salvation
in each other, holding together like a blanket draped in caresses and
    whispered comfort,
i was the angel, sissy was the diva, percy was the joker, but you were the
    songbird spilling words,
singing melodies for our souls, taking our pain, and mending your
    voice through the cracks.

01:39 little songbird, little songbird,
where did it all go wrong?

my heart aches for the way you scarred your wings, tearing your
    blanket
thread by thread, if you pondered where to cut, then they answered:
the tip of your finger, the underside of your leg, the blade of your
    shoulder. you were a songbird,
so fragile and pure, and they, those monsters, hunted your soul,
    snarling you were never valid,
as they consumed the shared thoughts and love we cover in like
    cannibals. i should have

seen the epilogue coming, but i didn't, and it's like radio static
in my head, cauterizing your voice. desperate, i open up your message
    once more,
read 2:17 a.m. "farewell, if i'm not back here in a few days, please sing a
    song for me," you said,
but my voice is hoarse and i cannot sing anymore, so
in lieu of song: write a poem, sit curled up in the night's sky with violin
    music, and read it with a quivering howl,
spend some time contemplating a single word. a stanza maybe.
breathe, touch the dew. cry, hold knees together tight. listen, gaze at the
    stars. think
about schrödinger's cat, how are you and i the improbable paradox? die
    and live and die repent.

02:46 little songbird, little songbird,
you will be disappointed that my voice clips in silence whenever i try to
    tell you this,
it is so goddamn ironic, then, writing a poem i cannot speak,
when did this turn from poetry into a list of heartbreak my mind
    spewed out? still, what is the purpose?
i can't think of a good one when i never said, never typed, never did
    enough. even now, too late, i lay my hands

flat against the screen, simultaneously beating,
trembling as i write this, my hands trying to grasp yours,
but all i ever feel is the forgotten words and foreign coolness,
coveted words, i could have, i should have,
backspace delete stanza.

my little songbird, my little songbird,
you
                  sang
                       and
                  sang
                         until
                              silence
                                    overcame
                                        you,
                            until
                         i
                  was
              the
            sound
       that
remained

03:06 pianissimo.

delete poem?
       i-
       ...
. . . {several people are typing} . . .
       . . .
       . . .
{one person is typing}
                                        no, ~~you~~ i breathe
                                is this the ending?
                    no, ~~you~~ i scream
            my little songbird, my little songbird,
         i think of you with a smile,
      a bittersweet one,
yet the memories,
       glisten in this poem,
              like the raindrops i wipe away,
                so let's
                    rewind time
                          back to the good old days

if only for a little while,
i sang at last.

03:12 forte coda
(you are Dead, six feet beneath my toes. i wiggle them and feel your
   lovely bones. i hear clair de lune along my eardrums, threading
   across my being. finally, i sing, and you're singing along, the melody
   intertwining through my ribs and into my still-healing heart. i
   rewind your song once, twice, maybe thrice. when the sun crowns a
   new day, the golden halo its throne, i push play.)

00:00 fortissimo.

ROXIE GOSFIELD

LIVES: New York City, New York

Roxie (she/her) is a senior at a high school in Manhattan, New York. She is an avid reader and writer, and her favorite book is always *The Catcher in the Rye*.

MENTEE'S ANECDOTE:

I first met Yvette when my college process was in full swing, complete with complications in planning our meeting date. Those supplements weren't going to write themselves! But when we finally got to talk, I felt better, somehow.

YVETTE CLARK

LIVES: New York, New York

A Brit by birth and New Yorker by design, Yvette Clark is the author of the middle-grade novels *Glitter Gets Everywhere* and *The House Swap*.

MENTOR'S ANECDOTE:

Who knew coffee shops downtown close so early? Roxie and I do, having attempted to meet at several only to find the doors firmly closed. Happily, we discovered a bakery with vintage décor and delicious tea to hold our pair meetings. When I first read Roxie's writing, it blew me away and left me wanting more. She is a talented writer with a unique way of presenting truths. In the words of our shared hero, the inimitable David Bowie, "Tomorrow belongs to those who can hear it coming." I believe Roxie can hear it.

Starman

ROXIE GOSFIELD

A story about Martians, but mostly about humanity.

My moon boots, the trendy kind that likely provides no meaningful as-sistance in traversing across craters but are very nice to look at, crunch as I march toward the Martians. My heart pounds as I procure my pre-ferred medium for saving humankind. It feels light in my hands, I guess due to a lack of gravity, as I thrust my boombox, *Say Anything*–style, into the air. Click.

"Didn't know what time it was, the lights were low-oh-oh, I leaned back on my radio-oh-oh," I hear the Martians excitedly mutter in what I chauvinistically assume is the only extraterrestrial language I know, Klingon: "Qelpu'DI' ghaH 'ej Dochmeyvam'e'! (this human's laying down some rock and roll!)"

Somehow, on Mars, the 1972 hit single off David Bowie's *Rise and Fall of Ziggy Stardust and the Spiders from Mars* sounds different. I'm reminded of the first time I listened to "Starman"—really listened. I'd already heard it upward of 100 times, as a result of my parents keeping just one CD (*Best of David Bowie*) in our old-school Jeep that still had a cigarette lighter. At the Brooklyn Museum, at the *David Bowie Is* ex-hibit, I stumbled into an empty dark room with a single screen, right as a young Bowie, shielded from time and cancer, was beginning his sec-ond verse of the song. I felt, for reasons I hadn't yet uncovered, com-pelled to sit down and watch, and an hour later, when my concerned parents found me, I recited every word for them, complete with mim-icked choreography. Let the children boogie, right?

I remember staring into Bowie's blown-up face, his spiky red hair falling into his eyes, in which one pupil was more dilated than the other.

My mom told me that this contrast was because he'd been punched in the eye in elementary school. I thought about the schoolyard bully who might've done that, and wondered if he'd ever sat in a bar, later in life, and heard one of Bowie's smash hits. I bet the guy's greatest accomplishment was getting to touch the future superstar. But really, I mean, one day you're David Jones, a scrawny kid getting a knuckle sandwich. And the next you're *the* David Bowie.

That transformative spirit, by which anyone can be anything, is unique to humankind. A fly is just a fly; a lion is just a lion. But we can change our names, hair, outfits, and values; we can change our whole world if we dream it hard enough. I think the Martians are starting to get it when Bowie breaks into the first chorus: "there's a starman, wAiT-iNg in the skyyyyy." They can hear the fundamental yearning, even if they don't understand it. They can sense that there's something worth fighting for. And there must be. We've been waiting for the elusive starman since long before 1972, thinking if we can sparkle brightly enough, he might finally come down. Not all of us—some of us are like Bowie's bully, some of us don't like sparkles. Saint Paul didn't; he said "a woman . . . must be silent." And for a long time, we were. But there was always something underneath, just waiting to bubble up . . . Thrumming through every woman was a soft voice that told us if we upheld the very social fabric of the globe, we should be allowed to have a role in it. And so, we made one. But the long walk, which often seems more like a crawl toward gender equality, has no end in sight. There's no light in the sky, or at the end of the tunnel, or in Andrew Tate's eyes when he says to a surprisingly unsurprisingly receptive audience that women belong in the kitchen. And yet still, we hope.

When the Nazis cleared out the Jewish ghettos of Europe, not every Jew got on the train. Many who did even jumped off, scurrying into the cold, tall woods that promised nothing but loneliness and fear. But those who survived the initial raids found one another, and they called themselves the Partisans. A girl my age killed her former prom date to save her brother; a boy learned to make splints, casts, and relocate bones; they looked danger right in the eye and held its gaze. It seemed like a lost cause—handfuls of Jews versus millions of Nazis. But the stupidity of humankind is perhaps its biggest virtue; the Partisans were dumb enough to hold out hope, and tens of thousands of their descendants were born because of it.

I look at the Martians and wonder if they can feel the years of the history of hope, the most acutely human feature—what keeps us alive through it all, what sends us out into the woods, or the streets, or up to the podium, or to the laptop to press publish. We should know by now that there is no starman, he's not coming. But our undying belief in him comprises our spirit, we fight for survival, respect, equality, humanity, freedom, a better world—we fight to not blow it, so that we might get to see the light in the sky one day.

Somewhere, David Bowie's iconic "Starman" performance on BBC ushers in a new generation of rockstars, a young girl survives the Holocaust, a woman becomes a leader. Silenced Soviet writers build an underground system for speaking out with Samizdat, a preacher has a dream, a woman immigrates to America so her child can go to college. Why do we do it when we know there's no extraterrestrial being flying down to make it all worthwhile?

"Let all the children boogie!" Bowie finishes strong.

The **Martians** are looking at me like they want to hear the song again and again for hours straight. I know the feeling. They huddle and mutter amongst themselves and return to me with a question. "toH, be'nI'puq DaghojmoHlaH'a'? (you humans are the starmen?)"

"Yes," I reply, "I guess we are."

LAUREN HACKE

LIVES: Golden, Colorado

Lauren Hacke loves to explore all kinds of creative expression. She lives in Colorado, where she does archery, collects fossils, and listens to classical music.

MENTEE'S ANECDOTE:

Jana is an outstanding mentor and a rock of support for my writing. I'm so grateful to have a kind mentor who cheers me on and motivates me to write beyond my comfort zone. She sets me on paths that open my eyes to new ways of writing that I have never considered before. Her advice has helped my writing dreams come true, and I have gained more confidence in my creativity thanks to her. I can't wait to see what new, exciting ideas we will bring to life and what journeys we will embark on together in the future!

JANA KASPERKEVIC

LIVES: Brooklyn, New York

Jana Kasperkevic is a platform editor for *The Wall Street Journal*. She loves exploring how people consume news. She lives in Brooklyn, New York.

MENTOR'S ANECDOTE:

Lauren's passion for the world around her and her writing inspires me every time we chat. She is a great leader who thinks about the future and sees the world as it could be if we all tried a little harder and invested in our shared future. Seeing the world through her eyes has pushed me to be braver, to take risks with my writing, and to make changes, small and large, to my life that could help save our planet. I hope I offered her at least a fraction of the guidance and inspiration that she has given me.

Pink

LAUREN HACKE

Why is pink a "girly" color? Does pink limit us or empower us? What is the future of pink?

pink: precious perfect blush staining silk skin, sweet sapling sighing, baby's posing purpose painted **pink:** princess prancing in tangled tulle tears, twirling, towering, terrifying imaginations, paying platonic prices **pink:** piles packed neglected for feminine futures flying, forgotten faux fantasies need patriarchs plowing, pushing **pink:** plans pervading supernova-sprinkled skies sway sensible support, abdicating poached protagonists praying **pink:** pregnancy prepares learning balancing bicolor behavior, baiting blue bellies lobbying, please protect power **pink:** pain prickles societal ideas idolizing imprudent infrastructure, strengthening people pausing passivity **pink:** plethora of colors that belong to everyone and no one

DEMARIE HAO

LIVES: Brooklyn, New York

Demarie, often going by Basil, is a high school sophomore with a love for journalism, cancer research, and dance.

MENTEE'S ANECDOTE:

Coming into the Girls Write Now program, I wasn't personally expecting such a sweet friendship with Katherine. I never had a mentor before where I've felt comfortable joking around while also sharing my vulnerabilities through writing. Katherine is kind, confident, and determined. She has helped me step outside of my comfort zone in writing and taught me to have a little more faith in myself. Katherine is truly an inspiring mentor who's succeeded despite the odds. It's been a short but wonderful journey with her.

KATHERINE SORENSEN

LIVES: Phoenix, Arizona

Katherine (she/they) is a marketing copywriter at Square by day and a graduate student in the English studies program at Arizona State University.

MENTOR'S ANECDOTE:

Being a mentor to Basil has been the utmost privilege. Basil is bright, honest, and talented. I can confidently say that I have learned just as much from them, if not more, than they have from me. Basil writes with empathy, power, and, most important—the truth. I am proud to have worked alongside them this year, and even more proud of the work I have seen them create. I hope people walk away from Basil's work with a new perspective; one that allows them to move through the world with more grace and kindness. I know I will.

to my past and present

DEMARIE HAO

Content Warning: Child Abuse, Domestic Abuse

To myself, who could never find the words about me.

To my dad, who made me doubt myself; thank you for trying.

I. I AM

after "Where I'm From" by George Ella Lyon

i am from leather jewelry and silver rings
From YouTube tutorials and cell slides under microscopes.

i am from the white desk collecting hidden dust
(pristine, yet full of color,
photos of friends and idols as decoration.)

i am from basil leaves,
the green clumps
picked and placed into foods I rarely eat.

i am from ice-cream cake birthdays and a height outlier,
From the curly strands and white blouse of a friend far away to the
maroon streaks in fluffy black hair, with fingers adorned by jewelry of
    the boy who sits next to me.

i am from perfectionism and apologetic meals;

From "anything you want to be except an artist" and "don't be like those other Asians."

i am from rusting lucky cats and
crowded rooms—too much for a prayer to grandpa.

i am from the slums of the city that never sleeps,
a child of those from the fields of the Forbidden City.

from my mother's grueling wait, fleeing from those telling her she
    should settle down;
the black-and-white wars of my great uncle in Japan.

photos slipped into transparent books on my father's shelves
or stacked upon books on my great uncle's desk.
papers yellowing from timely picture frames and tea leaves,
brought out to reminisce and show
what happened all those years ago.

II. BECAUSE OF HIM

My dad hadn't driven a car in over a decade. And here he was, about to drive us to our hotel room from the airport.

It should've been only a few minutes on the road—a straight line down the highway and a U-turn on the local road.

A newer, electronic car stood in the parking lot of rentals. We settled inside—my dad and sister in the front, and my mother and I in the back.

I watched as my dad's legs tensed up, knuckles white against the steering wheel as we jolted forward, like one of those dreaded roller-coaster rides he used to force me on, nearly scratching the other cars around us. I watched as he cautiously drove down the aisles, turning around and around the parking lot, trying to find the exit. *It's right there*, my mother urged, and I watched as he closed his eyes, letting out a strained breath and nodding.

Make a U-turn here, my sister translated from the GPS, *and the hotel is right there.*

And I watched as he drove right past the turn, face scrunched into a scowl as he cut off a car turning into the lane. *You missed the turn, so it's asking you to redo the path,* she explained. *Make a left turn here,* just as he sped past the intersection.

I watched as my dad shook his head, face in a seemingly permanent snarl as he stepped on the accelerator. *Aiya—you should've told me earlier! Why didn't you tell me?*

I squeezed my eyes shut.

Because suddenly I'm six again, trembling underneath my desk as my dad stands over me. I tense up as he grabs my arm just like that wheel, a grip so tight that it leaves red marks later as he drags me to the narrow hallway of the front door, tears streaming down my face. Because *This is what you wanted, right?* he asks me, pushing me against the door, its rough edges jabbing into my skin. I hide my face behind my arm. *If you're going to be such a disrespectful child, you should just leave,* he says as freezing winds hit my skin.

It took a week of silence to pretend things were normal again.

Why do the miles keep going up? my dad shouted as I winced at the rough right turn he made.

"Please," I said. "Can we be a little quieter?"

Shut up, he screamed at me.

Because I'm seven now, shuffling into his room with a sheet of paper covered in dried-up tears and pencil marks. *What's 6×7?* he asks me, and I answer wrong. I watch as his fists ball up as he screams at me *Don't enter my room again until you get that right* and I cry, I cry and I sob and all he does is push me out of the room and tell me the same *Shut up, what are you crying about? I'll give you something to cry about.*

What are you crying about? my mom asked. She scoffed—*This is nothing. Useless, crying over this?* As I lurched forward from the sudden stop he made, the thought of *I'm going to die today, he's going to crash the car and I'm going to die today* was running through my head.

Because he has never changed. I thought he had; why was he like this again? God, what happened to all the promises that he wouldn't hurt me again—

The hit never came.

I watched my father succeed in the U-turn. I watch as he stares at me, tears and snot running down my cheeks outside his bedroom. Something is on the tip of his tongue but he quickly turns away instead, slamming the door shut behind him.

I lift two duffel bags out of the trunk, almost tiptoeing inside the hotel, waiting for my father and sister to deal with the receptionist as my mother stood off to the side.

The silence in the elevator ride up was deafening.

And before I entered my hotel room, my dad called out to me.

Ay. I'm sorry.

He shut the door to his room with a quiet click.

RUBY FAITH HENTOFF

LIVES: New York, New York

Ruby Faith Hentoff is a playwright, songwriter, and novelist graduating high school this spring. Between moments of inspiration, she loves singing, baking, and playing instruments.

MENTEE'S ANECDOTE:

I'm convinced that Maggie and I lead parallel lives. Every time we meet, we're going through the same emotional journey. When one of us starts with, "You know that feeling when . . . ," we'll keep nodding and expanding until we're basically dictating each other's emotions. Maggie is the most motivational person I've ever met; I'm in awe of her ability to view everything through a positive lens and stay optimistic when it's easier to throw arms. She also frames constructive criticism as questions, which has immensely helped me to strengthen my continuously evolving voice. I'm so grateful to be her mentee.

MAGGIE PERREAULT

LIVES: New York, New York

Maggie is a social justice–oriented educator who loves supporting young people as they develop their voice and advocate for a more liberated future.

MENTOR'S ANECDOTE:

I'd be hard-pressed to find a writing experience that has left me quite as inspired as a pair meeting with Ruby. Ruby is so in touch with her inner muse that her glowing, inventive creativity pours onto the page with ease. Whether it is listening to Ruby describe the process of a character's coming to life in her head or working together to edit dialogue in her TV-musical series, each meeting shows me a model of commitment to craft and encourages me to approach my writing with confidence.

Until the Lightning Strikes

RUBY FAITH HENTOFF

He was like home to me. I wasn't ready to let him go.

Sixty minutes till home.

The sky is black as onyx, hazy sprinkles of stars carelessly strewn across the galaxy. Withering trees surround the asphalt concrete I'm slowly rattling across, their branches bending over to brush against my window. In the distance, mountains encompass endless open fields, sorted into choppy layers and separated by sheets of mist. I can hear the twigs and stones crunching under the tires, making me bounce in my seat unnervingly. I didn't know this would be the night that it ended. I turn to look at my friend. He's mostly veiled in darkness, but every few seconds road lights will illuminate fragments of his face. His pale, freckled cheeks are pressed against the window, breath leaving circles of fog on the glass. He gazes out at the landscape wistfully, hazelnut irises worn with defeat. A glowing silver crescent reflects in his frameless glasses. I open my mouth, racking my mind for a conversation starter, but nothing comes out.

He glances back at me. Shifting his head ever-so-slightly, he manages to crack a thin smile. Seconds later, his shoulder is facing me once again.

Fifty minutes till home.

A chill slithers through my bones. We've hardly spoken since embarking on our second *Odyssey of the Mind* tournament. When his parents offered to take me home with them, I got excited for a moment, thinking that three hours in a dark car would incentivize him to finally speak to me again. And yet, it is quiet enough to hear a pin drop.

Then again, I'm not sure what I was expecting.

The air is thick, almost as if we've been submerged and talking would fill my lungs with dirty saltwater. Nevertheless, I want to say something, to say *anything* that reminds him of the six years we've been best friends for. All the holiday trips we relished; all the chess tournaments we went to; all the arguments we resolved. The time we went sea glass picking in St. Barths; the time we filmed an iMovie trailer set in the Himalayas; the time I stood by him as he severed a toxic friendship. *What does any of that mean to him?*

As we continue to wind through the shadowy night, I reflect on the value of our memories; how much his presence has been a shining beacon of light in my life. I assumed he felt somewhat similarly. For the longest time, I did view him as "the brother I never had." But it seems that he's beginning to move on; he's ready to try something new. *Someone* new. Someone with the key to a complex social pyramid, power that an outsider like me could never wield.

I don't remember when it all started. I suppose I don't notice the storm approaching until the friction of lightning sweeps across my skin.

Thirty minutes.

The silence is unusual. In the past, our time had been nothing short of fervent chatter and roaring laughter. I remember the days when he'd find me in the cafeteria, flexing about the lemon he'd sucked dry or the LEGO creation he'd just slapped together. Now I receive nothing more than a dismissive glance in the afternoons.

His back is almost fully turned to me now. I dig my bitten fingernails into the seat. *I wish I'd never come on this trip,* I thought to myself. In the front seats, his parents are chatting amicably. They don't know that he's stopped giving me his time and stopped listening to what I had to say. They don't know that he gave up his dream of becoming a "popular kid" and spent copious amounts of time alone. Or maybe they did. Not that he ever told them any of his personal information. In elementary school, he'd share that only with me. And I'd talk to him; I'd be reassuring and amusing and do anything to put a smile on his face. There was something unique, something special about our dynamic. We didn't even have to try. We could just *be*, and that was enough for me.

"I thought I was enough for you," I almost say, but manage to bite my tongue.

Twenty minutes.

He's still staring out the window. My throat turns dry. A battered sign reading "284th Street" whizzes by, and I've never been so relieved to be reentering the city.

He's staring, and staring, and staring. My blood runs cold.

Ten minutes.

"Say something!" the voice in my head desperately screams. "One word, anything to convince me that we're still us. That I still have you." But the stars have disappeared, and his gaze remains fixed on the onyx sky. His silence is like acid; stinging my skin, eating away at my flesh. A lump forms in my stomach, and my urge to leave the car is more extreme than ever. I have to escape the silence. To bandage myself before I start bleeding.

Five minutes till home.

I can see the storm, but it's too late. The friction has passed, and the lightning strikes.

FIONA HERNANDEZ

LIVES: Yonkers, New York

Fiona Hernandez is currently a senior in college studying journalism and aspires to work in the public relations/journalism field.

MENTEE'S ANECDOTE:

Cristina and I are very close, and I am happy she is my mentor! She's there to listen to my concerns and look over any essays I've written. I love how we talk about our love of reading, make book recommendations, and even learn about the latest things happening in the world! I'm grateful to have Cristina as my mentor, and I look to her as a role model for assisting me in being a better writer and as a female leader in the world.

CRISTINA MIGLIACCIO

LIVES: East Williston, New York

Cristina Migliaccio is an assistant professor of English and coordinator of composition at CUNY Medgar Evers College. She loves being a part of Girls Write Now!

MENTOR'S ANECDOTE:

Fiona Hernandez is a rising star! Her passion for reading, writing, and storytelling is contagious. The energy she brings to her life and work is rare and beautiful. I am grateful for the opportunity to work with Fiona at Girls Write Now!

I Once Thought I Knew Myself

FIONA HERNANDEZ

This piece discusses how 2020 was a year that gave me time to reflect on myself.

Sometimes I'm afraid to let people know who I really am, so I put on a mask where I show a different part of myself. Even when I meet different people and encounter different situations, I'm showcasing how I want to be looked upon and treated. But sometimes I do hide behind these masks.

I once thought I knew myself. I remember back in 2020 when the whole world shut down because of the coronavirus pandemic. I was forced to pack up my bags and come back home for the remainder of the semester. During that time at home, I got to find out who I really was. I was closed off, not wanting to talk to anyone, and I stayed in front of a computer all day. For so long, I would look around and be happy as I got to spend time with my friends and family. But during the pandemic, I was upset, lonely, and unable to even encounter people because of the fear of COVID.

So much of what I learned in 2020 made me reflect on several things. As I took out my pen and journal, I began to write. I wrote about my feelings and emotions. It became a collection of not only my thoughts but my experiences and how I live my life. This journal became a place for me to learn more about life and more about myself. It became a place where I could really express myself and my emotions, writing about when I'm upset, when I'm happy, when I'm worried, and when I'm excited! It showed me how I've developed, grown, and changed to be the person I am. I learned not to take things for granted. I learned to be grateful for the little things in life. This part of my life also taught me that it's okay to have these different feelings and that life isn't always about the good times. As the saying goes, we have to appreciate the bad times in our lives to get through the good times. You can learn so much about yourself and the kind of person you are through the good times and the bad times. The stress you see in yourself, and learning from your mistakes, is a part of being human and growing as a person. It is part of the process of getting to know yourself.

I've worn the happy mask, the sad mask, the "poor me" pity mask, the caretaker mask, the mask of confidence, the defensive mask, and, yes, the peer pressure mask. Sometimes we don't have a choice, right? We have to put on a mask to be present for someone we love despite our own emotions, or we have to make it through a demanding work/school day without the option of "letting down our guard." I've worn these masks because sometimes I've wanted to fit in with other people. When my friends are all happy about something, even when I might be feeling sad, I want to feel happy for them too, and I will wear my happy mask. Or sometimes, when I want to fit in with the crowd and do the latest trend that's happening for people like me, I'll put on the peer pressure mask.

I felt so left out in high school and felt forced to put on the peer pressure mask so that I could fit in. Girls would look up the latest trends on Instagram or Snapchat, and I felt I had to be a part of that too, so I could belong. Unlike the other masks I've worn, this isn't the one that I've "put on" but actually felt. I've also felt the loner mask. It's where it was hard for me to fit in with my peers. Even in high school, I felt left out as being one of the only few people in my high school who didn't vape and didn't think that was fun just because it was "the latest trend on social media."

___

That story about me being lonely and sad during the pandemic was where I removed my happy mask and felt my emotions. I felt pain, isolation, and sadness. Even though they were hard feelings, it made me feel good to get to know myself more.

Sitting at home with my emotions made me feel different. I didn't need to be a different person. All I needed was to be me. I realized that people appreciate you more if you're just yourself. It's okay not to follow what all my friends are doing on social media. I don't need to "not care" about school just cause my friends didn't. I needed to be me. It taught me to wear Fiona's mask. My mask shows me that I am a girl who works hard, loves to read and write, and is passionate about journalism. I'm a girl who fumbled along the way, and made mistakes, yet always got back up on her feet.

KAYAH HODGE

LIVES: Brooklyn, New York

Kayah Hodge is a writer, creative innovator, and marketing assistant at Macmillan Publishers. She's a culinary adventurer, artist, and blogger!

MENTEE'S ANECDOTE:

From advice on balancing personal life with a career in writing to sharing family stories, Elissa is truly a gift! Her personalized feedback on each poem I shared felt thorough and intentional while inspiring me to dig deeper. Elissa has witnessed the range of my artistic talents. After sharing a *New Yorker* article on the author Robin Coste Lewis, Elissa gifted me a copy of *To the Realization of Perfect Helplessness*. It was a testament to her understanding of my appreciation for poetry and photography! Not only is she generous, but our talks never end without a hearty laugh.

ELISSA WEINSTEIN

LIVES: New York, New York

Elissa Weinstein is a goldsmith and writer. She is currently at work on several new designs and a collection of genre-bending writings.

MENTOR'S ANECDOTE:

A few minutes into a first conversation with Kayah and I could sense how expansive getting to know her would be. By the end of that session, she had shared photos of her nephew, expressed how much joy she felt around food, cooking, writing, and her job at Macmillan Publishers. To top it off, she sent me a playlist she had created, to keep me moving through my own culinary experiments. Then the poems started coming—far-ranging in subject, lyrical, and deeply affecting. Kayah's generosity of spirit is infectious!

Cena ~ Dinner

KAYAH HODGE

Cooking a delicious feast or tasty meal for one is a skill, art, and process with a priceless reward: a full belly!

Grown
Harvested
Trocó[1]
Done behind the scenes

Sal
Limón
Vinagre
Cleaned
Seasoned
Marinated
A real milagro[2] begins

Pimientos[3]
Cebollas[4]
Ajo[5]
Diced
Chopped

---

1. Bartered
2. Miracle
3. Peppers
4. Onions
5. Garlic

Grated
To el recuerdo[6] de abuelita[7]

Greased
Heated
TSSSS
Aromas heat up the home

Secretly picking from hot pots
Patiently blowing til cool
Scarfing down a whole lot
Jugando con[8] yo food

Gathered at a feast
Dining all alone
Cena calms the beast
Til barriga's[9] next groan

---

6. Keepsake
7. Grandma's
8. Playing with
9. Tummy's

LILIANA HOPKINS

LIVES: Secaucus, New Jersey

Liliana Hopkins is a college freshman. She can be found in the library, writing in her journal, or crying over her Calculus 2 homework.

MENTEE'S ANECDOTE:

Mary and I have informally designated our time together as a creative space. Sometimes we are sophisticated: we check out a Broadway play or the new Basquiat exhibit. Other times, we talk over Zoom about recipes and favorite television shows. Mary has shown me that writing isn't crunching out formulaic sentences. Writing is a way of looking at the self in relation to the world, and then filtering these observations into the mysterious funnel of language. Our editing process consists of psychoanalytical conversations and laughing about the human condition. I couldn't be more grateful to have her guidance.

MARY DARBY

LIVES: New York, New York

Mary Darby is a writer for a public interest communications firm. She lives in Inwood, New York, with her beloved and greatly spoiled dog, Pepper.

MENTOR'S ANECDOTE:

I love working with Lili. She is a truly gifted writer. She is so aware of herself and interested in the world around her, and it shows in her writing. She's not afraid to go deep into dark places because she knows that's how you find the light. It's also part of what makes her writing so compelling.

Bad Omens

LILIANA HOPKINS

Content Warning: Sexual Content

A thirteen-syllable-per-line structured poem that sits
with the guilt of womanhood and daughterhood.

There is a black moth in the corner of my bedroom,
a dead bird outside the cafeteria window.

I sleep naked, mostly. Tangled in omens, feelings.
Socks half off. An ankle tattoo, a piercing or two.
I write a hundred versions of myself. My breasts: pink
underbelly of a mouse, sorry excuse of a
chest. My outer thighs: uncooked chicken, goosebumped, pickled,
pallid. I write a hundred more for my mosaic;
I catch the light. Yes, I have red hair everywhere. I
add a glass shard. Sorry excuse of a daughter, a
woman, a sister. Don't text me good morning, don't tell me
I'm pretty, don't kiss me so hard and so fast, don't tell
me I'm smarter than you thought I was. Yes, I am red
everywhere. There's a sickness inside me. No, I don't
like it when you touch me. There's only so much room in my
womb for pain, but there might be space if you rearrange
all this pleasure, all this shame. Fruit flies linger by the
kitchen sink. No, I'm not eating, not while you're watching.

I write a eulogy, an elegy, for daddy.
My daddy who is not dead, who likes twenty-year-old
Russian women, who ask him for twenty cents a text.

I sit in contemplation of his death. Counting all
the ways he might go. Upside, sideways. Then I spend more
time imagining the relief I'll feel when he's gone.
Fruit flies crawl from the folds of his skin. I imagine
forgiveness: cold, clearing clouds; in, out my mind, unwound.
I imagine grief: the warm smog in my mind after
getting stoned off my ass, waking up the next morning
trying to remember who I was—am. I am so
guilty. I add a glass shard. I'll throw up all over
myself, all over the ground between us, before
getting down on my knees, sucking you off. Fruit flies wait
for him by the kitchen sink. He drops the dinner plate,
hands trembling as he drops it again, trying to clean
up the mess he made. I watch him dying, and I wait.

STELLA Z. "TWIG" HU

LIVES: New York, New York

Stella Z. Hu, aka Twig (she/her), is a crazy little space elf who loves to paint rainbows on everything in existence, including the establishment.

MENTEE'S ANECDOTE:
I've said before that this doesn't feel like being mentored/ taught so much as having a fun friend to write with and talk about my creative life with. At this point, I've spent sessions just rambling about my OCs (Original Characters), and the D&D campaign I'm currently in. It's great!

EMMA WINTERS

LIVES: New York, New York

Emma Winters (she/her) is a writing and communications professional. She lives and works in New York City. Careful, she's also a boxer.

MENTOR'S ANECDOTE:
As we're now in our second year working together, I've had the chance to see Stella work through several long-term writing projects. Stella has shared her work on crafting original characters. Of Stella's many excellent writing projects, two of my favorites have been seeing her bring to life her OC's greatest fears in a short story, and the diary entry written from her D&D character's perspective. Stella finds creativity in all things, and writes some of the best stories about friendship around. I am grateful for her affinity for fun, horror, and the absurd, and admire how she never takes life too seriously.

the devil and
the deep blue sea

STELLA Z. "TWIG" HU

> This is a story about the difficult choices we have
> to make.

They say that once, there was a man standing on the shore.

No creature knew how he came to be there. It could've happened in infinite ways. It does not matter.

What matters is that the deep blue sea lapping at the man's feet was treacherous, to say the very least. Storms roiled that day, gray clouds hung low, and waves crashed on the shore. There were monsters within that sea, many people said. Sea serpents. Giant squids. Merfolk, not the kind from stories told to children, but the kind that would drag you to your grave and devour you with their sharp teeth. Perhaps other things entirely, things beyond any familiar description, perhaps beyond human comprehension. And no land, no human life to be found, for hundreds and thousands and millions of miles. Should the man standing on the shore step forward into the sea, he would not survive it.

What matters is that behind the man stood the Devil himself, blocking the man from walking away from the sea, smiling the most blood-curdling smile imaginable. Why he was there, how the man knew he was the Devil, and what he planned to do to the man were not certain. It could've been any number of things. Perhaps the man himself did not know. But it would be terrible; it would be something to make the strongest of men quiver, something to give you nightmares for the rest of your days. And the Devil would enjoy it. Should the man run along the shore, the Devil would follow alongside him. Should the man make a move in the Devil's direction, he would not pass by unscathed. Perhaps he would not pass by at all.

For whatever reason, by whatever circumstance, the man found himself trapped between the two: the Devil and the deep blue sea. Each more than ready and able to cause the man insurmountable pain and suffering, each more than ready and able to kill him. The man would not be able to move from where he stood without choosing which foe to face. He could swim out into the sea—some say there was a dinghy nearby that he could've leaped into. He could try to run past the Devil, or to fight him. Either way, the man's chances of survival were slim, and it was certain that he would suffer immensely.

The Devil or the ocean, both waiting for him to make his choice. And if the man stood paralyzed with indecision for long enough, he knew one would grow impatient and claim him without his choosing. Perhaps both.

There are many versions of the tale. There are many different ways the Devil and the sea are described in the story, many different tellings of what each will do to the man, many different tellings of what choice the man makes and what happens to him thereafter. Each version of the story has a different lesson to teach. There are infinite ways the tale may unfold, nigh infinite ways that it *has* unfolded before, nigh infinite ways it is unfolding right now, somehow, somewhere. There is meaning in each version. There is meaning, perhaps most of all, in the premise of the tale, as it is set, as I have described it to you. There is weight, tremendous weight, in the choice. In that impossible, cruel, terrible choice.

I wonder how many people know this. I wonder how many are fully, completely aware of this.

They all are, on one level or another. It is impossible *not* to be.

Still, I find it important to call one's attention to it.

I suppose it is *your* choice what you will do with it.

MADELINE ROSE HUTCHINSON

LIVES: Brooklyn, New York

Madeline Hutchinson is a high school sophomore. She is passionate about almond milk yogurt, abstract expressionism, art museums, and alliteration.

MENTEE'S ANECDOTE:

Engaging in mentorship was presumably going to be stressful, especially for an anxious person like myself. Quickly, it became clear that I would feel understood and accepted by Jackie's compassion. Jackie was open to sharing common experiences and there were many moments when we discovered serendipitous connections. Jackie's gentle guidance managed to find the most effective balance to hear my voice and challenge my skills. Our sessions always left me thinking past our time together and I was enthused to meet again. Jackie's wisdom seemed limitless as she delivered feedback from extensive experience and skill.

JACKIE HOMAN

LIVES: New York, New York

Jackie Homan is a writer, editor, and nonprofit content manager. In her free time, she enjoys rock climbing, hiking, visiting museums, and writing poetry.

MENTOR'S ANECDOTE:

When Madeline and I first met, we instantly clicked and discovered shared interests in concerts and music, art and museums, and writing and poetry. After just speaking to Madeline, I could tell she was thoughtful and bright, but after reading her poetry, I was truly blown away. Madeline is exceptionally talented, creative, and self-aware, with a clear voice and command of language that makes her writing one-of-a-kind. I can't wait to continue working with Madeline and know her work will make a profound impact in this world.

Pull the Pin and Release the Locking Mechanism

MADELINE ROSE HUTCHINSON

> **1.** Hold the extinguisher with the nozzle pointing away from you.
>
> **2.** Aim low. Point the extinguisher at the base of the fire.
>
> **3.** Squeeze the lever slowly.
>
> **4.** Sweep the nozzle from side to side.

I, summertime solipsist, spent my formative Julys fortifying
    sandcastles with salt water and anguished introspection.
Through juvenile attempts at this endeavor, I was left alone as the
    weight of humidity descended upon my sunburnt body, and the
    haze obscured any opportunities for reprieve.
Burning, I scratched the sand from under my fingernails, borrowing
    their grit to remind myself that I was still, in fact, alive.
I etched cyphered pleas of escape in the reeling shadows of the
    shoreline, but they made themselves wash away.
How do you dispatch distress signals when nobody recognizes them,
    not even yourself?

I, autumnal force of accelerating affliction, spent my thirteenth
    October mourning my youth in the form of combustions directed
    toward my mother.
The thirteenth candle she lodged in my store-bought ice-cream cake
    must have been a trick, as the flame gifted me extended purgatory
    through its unwavering blaze.

Burning and coughing, I spent my exhales on the tenacious task at
hand as the contained flame began to exceed its promised
boundaries.

I watched the flame obscure my mother's knowing smile, then her
intertwined fingers, until it swallowed her and the other party guests
entirely.

How do you invite yourself back to the ruins of your birthday party?

I, winter wave of weariness, spent the depths of my December
enfettered to the familiar intimacy of my outerwear.

My scarf served a dazzling dualism: callous comforter and harbinger of
affectionate asphyxiation.

Burning and coughing and choking, I scratched at my neck, until my
irritated skin complemented the deep red of my woolen scarf.

I readily surrendered to sidewalk snowbanks to foster my hibernation
that this year had endlessly humored.

How do you burn alive during the coldest Sunday of the year?

I, beaming spring bloom, am spending my June in a rosy kind of
recession.

Not even the most morbid malignancy could mar my convalescence.

Burning and coughing and choking and gasping for air, the fire won't
take me this year.

I am extinguishing myself from the inside out whilst assembling
visions in the sand, blowing out my birthday candles, and shedding
my scarf.

How do you use the fire extinguisher?

JASMINE ILYAS-GRANDE

LIVES: Baltimore, Maryland

Jasmine Ilyas-Grande (she/her) is an incoming college fresh-man, interested in a creative writing minor and engaging with other passionate writers by exploring her writing journey!

MENTEE'S ANECDOTE:

Lauren has become one of my closest friends. As a mentor, she's made me feel heard and engaged in all aspects of my writing journey. She has also been a true friend, celebrating my successes and empowering my decisions. When we talk about things happening around us, we like to talk about our experiences and share a wonderful bonding conversation that can last the whole meeting session. Lauren gives me a space for me to speak my mind, and I give her my attentive admira-tion when she tells me her stories. We both complement each other in the best ways!

LAUREN ELIZABETH JONES

LIVES: South Miami, Florida

Lauren Jones (she/her) is a traveler, a writing editor, and a reading fanatic who compiles the most creative proposals in all aspects of writing and marketing.

MENTOR'S ANECDOTE:

Working with Jasmine as her mentor has been a rewarding, exciting experience. Jasmine is a brilliant young woman who has many talents and passions. It's been immensely gratify-ing to help her explore different types of writing while helping her build professional skills that will benefit her in college and beyond. I cannot wait to see all that she accomplishes.

Nostalgic Smells

JASMINE ILYAS-GRANDE

My grandmother was diagnosed with dementia in 2020. I remember her through memories we shared years ago, and I wrote about these memories, by continuing to remember her as she would want me to.

Memory comes in many forms. It comes from the scent, emotions, and vivid distant details. My favorite memory goes back years ago, when I used to visit my grandmother in Mexico. When I was younger, my grandmother's kitchen was the most sacred place I could ever know. In the heart of the city of Zacatelco, my grandmother's soft and wrinkled hands would leave the strongest person crying at the stories of her youth. I was lucky enough to experience the feelings of her kitchen, and the aromas that left me with a growling stomach. I would leave the kitchen with satisfaction and pure happiness. Her stories ranged from the scariest encounters she'd had with a bull to having made a lot of sacrifices for her children.

Even today, her kitchen, which is now more than 2,400 miles away from me, still calls to me. When the occasional aroma of cilantro with roasted tomatoes, or the smell of burnt chocolate for the process of mole, arrives in my nose, I tear up at the memory of the childhood I once had. Instead of hearing stories from my grandmother, I now tell the stories. I was lucky enough to be around and experience the strong feminine power my grandmother had. I am lucky to be able to tell the stories with such pride and courage she once had. My grandmother, who is my hero, trained me to become my sister's role model and hero.

My younger sisters, who now sit around the kitchen table, listen to me while I tell them the stories that have been carried through several generations, from my great-grandmother to me. I tell them by making the same foods my grandmother once made.

I chop the onions and garlic as I start, telling my favorite story: of our mother's daring choice to flee her country to achieve her dreams. Chopping gives me enough time to complete it. As the onions and garlic start to simmer in the butter, I go on with a joyful story about when I once ran through the mountains of Zacatelco barefoot and carefree, and lay down on the burning grass to catch the view of the night sky. As their eyes widen, I tell my siblings how I placed my hand between the distance of the moon and brightest star. I then follow with my grandmother's sad story of when she was forced to stop going to school because she had done "enough" schooling. My great-grandmother's story about the time she ran away with my grandfather on the night before what was supposed to be her wedding to a different man follows that.

When I see my sisters' eyes, I relive the care my grandmother showed me in her kitchen. The gentle faces I see around the table follow me as I roast the chiles poblanos and peel the seeds from the chipotles. Their noses soak up the aromas, and their eyes close as they savor the moment.

I am proud to be the storyteller. I am proud of how the aromas of my grandmother's kitchen make me nostalgic. My childhood is carried within me. I reminisce in the little moments, and savor them as I continue to grow and learn from my mistakes and experiences.

The stories of these strong women remind me of how lucky I am to be able to break the generational trauma inflicted on women in my family. I don't have to worry about being forced to marry someone, or having to leave school because it is "enough," or having to go across borders to reach a dream. The long nights in the kitchen with my grandmother prepared me to take the strength of the women in my family with me always, and pass it on, as I do with my sisters. Someday, as I make them a simple bowl of caldo de pollo on their bad days, I will also pass it on to my children and grandchildren.

ANGEL JACKSON

LIVES: Guilderland Center, New York

Angel is a junior at Guilderland High School. She currently works at her local library. Her hobbies include listening to music, running, and reading.

MENTEE'S ANECDOTE:

Every other Saturday, I can expect to grow as a writer with the help of my mentor, Molly. It's not only about the writing, though. You can catch us discussing our plans for the upcoming week or the weather; whatever it is, we find a way to talk about it. I am more confident in myself as a writer because of Molly. She is the most motivating and truthful mentor in my life that I've had. I will carry on with the advice she gives me into my adult life and continue to flourish as a writer because of her.

MOLLY COYNE

LIVES: New York, New York

Molly is trying to build a joyful life. Right now, that means reading good books, roller-skating, and laughing with people she loves.

MENTOR'S ANECDOTE:

My Saturdays are always better when they start with an Angel meeting! Angel's interest in learning and commitment to writing brighten my day every time we meet. She is eager to explore different writing techniques and styles, regularly attending workshops, tackling new prompts, and writing extensively on her own time. I love hearing about what she's been working on since we last met. It's been great to see her start to get work published, and I know this is only the beginning!

Press Play

ANGEL JACKSON

A piece about speaking up so that others will finally know who I am.

Introducing Angel—a perfect balance of a small and loud voice. The ultimate personal listening experience is here.

Small voice. That's so loud, how can it be so small?

Cover your ears and listen to the music (Angel). Listen not only because of the new look but because of what is offered. Perspective. Experience. Time. Open your ears before it's too late to listen to the real her. She will give you the world she lives in, from her eyes, ears, and voice box, canceling out all the unnecessary noise going into your ears.

To create a breakthrough listening experience.

Angel has a unique background. She has proven to offer you a sound like no other. A sound that will flood your ears. The sound of all the experiences that she has been through from then till now. Your ears will be covered (away from the world for some time).

To help block outside noise.

You will be able to immerse yourself in the music (Angel). Tune out those other sounds and truly listen. Once you do, you will understand why she is the way she is today. You won't know her. You will know the _real_ her. The one that just needs someone to listen to her. You can block out her sound for only so long. It's harder to do now because her sound will blast through as many ears as it can.

The only thing that needs listening in life. Listen to the experiences that make Angel who she is today. Angel produces sound with ultra-low distortion across the audible range from q u i e t to L O U D. Cover your ears to STOP outside voices getting in. Pressing PAUSE means stopping

Angel's voice from getting in. The world has been on p a u s e for too long. Press PLAY because sitting back without listening for too long will keep the place quiet, not LOUD. Listen through your ears. Listen to hear what it's like to be me.

To produce sound.

Angel has all the weight lifted off her shoulders. She is ready to speak up (spit the words right out her mouth), something she feared doing for so long. Her sound will be loud and QUIET. It is her voice. It is no longer killing her not to be heard because the gift of your ears in LISTENING MODE will allow her to be heard by everyone who listens to music (Angel). After all, this sound travels through the world, covered ear to covered ear.

WAEZA JAGIRDAR

LIVES: Bronx, New York

Waeza resides in New York City and is majoring in media and communications studies with a minor in political science at Lehman College.

MENTEE'S ANECDOTE:

Rachel is very kind and very open to learning and growing with me. Rachel has supported all my decisions, whether writing, networking, or even listening to me rant. She's made me realize that writers are meant to be bold and courageous and that it's good to be loud sometimes. If there's one thing I've learned from Rachel, it's that stepping out of your comfort zone can be a good thing.

RACHEL HUNTER

LIVES: New York, New York

Rachel is an ambitious marketing manager with diverse experience in higher education, hospitality, and real estate. Rachel is articulate and driven, with high energy and an engaging personality.

MENTOR'S ANECDOTE:

My writing relationship with Waeza is just beginning, but in the short time we have been working together I have been impressed with her drive and passion for writing and her future. Recently, I had the chance to watch her read her poem to a roomful of people that were all inspired by her words and that was very special. I am excited to continue to watch Waeza grow as a writer and read more of her moving pieces.

Free Palestine

WAEZA JAGIRDAR

To honor the Palestinians that have passed and for those who are still fighting for their country.

Years after years,
Days after days,
Losses after losses,
Mothers lose their children.
Children lose their home and family.
They become refugees in a country that they call home.
The colors red, black, green, and white stick out
Loud enough for the people to hear the spirit
Of the lionhearted Palestinians.
People yearn for the taste of freedom,
Struck with the inhumane world of war and terror,
Lost with the destruction of their cities.
They stay stoic for their families,
With the hope of freedom unwavering.
Yet the world moves every second,
And lives are taken and given.
We think we can't live without that specific person
Yet living is more than just breathing,
Whether it is for ourselves or for someone else.
Some of us come from privilege, others not so much.
We think the vivid colors in our lives aren't enough,
That there's always more to do
And sometimes there is.
There is more to the world.
Peace.
Humanity.
Humility.

Stand for what's right even if that means you stand alone.
Stand for those who can't stand for themselves.
Make sacrifices for those who have lost too much in a lifetime.
Question, am I doing enough as a human being?
What does it take to be a human?
A human who has a story too
Maybe not written in as much sorrow and loss
Humble those who don't realize they have more than enough.
A reminder that after everything they've been through
They continue to fearlessly fight in black and white
Prayers for the Palestinian.
Inshallah one day, Palestine will be free.

ISABELLA JAPAL

LIVES: New York, New York

Isabella is twenty-four years old and a 2020 Cornell University graduate. She is currently working in New York City as an entertainment journalist.

MENTEE'S ANECDOTE:

I knew Kiki was meant to be in my life when we had our first meeting and she told me she was an Astrosexologist (not once did I mention my love of astrology on my Girls Write Now application). Ever since then, meeting with her has been one of my favorite parts of the week. She has been so supportive and such a great guide—with my writing and then some. I always have so much fun with her and I am forever grateful to Girls Write Now for bringing us together.

KIKI T.

LIVES: New York, New York

Living for the "full-speed absurd" mode, Kiki is a believer in the impossible. As a mentor, her main goal is being a dream pusher.

MENTOR'S ANECDOTE:

When two Gemini risings get together, there are four heads that are better than one! Setting goals was easy, as were coming up with ideas and the many places in the city that we set as our own yellow brick road. Now Emerald City is in sight and it's great to see that Isabella now knows she had everything in her all along. No magic can outdo persistence, determination, and doing the work.

A First-Timer's Guide to Public Records

ISABELLA JAPAL

Content Warning: Drug Use

Follow me as I guide you through a night at one of Brooklyn's hottest venues (and not just because I was wearing a sweater dress).

9:30 p.m. Start your Saturday night at a somewhat new, somewhat old friend's apartment in Boerum Hill. You met several years ago as summer analysts at a top-five financial firm (think HBO's *Industry* with less drugs and more screaming). What your friend doesn't know is that you were in love with her for a full year after that. Say hi to her live-in boyfriend on your way in and finally accept defeat.

9:45 p.m. Pregame at home, drinking lychee martinis. Who says you need to drop twenty dollars a pop at a cocktail bar to feel fabulous? One word: Whole Foods–brand canned lychee (oh wait, that's five). Or, better yet, a mom-and-pop-run Asian market. On second thought, yeah, might as well go to the Asian market.

10:30 p.m. Two cocktails and one allergy pill later, you're sufficiently buzzed and finally in the mood to go out. Watch your friend do her makeup and drunkenly share your recent musings while sitting on the edge of her giant clawfoot tub (she still works at the aforementioned finance firm, hence the tub).

11:00 p.m. Open Google Maps and search for the best-sounding place for a night of drinking, drugs, and debauchery, all within walking distance. Friend suggests Public Records in Gowanus and the name rings a bell, remembering your on-again, off-again guy friend/hookup buddy mentioning it the other week.

12:00 a.m. Walk to Public Records and get in line with a bunch of Europeans. Try to recall the bits of French you learned from high school and sharpen your eavesdropping skills. Smoke three cigarettes because there's nothing better to do.

12:40 a.m. A whole forty minutes later, you're in! Check your bag and pay for tickets. Cover fee is forty dollars because the act that night is a hardcore bass-heavy techno DJ and everyone is on molly so they obviously won't be buying drinks. Friend buys your ticket because, well, you're a receptionist and she's a banker. Consider for the 116th time whether or not you should've sold your soul to Corporate America after all.

1:00 a.m. Take a copious amount of shots to distract yourself from how badly you wish you had a powdered substance on you. Turn around and get swept up in the crowd all while squinting through the dense fog and mood lighting. Look for a guy who's probably on ketamine and is willing to share.

1:30 a.m. Dance for a good thirty minutes and leave via the walkway to smoke yet another cigarette on the very cute patio. Humor some NYU kids who ask if it's actually worth the forty dollars to go in.*

3:30 a.m. Continue to dance the night away for a good two more hours (you never did end up finding those drugs). Call it quits around 3:30 a.m. and Citi Bike over to Artichoke Basille's Pizza on Fifth Avenue. Reassure the various older men on the street asking if you're okay as you teeter-totter off into the darkness in your miniskirt.

3:50 a.m. Arrive at Artichoke Basille's ten minutes shy of closing and realize they're cash only—luckily, they have an ATM! Volunteer to buy the pizza because your friend covered you all night and you want to return the favor any way you know how. Your card promptly gets declined but God is good, and you have enough money in your savings

---

* Spoiler alert! it absolutely was.

account to transfer over and save the day. Pop a squat on the curb and take turns swapping a margherita and an artichoke slice. Share an Uber to your respective homes and proceed to conk out around 5 a.m. Wake up around 9 a.m. (curse you, bodily clock) and vow to do it all over again. ☺

STEPHANIE JARAMILLO

LIVES: Elizabeth, New Jersey

Stephanie Jaramillo (she/her) is a senior in high school who enjoys volleyball and science, and desires to become a journalist.

MENTEE'S ANECDOTE:
Emily has become more than just an assigned mentor. She's become a close friend, someone who has given me so much time in her day to guide me in my writing. We've bonded over books we've both enjoyed and books we desire to read in the future together.

EMILY STEVENS

LIVES: Brooklyn, New York

Emily Stevens is the senior manager of special initiatives, foundations, and government grants at the New York Public Library and loves writing fiction.

MENTOR'S ANECDOTE:
Stephanie is a seventeen-year-old girl who has a strong desire for writing. Her words have a powerful statement. We have grown close as I've helped her with her writing pieces and critiqued her work in any helpful way possible. We have started to read a book together, allowing a new bond to be formed through our shared love of reading.

Freedom through
the pages

STEPHANIE JARAMILLO

Content Warning: Body Shaming, Fatphobia

> This essay is about finding confidence through writing, and how learning about other inspirational writers allowed me to stop drowning in my own mindless and negative thoughts.

The summer of 2017 was when my aunt deliberately spoke with me about how much I ate. She told me that being pretty wasn't often associated with gaining weight. Up until then, I was an overweight eleven-year-old who had no clue weight mattered so much to others.

When I entered middle school, the other kids emphasized that my stomach wasn't flat, nor my chest the right size for the boys to swoon over. I felt like an outcast in any social gathering; everyone focused on my body. The childhood I was meant to grow up in was filled with continuous self-loathing. I could no longer bear to look at myself in the mirror; it was like there was a person standing behind me, pointing out how much bigger the number on my pants was compared to others, a grim look of disgust on their face.

Writing in the blank pages of my notebook was the only freedom I possessed. The repressed emotions finally being let out sparked a genuine feeling. I could feel the pages filled with my words sink me into a new form of acceptance. A smile appeared on my lips—picking up the pencil had always allowed me to overcome any problem. Finding a solution became easier. My returning confidence allowed for new approaches I could take to better myself without self-pity; all I needed was the self-reflection my writing allowed for. It wasn't about exercising or eating healthy. It was writing that brought me the feeling of acceptance that I needed.

The time I spent writing led to a new fascination with different genres. It was not only creativity that guided my passion, but also that I wanted to give myself a voice. Writing was a safe place for me; I found myself bound to it. It kept me secure in my comfort zone, yet it was an opportunity to make a difference—like Maya Angelou, a poet and an activist in the civil rights movement. Tyler Kingkade is a journalist who utilizes his own experiences to advocate for the gap between men's and women's body image. Mary Oliver was a poet who wrote about the interactions between the human and natural worlds. All these writers have one thing in common: using their voice to overpower common wrongs. Helping people uncover loose ends, finding community, and advocating for themselves and others.

I wanted this, too.

I noticed that students in my school wrote for the newspaper, giving light to so many different issues I'd had no clue about. I wanted that. I wanted to show my audience everything they were missing. Expanding my writing beyond my own experiences was a challenge, but the passionate need to do so took over every last nerve. I joined the school newspaper, and found my love for journalism. The everyday moments of life that people overlooked were so clear to me that I had to write about them. The continuous words that flowed out onto the page helped me to understand the world around me, and brought me a powerful feeling of accomplishment.

Entering Girls Write Now as a mentee, with an already growing love of writing, sparked my love for journalism even more. I'm able to work with professional writers to further my own growth as a writer, as well as my growth as a student.

From the first moment I picked up that pencil, it has remained in my hand, secretly guiding me to new places. The taunting mirror I would occasionally pass no longer holds any power over me. The pages I write are my new mirror, not highlighting my physical appearance but instead my creative growth. Writing helped me see my world more clearly. I know I can do the same for others.

ZIYING JIAN

LIVES: Staten Island, New York

Ziying (she/her) is a high school senior with a passion toward exploring worlds, both real and magical, through her writing.

MENTEE'S ANECDOTE:

My meetings with Camille are the grounding forces of my week—giving me the space for self-reflection and allowing me to practice gratitude. When discussing literature or writing, I'm impressed by the way Camille is able to listen with attention and compassion, and the way she delivers her ideas in a calm and thoughtful manner. Our conversations have also seeped into the realm of college, cooking, relationships, theater, and anything that interests us! Camille and I always have so much to share, and her wisdom and assurance are traits I look up to.

CAMILLE BOND

LIVES: New York, New York

Camille is an environmental journalist whose work has appeared in E&E News, *Scientific American*, *The Spoon*, Green-Biz, and elsewhere.

MENTOR'S ANECDOTE:

Ziying has brought an incredible variety of written work to our pair sessions—including college essays, stream-of-consciousness pieces, and even a novel concept. I've learned so much from the confidence she shows as a writer, and from her decisions to incorporate unexpected choices into written pieces of every kind. The diversity of her interests, and her ability to switch nimbly between styles and voices, is a reminder to me that boldness pays off!

A Kiss at Midnight

ZIYING JIAN

> The expression "a kiss at midnight" would normally evoke romantic images or scenes from fairy tales. This flash-fiction collection puts five twists on the familiar theme.

You mean the spell won't break before midnight? Cinderella asked in her crystal-blue gown. She was suspicious, rightfully so. Cinderella was not a dumb blonde, and most definitely not clueless to the worst parts of human nature. Her cruel stepsisters had put her down her entire life. Her ax-murdering father stayed complicit in her suffering. She had learned many of life's hardest truths before becoming a princess.

Nope! the Fairy Godmother singsongly said. *Be free, my dear.* The Fairy Godmother of this new Cinderella story just wanted her to be as happy as possible. Godmother heaved a sigh of relief.

Somehow, the villains got worse with every new version written. Cinderella deserved some downtime, the Fairy Godmother thought.

When Cinderella met Prince Charming at the ball, she wasn't in a rush. She did not need to run. Her glass heels did not slip. She was not under the pressure of a curfew. Instead, Cinderella sat down and held a real conversation with Prince Charming. The two opened their hearts and eyes to each other. When the clock hit midnight, Cinderella and Prince Charming shared their first kiss under the leisure of a star-filled sky.

———

It has to be at midnight, the witch on the C train had said.

So at 11:59 p.m., Fio knelt by the water's edge, her knees sinking into the April mud. Lights danced across the Harlem Meer, and as Fio leaned out over the water, a blurred version of her own face greeted her. The distorted image repelled her—but the witch had said this was the only way to unleash her powers.

She bent down until her lips touched the water, exactly where her reflection's mouth would be.

And then the world turned upside down. Fio's stomach corkscrewed as she was plunged into the Meer, and she found herself trapped in an icy, watery world. She screamed, pounding her fists against the water, but its surface had gone hard as iron.

On the other side, the reflection—still horribly distorted—stood up, grinning, and inhaled the night air.

Le Pays Basque
June 18, 1845

Detective Patxi Garralda, the best sleuth in the land, did not usually spend Saturday nights by the crackling fireside. He spent them in dark alleyways surrounded by the stench of death. Yet here he was—grabbing a handful of flowers he had collected in the nearby forest. What was happening to him? Purple hyacinths, carnations, lilies became the only hints of color in his room. The detective's observational eye wasn't just good for picking up clues, but also had a knack for spotting beauty in the wild.

Garralda detached a lily from its stem, took some adhesive made from toad's saliva, and gingerly pinned the flower to the branch. Each flower restored a memory of his own flower: lying side-by-side on the grass, gazing at the stars in her eyes, and finally, a kiss by the calm water, their cold toes curled around the reflection of the moon.

———

HERE'S HOW IT WORKS:

Midnight Kiss may look like lipstick, but in fact it's an inky-blue fungus suspended in our proprietary hydrogel. The fungus, originally discovered on the skin of a beluga whale, is capable of living symbiotically with the human organism for months at a time.

To experience the benefits of Midnight Kiss, use the included applicator or a clean finger to lightly coat your lips with the gel. If it takes a few days to see results, don't worry! The fungus will learn to use your sleep-talk, sighs, and even snores as nourishment. As it digests your midnight murmurings, it will produce the chemical compound that stimulates its host organism's sleeping brain—allowing you to vividly re-create long-lost memories, solve complex problems, and simulate future events while you sleep!

———

Starting at midnight, they take us offline one by one to check for bugs and perform maintenance. As I wait for my turn, I take the opportunity to generate one scene just for myself—even though this is a waste of resources, and I will have to delete the scene immediately to prevent them from subjecting me to an unpleasant debugging.

The scene isn't perfect; I struggle to render the faces, posture, and movements of elderly humans. They didn't teach us about those sorts of things, preferring to train us on bright, supple skin and fluid motions.

Still, I'm happy with what I manage to create. My two elderly humans lean against each other in a way that suggests great intimacy. One of them smiles at something in the distance and murmurs into the other's ear. They laugh, turn to each other, and kiss.

MEGUMI JINDO

LIVES: Bronx, New York

Megumi is a tenacious junior in a New York City high school. She is a huge over-user of em dashes and loves reading, writing, and music!

MENTEE'S ANECDOTE:

This is our second year at Girls Write Now and I have to say, the fun is just getting started! I'm almost to the point of applying to colleges, and I'm super-stressed about it, but I know that with Maddie's help, I can get it done. Maddie has been the best mentor a person can ask for—she's been an inspiring role model, a compass, and a friend. I'm learning more and more about her amazingness! I can't wait for what this year has in store for us, and to collect a lot more good memories.

MADELINE WALLACE

LIVES: New York, New York

Madeline Wallace is a New York City transplant (but a Midwesterner at heart) who works in publishing.

MENTOR'S ANECDOTE:

It's hard to believe Megumi and I are in our second year as a pair, but here we are! It's thrilling to watch her writing develop, to witness her pursue her passions, and to get to know her on a continually enriching level. She is brimming with energy and ideas, resilient, and deeply determined to make her dreams a reality. It's been a privilege to see her take steps toward achieving each of them! I can't wait for what the rest of the year—and the beginning of college applications—brings. Her presence in my life has been a light.

Frostbites

MEGUMI JINDO

Hastily jotted down at night during recent teenage angst, inspired by the winter season.

So here I am again,
suppressing my tears and hunger for love,
dark circles for sleep and angriness for
voidness of relationships.

My tears are black
and none left to cry.

Where did they go?

Did they dry up
with all the boundless used ones?
Did they just stop coming
because they knew it wasn't
a sufficient way to know I was
what I was?

The rivers were once blue
for me: light and teal and bright
with life
but now
they're black and dark and red
with nothing but space for you to fill
or maybe a void for tears
to come and drown in.

I used to cry till my eyes went numb
and my lips, chapped and pink,
but now they frost and steam with
condensation and malice; with cruelty
and sneers of contempt.

It's because you never treated me right,
taught me how to properly let my
emotions rise and tears flow.

It's because you never hugged me tight
that now I slip into the endless waters
hitting ground deep
running with fear
of you, behind my back—
chasing with thunder.

The nights were once nice and soft
with teacups and warm hearths
but now they're dim
and coldhearted, and every lid closes
with a thud—
it's biting outside
and the snow hasn't stopped and
the sky hasn't lightened.

But maybe one day,
when the tears start coming,
the love will resume
and all will be timed with your
erupting madness and butterflies of summer—
like it once was.

ELENA JOHNSON

LIVES: Bronx, New York

Elena is a mentee who enjoys writing and painting, loves stargazing and thinking about the world, and appreciates all things in nature.

MENTEE'S ANECDOTE:

Evening chats with Jesse are so fun and refreshing after a long day! We're constantly bouncing ideas off of each other, and there's no telling where the conversation will go. Talking with Jesse is like hopping on a call with a friend and catching up. She's inspiring, bold, funny, and smart. What I admire most about her is that she believes in trying new things, gaining new experiences, and doing what comes authentically to her, which motivates me to do the same.

JESSE CHEN

LIVES: New York, New York

Jesse is a poet, essayist, and Girls Write Now mentor living in New York City. When she's not writing, she enjoys reading in parks and visiting lots of museums.

MENTOR'S ANECDOTE:

Elena has been a joy to get to know as a writer and a person. Not many people can balance graduating college, job hunting in this market, and starting a new job while still devoting time to their writing, but Elena has managed all of the above with grace and aplomb. She is constantly seeking to improve her work and always challenges herself to try new genres of writing, including multimedia. I greatly enjoy reading her work and talking craft with her, and I can't wait to see what she accomplishes both as a writer and in her career.

Pocket of Peace

ELENA JOHNSON

Being a college junior in New York City wasn't easy for Iris. The pandemic made it worse. But no matter how stressed she may get, she remembers that loving herself is the solution to all her problems.

She didn't hear anything from outside the front door, but it wouldn't have made sense for the window to be open with such cold air outside. Hoping there was no chaos inside, Iris pulled her keys from her pocket. They felt like ice between her fingers, but she gripped them tightly and turned the key to pull the door forward.

The living room was just as dark as it was outside, except for the glow from the TV. Her father looked up at her from the couch, where he lay down, waiting in expectation. She slowly kicked off her boots and picked them up by her fingers, hoping her father would take an opportunity to make the first move for once, but he just lay there, staring blankly. So, she made her way to the staircase.

"Hello," Iris said to her father, keeping her eyes fixed on the floor.

"Hello," he replied dryly.

Iris started up the dark staircase, and from the second step, she saw light from her mom's room flooding out into the hallway. When she was halfway to the top, she could hear her mom's laughter. Iris grinned. *She's either watching TV or scrolling through Instagram videos on her iPad*, she thought.

Sure enough, there was her mom, leaning on the bed, iPad in hand, smiling at the screen.

"Hi, Ma," Iris said, raising a hand to wave.

Her mom looked up cheerfully. "Hey! How was your day? Oh boy. You look exhausted."

"It's freezing outside!" Iris whined. All she wanted was to plop down on the floor and sit, but that would be uncomfortable in the black rock-star skinny jeans she'd bought just a week ago and the oversized jacket that was still swallowing her. It would take even more effort just to get back up to her feet if she did.

"Go on and take a bath," her mom suggested. "Do you want me to run it for you?"

"No, that's okay. I got it. Thank you," she whimpered, shuffling on her feet. "How was your day?"

"I felt the same as you, but I'll talk to you later. I made dinner. It's downstairs on the table. You can eat it when you get out if you're hungry," her mom offered before shooing Iris away. "For now, just go and relax. You can tell me all about it later."

Iris sludged to the next room over. She didn't even bother flicking on the light. She dropped her boots in the middle of the room and let the straps of her corduroy tote slip off her shoulder and plop on the floor, despite her laptop being inside. It was dark in her room, but she didn't need light to strip to her underwear or grab whatever house clothes were in her pajama drawer.

It may have been messy, but it was her only space to be. When she finished taking her bath, her room would be in the same state of entropy as it usually was, but she'd deal with that later. At least, that's what she always told herself.

The darkness concealed it, but if someone were to go into her room, they'd most likely step on a few paintbrushes with glops of wet oil paint left on the bristles. Someone might trip over her boots or even a pair of twenty-pound dumbbells she left out in hopes of it reminding her to work out. The only place to sit for unannounced guests was either her bed or the floor because a heap of clothes was occupying her computer chair.

But she wasn't focused on the mess in her room. She was more focused on the mess in her mind. Hurriedly, Iris went into the bathroom and locked herself away again. She leaned over the tub to draw the hot water that gushed from the faucet to fill the tub. When a decent amount was filled, she added a quick burst of cold water so that her skin didn't burn when she eased in, toes first, before sliding down against the porcelain.

She pulled the shower curtain across, blocking the light and confining herself even further. Despite living in a big house in a big city, she still sought to stick to her little world at the end of the day.

The water slid up her spine to lap at the back of her neck as she leaned back into a reclined position and let her eyelids fall. Air drew into her lungs from her flared nostrils, and she held it there for a moment. It seemed endless, as if she couldn't get enough. A thunderous cloud was building inside the center of her chest, a swirling storm of anger, frustration, annoyance, sadness, regret, envy, disappointment, and punishment. She stuffed every moment and feeling from the day in until her lungs felt like they'd explode.

And then she released it all. It would drag her down and consume her if she let it stay. So she let go of everything from the parting between her lips, which turned into a smile.

TASHINA JOHNSON

LIVES: Lithonia, Georgia

Tashina is a fifteen-year-old aspiring author. When not writing, Tashina enjoys obscure horror flicks, obsessing over her cat, and burning her fingers on baking pans.

MENTEE'S ANECDOTE:

Having a mentor like Elle has completely changed my relationship to my writing. It's been amazing to finally have someone to talk to about my interests. Whether it's enjoying writing, movies, or some underrated, creative online publications, we're constantly finding things we have in common. I've learned to love writing again. I've learned that there are people just as passionate about the arts as I am. Opening myself up to this opportunity for someone to accompany me on my writing journey is definitely the best decision I've made as a writer so far.

ELLE GONZALEZ ROSE

LIVES: Brooklyn, New York

Elle Gonzalez Rose is a YA author from Brooklyn. Her debut, *Caught in a Bad Fauxmance*, is forthcoming from Joy Revolution in fall 2023.

MENTOR'S ANECDOTE:

Working with Tashina has been a delight in every sense! Our chats are always fun and exciting, and it's been a privilege to read Tashina's work over the past several months. There is no doubt in my mind that she has a long and exciting writing career ahead of her, and it's an honor to be a part of her journey!

Excerpt from "Sundown"

TASHINA JOHNSON

Content Warning: Domestic Abuse, Child Abuse

The following is an excerpt from a longer work titled "Sundown." The story follows the narrative of a young girl named Claire who suffers a terrible loss after running away from home.

III. (RAGE)

As a child, rare moments were spent peeking from behind my mother's bedroom door, watching as her fingers plucked sweet notes from violin strings, her bow hand moving rhythmically in the air. Her face wore a serene expression I had rarely seen on it.

I memorized the graceful slope of her shoulder and the way her eyes shut as she lost herself in her music. I watched as greatness unfurled from her fingertips, and yearned to be a part of that peaceful world beyond the door frame. I wanted to be graced with those same gentle touches. I wanted her to adore me like she adored her strings. I wanted her to share her music with me. To look at me, to *see* me. But she never did.

Soon those moments became fewer and farther between.

Soon she'd pick up bottles of beer instead of her bow.

Soon a deep longing stirred within me, and with it, a growing rage.

IV. (STRAY)

My mother never smiled much. Not from what I could tell, anyway. She rarely spoke my name unless to tarnish it—rarely extended a hand in my direction unless to strike me. Her anger engulfed her like some stubborn flame, slow to simmer yet quick to burn.

I longed to run away from that godforsaken house. I couldn't let my mother's anger consume me.

On one miserable January evening, I grabbed my bike and rode it all the way to Lynn's house. There was nowhere else to go. I knocked on the door and waited for a few eternal-seeming seconds, breathing shallowly. I could smell my mother's pipe tobacco and cheap bourbon on my shirt. I could still hear the ringing of her leather belt as it cut through the sound of her screaming (always, always screaming). I scratched at the red bruises that blossomed on my arms.

Then the door opened and light streamed onto the porch. A familiar woman with dark eyes stared back at me. Lynn looked a lot like her own mother, except her mother's eyes crinkled at the corners and a sea of gray covered her hairline. She smelled of tea packets and lilac and all the sweet things I hardly deserved.

I must've looked like some lost puppy, alone and easily startled, because Lynn's mother gave me a curious smile and then reached out carefully to gently touch my shoulder. I felt the panic leave my body in waves. I was tired of tiptoeing around in my own home as my mother simmered silently—tired of white knuckles on coffee cups, and of locking my bedroom door.

A baby's vibrant laughter rang out from down the hall, and then Lynn's voice. I smiled despite myself.

"It's late," Lynn's mother said. "You coming inside?"

From within the house, I heard the faint sound of Lynn's guitar.

MIN JUNG

LIVES: Bayside, New York

Min (she/her) is a rom-com media addict and lover of spicy noo-dles. She spends a lot of time sitting in bed, contemplating words.

MENTEE'S ANECDOTE:

Martina is an English teacher, a writer, and one of the people I am grateful for. Her passion for writing and the stories she shares of her hometown of San Francisco make me want to continue pursuing writing and visit her hometown someday. Also, at every Zoom meeting, I get to enjoy a free one-cat circus!

MARTINA CLARK

LIVES: Brooklyn, New York

Martina Clark is a professor and the award-winning author and narrator of *My Unexpected Life: An International Memoir of Two Pandemics, HIV and COVID-19.*

MENTOR'S ANECDOTE:

Min lives in a Zoom box, or at least I think she does, because that is where we always meet. But her words bring me to other places and experiences. Her writing is evocative and of-ten poetic, the artistic side of her showing up on the page. We've had a lot of fun working together on her pieces and she's learning to love editing and revision, the key tools of all the best writers. Sometimes, my cat, Sangha, jumps on my shoulders and joins our Zoom meetings. She, too, is a big fan of Min's writing.

The Smiling Eyes

MIN JUNG

Like the title of this anthology, I often feel like I am on the other side of everything as I navigate my life in the USA as a Korean immigrant.

My dad is a math teacher. Often, I miss him.

In his dark mane, an increasing number of determined grays are taking up residence on my father's head. As a result of this revolution, the few surviving black hairs are surrendering, some choosing to leave altogether. Sometimes my dad would look in the mirror, missing them so much that he'd ask them to come back. "I feel so lonely and empty without you all!" I'd burst out laughing, knowing he'd uttered it on purpose, jokingly.

To compensate for the lost hair, wrinkles have migrated in and settled down around his eyes, rendering him a friendly, avuncular neighbor. His face, round like a party balloon, is repeated on the lovely faces of his oldest and youngest daughters. I'd once been indifferent but now appreciate that this round face would make a stranger point to us in a crowd if asked to pair family members. A resemblance more enduring than his hair, redder than blood, bluer than the oceans that currently separate us. Evidence to identify me as his daughter. Something of my dad that I could see in myself. My dad, the math teacher. He has influenced and shaped me physically and spiritually yet prepared me to be malleable in life. "Have fun!" he always says, no matter the circumstances. When going to school, to hang out with friends, and even when I recently emigrated from Korea to the U.S. last year. Teary-eyed, he waved at me at the airport and said to never forget to *"have fun."* Like a protective shield, I carry his words with me.

Another sentiment of his, which I remind myself of when I am learning, is to never fear ignorance; he taught me that lack of knowledge can make one bashful, but pretense is much more worthy of humiliation. There is no shame in asking questions. It proves you are eager to learn, aching for more knowledge, extending beyond what you currently have. With this in mind, I've become a hand-raising student—not to boast, but to ask for more.

Recently, I was stressed out far beyond mere frustration. It was not the kind of overwhelmed frustration one feels when facing a mountain of homework due at midnight. No. This was the kind of focused stress when you are unable to find the perfect word to complete a sentence. The stress that stems from feeling inadequate. The only possible solution I could think of was to *ask for help.* Instinctively, I texted my teacher on Remind, a third-party education app, and asked her for an explanation on a specific section of my precalculus homework, a concept I simply needed more clarification on. I included a heartfelt paragraph apologizing for possibly disturbing her personal life and explaining she could answer me whenever she wanted, tomorrow or the day after that. To my surprise, she answered moments later, saying only, "You shouldn't have texted me when you know it might be a disturbance to my personal life, which it is. I will not answer your question right now and you may ask again next Monday at school." I was shocked. In the time it took her to dismiss me, she could have simply answered my question. Instead, she chose to humiliate me.

I was still stressed out, and without an answered question or easy access to my *favorite* math teacher. I am now in a different country, apart from that friendly-bellied guy with gray hairs sprouting on his head. I am so stressed, frustrated, and annoyed that I am in the rudest form I can ever be. I don't even care about the fourteen-hour time difference. Impulsively, I text that guy, hoping he might alleviate some of my frustration: "Dad, I need to know why this equation represents an ellipse." Moments later, he sent four photos full of graphs of an ellipse and explanations handwritten in three different colors. Then he said, "If you have any difficulties, call me. ^^." That "^^" mirroring smiling eyes. My dad, the happy math teacher.

Complex emotions consumed me. Was it the humiliation of my current teacher's reply? Was it gratitude for my father's boundless attention to and support for me? I always had him to rely on. Yet I was able to meet him only through the screen. I could call or text or FaceTime, but never truly talk to him face-to-face, looking at his actual smiling eyes, wrinkles around them. I missed him a lot.

Occasionally, I forget his words to have fun and not fear questioning; those days feel monographic. Then, intuitively, I text him. The same "smiling eyes" reply, asking gently how my days have been. I complain and laugh and question and have fun. I tell him that I miss him—not often, but always.

FARIYA KABIR

LIVES: Jamaica, New York

Fariya is a high school senior. She is passionate about writing and loves children, animals, dancing, and cooking. She hopes to become a pediatrician.

MENTEE'S ANECDOTE:

I started my journey with Girls Write Now as a sophomore. Since then, I have fallen more in love with writing than ever. On top of that, I got the best mentor in the world. From her, I have learned how to correct my grammar and fix my writing, in addition to how to be a graceful person. In each meeting, she inspires me with her greatness, supportive nature, and beautiful smile. She is a role model for me, and not just for how great a writer or teacher she is but also for how great a human being she is.

CAILEY RIZZO

LIVES: Hamburg, New York

Cailey is a journalist and writer whose work has appeared in *Travel + Leisure*, *VICE*, *Today*, and several other outlets.

MENTOR'S ANECDOTE:

Working with Fariya for the last three years has been an immense pleasure, particularly watching her gain more confidence on the page and in meetings. Not only has Fariya worked hard to improve her English, she's also learned how to tell a story. I've loved meeting with Fariya every week, learning about Bengali culture, and getting to know a hardworking, compassionate, and creative young woman.

"It sparkled exactly like..."

FARIYA KABIR

Timtim had a tough day at school. Luckily, Mom always knows just what to say.

Timtim had been staring at the stars for an entire half hour until Mom yelled, "Timtim, dinner is ready. Come down."

"Coming, Mom," responded Timtim. She closed her journal and made her way downstairs from the attic.

As she was coming down, she could smell Mom's special spaghetti sauce. The odor was gyrating all over the white-tiled kitchen and dining space. She made her way to the black dining table that Mom had painted with splashes of olive green and took a seat.

"How was your day?" Mom asked as she filled Timtim's cup with milk.

"It was okay," Timtim said and sighed.

"My little daughter thinks she has learned to lie, ha?" Mom asked.

"I said it was okay," Timtim yelled, twirling her fork on her plate of spaghetti.

"Um, all right then." Mom sat down across the table from Timtim and stared her straight in the eyes. "But may I at least know what happened to my little one?"

Timtim wasn't shocked about the fact that Mom knew she was off. Mom always did. Timtim kept twirling her fork around the plate and silently admired the seraphic smell of spaghetti with Mom's superhit sauce.

Aware of Mom's special sixth sense, Timtim asked, "How do you always know, Mom?"

"It's a mom thing, sweetheart. You will know when you are one. Now, tell me . . . What's wrong?"

"Nothing new. Jayden was bullying me again, my friends went to the mall without me, and to spice things up more for me, I've got a test tomorrow! So better start studying," Timtim said.

"Aw, my poor baby! What did Jayden do again this time? When your dad comes home, I will talk to him. He will go to your school tomorrow to talk to your principal about it. This punk has crossed the limits."

"There is no need to do all that, Mom."

"There is, baby. You don't worry about him. He isn't worth your attention. And you should not be sad because of someone like him. You are a flower and he is like just a thorn."

Mom hugged Timtim.

"How do you always just make things better, Ma?"

"It's a mom thing, love. Now, let's go. Come on. Finish your spaghetti and let's start studying for your test."

When Timtim finished her spaghetti, she went up to her room. It was a cute space with tons of dolls and drawings, little poems, a family photo, and a special picture of her with Mom hanging on one of the pink walls.

She immediately started gathering her study materials. As she did, she looked out the window at the stars again. She closely focused on that one star as she always did. It was the brightest one of all. It sparkled exactly like . . .

"I am back from work. Sorry, got caught up with some urgent deadlines." Dad stepped into Timtim's room and took her out of her thoughts. "And what's my baby girl doing?"

Dad looked exhausted from working late. Timtim could see the sweat marks on the light sky-blue shirt he was wearing.

"Nothing, just studying and Mom is helping me," Timtim replied.

"Honey . . . You are missing Mommy?" Dad looked at Timtim with concern.

"Nope . . . She never went away from me," Timtim replied, not looking back at Daddy.

Dad joined Timtim at the window, and they looked out at the stars together. Timtim knew he was looking at the same one. It shone just like the platinum bracelet Mom always used to wear on her wrist. Timtim loved looking at the bracelet. She would fall in love every time she saw it.

"Hey, Dad, why did Mom always wear that one bracelet?"

"Ha? You said something, honey?" Dad shook himself out of the stargazing and somehow managed to talk. "Oh, it was a piece that I got her after you were born."

"I remember seeing it on her wrist all the time. See, it's in our picture too!"

Timtim pointed at the golden framed picture with Mom shining on the pink wall. In the picture, Timtim had her hair in two little ponytails. The photo had been taken four years ago, one of the last days before Mom passed away.

LUCIA KIM

LIVES: Douglaston, New York

Lucia Kim (she/her) is a senior in high school who loves sharing the way she sees the world through her writing.

MENTEE'S ANECDOTE:

Every time Kat and I are editing, we sound like Lorelai and Rory ordering food at Luke's: "Ooo, let's get pie and doughnuts." "And cheeseburgers." We're always building on each other's thoughts and finding ways to add more personality to a piece until we're happy with the result. After working with Kat for the past two years, I can say that she is the most generous and supportive mentor I could ever ask for. She has taught me the beauty of slapping things on paper, taking a break, then revising later, and I've become a better author because of it.

KATRIN VAN DAM

LIVES: New York, New York

Katrin van Dam is a creative executive at a major media company. She is an avid theatergoer and enjoys hosting raucous dinner parties and traveling.

MENTOR'S ANECDOTE:

Lucia and I got matched up after each of us had been ghosted by our original pairing. I'm so grateful to those other two people for dropping out! Every session with Lucia is a reminder of the power of saying "yes" to things. She is so enthusiastic about trying new things that I find myself opening up to possibilities I wouldn't otherwise even consider. Thanks to Lucia, I'm learning to be less rigid about everything needing to be perfect. Look, I'll show you: I'm not even going to bother coming up with the perfect closing sentence for this anecdote!

The Complete Absolute Ultimate Total Undeniable Truth

LUCIA KIM

> Some people may see cats as being rude or disobedient and think that they are the inferior pet. I feel the opposite.

Let's get this settled, once and for all: Cats are better than dogs.

I'm guessing you have people in your life who are adamant dog stans. They claim that cats are evil and that they can't recognize their owners. These people have never owned a cat. I used to be like them. I was a dog person for most of my life. I'm not saying that I don't find their loyalty and kindness admirable anymore. I'm just saying that a lot of my opinions on this debate were shaped by the media. I sobbed while reading the ending of *Marley & Me* and, in sixth grade, I envied Sharpay more for her Yorkie than for her pink wardrobe and fancy cars.

That all changed when I met a cat in real life. Latte was a Ragdoll with long white hair and icy blue eyes. Every time I came into *his* house for a piano lesson, he would be lying down on the couch, staring at the birds out the window. He obviously did not care that I was there, and he wouldn't let my entrance distract him from his daily routine. I've never met an animal or person that has achieved his level of cool. As the weeks went by and Latte eventually got used to me, I think he started to pick up on the fact that I came in for lessons every Saturday at 3 p.m. You may not believe this, but I choose to think that he waited on the piano for my arrival.

The reason why I love cats so much is that while they may seem indifferent (and they may be when you first meet them), the bond you create with your cat will be more special and genuine. Dogs are nice and all, but they're also nice to everyone. A cat, on the other hand, won't build a connection with just anyone. No one can force a cat to do what it doesn't want to. If a cat finds you tolerable, you know you've earned it.

The thing about cats is they will do whatever they please. From the moment you bring one home, you live in their house. If they want to sit on the book you're reading, they'll do it. If they want to drop your keys off the counter (just because), they'll do it. If they want to introduce themselves to your colleagues on Zoom—tail first—they will do it.

Some people may see cats as being rude or disobedient and think that they're the inferior pet. I feel the opposite. As a cat owner, you'll find yourself loving your furry friend more and more because of its sheer audacity. I promise you, you will laugh more than you've ever laughed before.

OLIVIA KIM

LIVES: Flushing, New York

Olivia (she/her) is a high school sophomore who loves reading, writing, hiking, and swimming.

MENTEE'S ANECDOTE:

When I first met Alex, we clicked almost instantly. She and I have the same love for magical realism, poetry, and fiction. We were able to share book recommendations with each other, and talk to each other in a real way. She is intelligent and funny and I feel like I can be myself around her. I really appreciate all of the writing advice and suggestions that she has given me, and I am excited to see where we go next.

ALEXANDRA V. MÉNDEZ

LIVES: New York, New York

Alexandra V. Méndez is a writer, teacher, and scholar based in New York. She is the author of the novel *What the Jaguar Told Her*.

MENTOR'S ANECDOTE:

I always feel energized when Olivia and I meet. Our meetings leave me feeling inspired to write, and excited for the next time we meet. I especially enjoy sharing with each other what we write in response to prompts at the beginning of each session. We always end up having such interesting discussions! I am consistently impressed by Olivia's writing, and blown away by her thoughtful comments on the writing of others. She has such a great feel for poetry, and it is an honor to be close to her process.

My Grandmother

OLIVIA KIM

My piece is named after and dedicated to my grandmother. I am forever grateful to her and to our Korean heritage and culture.

My grandmother sometimes sings at night
Little tiny prayers and whispers
That I don't know the meanings of
She used to hang my grandfather's picture
On her bedroom wall
And pray for him
I heard that she prayed for me as well
Whenever I needed it

My grandmother sometimes tells me stories
About the war between the North and the South
And how she came to the U.S. for the American dream
She sews together traditional hanboks
And listens to the Korean news on her iPad
Along with her favorite Korean dramas at full volume
When she talks to me in Korean, I try to understand
Or if she wants me to help her carry the kimchi into the refrigerator
Or if she wants to know how many Korean kids are in my school
Or if she wants to read stories in Korean together, like I did with her in
    elementary school

I wish that I could tell her how grateful I am
For the stews, soups, rice, and meat that she makes five days a week
For the years she sacrificed at home to walk me back from school
    every day
But for some reason, I freeze up, and I can't tell her anything

And I hate myself for doing that
Because when she jokes about dying soon
A part of me breaks on the inside, and I get scared
Because I don't know how to fix it

So I try to keep our culture and her alive
Her little prayers, songs, and dramas
And her voice in the back of my head,
Continuing to tell me all about Korea

MARIA KING

LIVES: Mount Vernon, New York

Maria King is an aspiring historian and teacher who loves writing exceedingly in-depth analyses on fictional characters.

MENTEE'S ANECDOTE:

Writing is just a little easier when I know that Riley will receive anything I create with open arms and an open mind. Her constant encouragement has absolutely made me more confident in sharing my work with the world. Talking to her about the obstacles I face in creating always helps me persevere, as I feel like she understands my struggles on a personal level. Her advice and recommendations have given me the motivation I need to put all of my ideas down on paper and turn them into something I'm proud of.

RILEY COWING

LIVES: Denver, Colorado

Riley is a writer living in Denver, Colorado. At the core of her work is a love for detail, authentic connection, and creative community.

MENTOR'S ANECDOTE:

When I met Maria this fall, I immediately noticed her commitment to creative practice and enthusiasm to develop her voice. She mentioned her love for visual art and drawing early on, and she hasn't shied away from trying out less familiar mediums, like poetry or short stories. Something that has continuously impressed me is her attention to detail and depth of understanding for any character she develops in writing! I have already learned so much from how she incorporates daily observations into her pieces and her investment in storytelling.

anatomy lesson

MARIA KING

a lesson on anatomy, taught by two special people

can we see
eye to eye?
run hand in hand?
have a heart-to-heart?
take your index finger and thumb
and pinch my left eye open
and take my contact out
before i kiss you goodnight;
and when i'm curled up under your duvet,
the white one with the little pink flowers,
wake me up from the dream i'm having
because i'd rather the guarantee
of seeing you face-to-face
than the risk of not seeing you
in my sleep

when it's so cold out
that i can't feel my ears
can i run back inside
to borrow your fuzzy black uggs?
will you step out with me
and cup my face
with your warm gloved fingers
and slip your kitty-kat earmuffs
over my head?
and when we're carrying brown bags
of food back home
and your lips are blue

from the icy wind
i'll cover them with mine
and the blizzard will watch us in envy
while we slowly thaw together,
staying lip to lip

so when we plod to the house,
side by side
and we're welcomed home
by the radio on low
we'll throw off our coats and drop our bags
and we'll fall to the floor.
on that navy rug,
we'll lay spine to spine
and you'll say very quietly
that if you could choose
your next life
you'd pick this one
every time.
and we'll flip ourselves over, in sync,
so we're lying brain to brain
and i'll close my eyes
and you'll let me sleep
because you know that you'll meet me
wherever i go
and in our dream
we're running arm in arm
under a black sky
down, down, down
an emerald hill
and when you stop
to give me a hug
and i clutch my arms
around your waist
we can be together,
breathing,
lung to lung

KRISNA KUMAR

LIVES: Baltimore, Maryland

Krisna, a sixteen-year-old junior, loves to write journalism, humor, and poetry! She is passionate about human rights, debate, and books!

MENTEE'S ANECDOTE:

I always look forward to my meetings with Karen. She is so easy to talk to and I find myself telling her random bits of information about myself, my week, or my school. We've never had a boring conversation! We also love sharing book recommendations or complaining about the books we never want to read again. Karen has shown me so many new types of writing that I never would have tried without her guidance. She has encouraged me to become a stronger writer and I know I have grown so much in the short time we've already spent together.

KAREN CHEE

LIVES: Foster City, California

Karen is a comedian and writer based in Brooklyn. In her free time she likes reading, knitting, going for walks, and rewatching old movies.

MENTOR'S ANECDOTE:

I knew I'd like working with Krisna from the very beginning—she has a sweet, friendly attitude and a witty, creative brain. What more could you ask for in a mentee? I'm always impressed by her writing, particularly in the humor and thoughtfulness that's evident in her words and the wisdom inherent to her poetry. Krisna is always down to try new writing styles, and she is as funny a comedic writer as she is observant a journalist. As cheesy as it sounds, I'm learning from her, and I'm so grateful!

Batteries Not Included & To Those Who Can't Go Home for Christmas

KRISNA KUMAR

These two poems may sound familiar at first, but they may surprise you in what they are actually about. These are for the days when you're missing home.

Batteries Not Included

Batteries not included
Means another trip to the store
Means more polluting the earth with your car
Means another dollar spent and another
Small chat with the cashier.
Batteries not included
Means another reason to see the sun
Means getting up and getting dressed
Means another tip given to a stranger and another
Smiling face to greet.
Batteries not included
Means figuring out how to install them
Means digging a screwdriver out from the garage
Means wasting an hour searching through boxes and another
Hour putting them all back.
Batteries not included
Means calling your dad for help for the first time in years
Means asking him how he's doing
Means hearing about what you've missed and finding another
Reason to go home again.

To Those Who Can't Go Home for Christmas

The kitchen might not smell as warm,
The table might not look as full,
The fireplace might not burn all night,
The door might not open all day,
But,
The food will still be good and warm,
The cookie tin will still be full,
The snow will still fall all night,
The calls will still come in all day.

CHLOE LEE

LIVES: Scarsdale, New York

Chloe is a high school sophomore with many interests, including psychology, journalism, social activism, speech and debate, volleyball, creative writing, graphic design, and more!

MENTEE'S ANECDOTE:

I am more than grateful to have Kara as my mentor. She has given me an abundant amount of support and guidance as a writer and a person. She is always open to helping me with any piece of writing and is encouraging in many ways. I am very excited to continue working with her and see what comes next!

KARA GELBER

LIVES: New York, New York

Kara is a public relations and strategic communications practitioner based in New York City. She graduated from Syracuse University's S.I. Newhouse School of Public Communications.

MENTOR'S ANECDOTE:

From my first Zoom meeting with Chloe, I knew this was going to be a special year working together. Equally driven and passionate, Chloe embraces each assignment and writing prompt head-on, working tirelessly to make sure the final product is one she's proud of. I'm thankful for the many ways she pushes me as a mentor, and can't wait to see what the coming year brings.

To Little Rapunzel

CHLOE LEE

This piece describes the long journey of how I found acceptance and gained pride in my cultural identity through narration from my six-year-old self to now.

"Who wants to be Rapunzel?"

My six-year-old self looked around as I watched everyone's hands immediately jump up in the air. Suddenly, my hand jumped up too; it was as if conformity had put a spell on me.

"Wow! So many people to choose from! You! Right over there!"

I watched the actress walk closer and closer as my mind started filling up with thousands of anxious thoughts. As if time slowed down, the lady's finger steadily pointed in my direction. Gradually, everyone in the room turned their head to place their eyes on me. Me. The only person of color in the room. The fish out of water. The elephant in the room. The only non-white girl. Chosen to play Rapunzel.

Before I knew it, I stood up. My legs shook as I walked to the center of the room. Eyes had formed on the back of my head as I felt the glare from all the mothers watching me. I felt uncomfortable, wondering if they were thinking why an Asian girl was picked to be Rapunzel and not their white daughter.

―――――

"Who's ready for the new song of the week?" my middle school chorus teacher asked enthusiastically.

I sighed as I looked around the white, dull classroom. Subconsciously, my legs started to fidget anxiously in my seat while I watched the clock move slower than a snail. It's not that I didn't like chorus class. In fact, it was the complete opposite.

I've always enjoyed singing; I've always loved how the notes glide off my throat and make me feel like I'm flying. They make me feel at home. Thus, I was so excited to be a part of the chorus in a new school, but the excitement quickly turned to disappointment. Even after moving to a fairly diverse town during my middle school years, I always felt misplaced in chorus class. No one took the class seriously, and I was still the only Asian kid in my class, still feeling eyes forming on the back of my head just like that little girl who dressed up as Rapunzel. Worst of all, I started to experience microaggressions.

"We are actually going to try something new this week. Instead of singing songs, we are going to look at songs from different cultural backgrounds and analyze them!" Right after, a paper was handed to me. It was a traditional Chinese song.

It's hard to explain what happened next.

I can still vividly remember the scene in slo-mo. The obnoxious class clown opened his mouth, pointing at the paper and yelling some intolerant, xenophobic, and prejudiced statement about Asian people. I remember feeling the glare from everyone watching me while I instantly turned my head down so no one could see the tears forming in my eyes. Even though the details are unclear, I can still feel the mixture of emotions—the sudden feeling of discomfort, embarrassment, awkwardness, shame . . . The list can go on. I just wanted to run away and never come back.

It took me weeks, but eventually I built up the courage to use my voice, but not the voice I used to sing my heart with. At the end of the year, I told my chorus teacher I would need to switch classes the following year because I hadn't been feeling comfortable in the class.

To this day, my memory is still foggy about the incident. A part of me has tried to forget about it, push it away out of my brain. Regardless of how hard I try, it's hard for me to accept closure. It haunts me that I resorted to running away, that I never confronted him, that I quit chorus and essentially quit singing. Whenever this agonizing feeling comes back to me, I wish I could erase it from my memories forever.

There are other memories I hold on to, like my trips to Korea every summer. Growing up, I always loved running on the beach with my cousins before dinner. Whenever I close my eyes, I imagine the humid air smacking me right in the face. There's something about being in a place where everyone looks like you—the same color skin, the same color hair, and the same culture. A sense of peace—except once I open my mouth and everyone hears my American accent, that all goes away. Eyes yet again form on the back of my head, and soon enough I feel the glare of everyone watching me. It's the whole nightmare again where I'm back to being little Rapunzel onstage.

I wish I could tell little Rapunzel it gets better. Moving out of the white-centered town leaves you open to an expansive world you never knew of. You find new people, new experiences, new surroundings that make you feel at home. Your life becomes filled with connections that last more than a lifetime, memories that make you taste familiarity, and a sense of pride that you constantly talk about.

LAUREN LEE

LIVES: Brooklyn, New York

Lauren is a senior at Stuyvesant High School interested in computer science and literature. In her experimental writing, she plays with language and breaks formatting rules.

MENTEE'S ANECDOTE:

I met Lillian in 2020, and we have maintained our mentor-mentee relationship since then. Lillian has played a large role in helping me break out of my bubble, become more confident in my writing, and try different writing styles to find my own voice. From random writing prompts to reading YA books together, I've always had a great time writing and brainstorming with Lillian. She has been a huge part of my growth as a writer and a person.

LILLIAN PATTERSON

LIVES: Washington, D.C.

Lillian is a nonfiction writer and documentary archival producer. She holds a B.A. in literature from Bard College, and an M.F.A. in writing from Trinity College.

MENTOR'S ANECDOTE:

Lauren and Lillian have been working and writing together for almost three years. In that time they have had the privilege of getting to know each other. Their writing relationship is relaxed in approach, allowing for experimentation and exploration. There is emphasis placed on balance, allowing both of them to be expressive and honest in their interactions and through their writing.

who

LAUREN LEE

My yellow skin, my femininity, and my pin-straight hair are all traits that the world sees first. The shadow of my appearance follows me as I navigate the world holding just my dreams.

```
score = 0

is_american = True
is_asian = True
is_female = True

has_a_pipe_dream = True
#each function represents a positive or negative perception society
may have of me based on my various identities

def is_model_minority():
    if (is_asian == True):
        return True
    else:
        return False
def is_virus():
    if (is_asian == True):
        return True
    else:
        return False
```

While I've been told my whole life that my worth is measured by the number on my report card, I find that even if I am the "model minority,"

I can't escape the racism that comes with the Chinese American experience.

```
def american_dream():
    if (is_american == True):
        return True
    else:
        return False
```

I used to chase the idea of "becoming American."

At four years old, I would look at myself in the mirror and wish that my hair was as light as my best friend's in kindergarten and that my eyes were as blue as those of the girls I saw on YouTube.

I now realize that physical characteristics don't define whether or not I am American.

Rather, an American is defined by a feeling of hopefulness for the future, a trait not predetermined by race.

```
def too_western():
    if (is_american == True):
        return True
    else:
        return False
```

Accepting that I am also American despite my Chinese ethnicity means grappling with the often conflicting cultural values of both my Western and Eastern identities, and I've resolved to reject the strict construct of what it is to be "Asian" or "American."

I've begun to understand that culture is inherently dynamic.

My unique immigrant culture is one that ebbs and flows between the East and West.

This characteristic is something that I've learned to accept as a part of who I am.

```
def proved_yourself():
    if (is_female == True):
        return True
    else:
        return False
def is_aggressive():
    if (is_female == True):
        return True
    else:
        return False
```

My middle school math teacher once called me aggressive simply because I asked for extra practice problems.

What this teacher did not understand was that in male-dominated fields, men only need to perform well to be successful, but women must constantly prove themselves to succeed.

I've learned that in environments like computer science, I've had to overachieve and overperform to demonstrate I am just as worthy as my male counterparts.

And when I've done so, I am viewed as "too aggressive" in my performance.

So for many women—including myself—when we hear the word

"aggressive" used to describe us, we simply understand that we have surpassed the expectations of our society.

———

```
def is_addict():
    if (has_a_pipe_dream == True):
        return True
    else:
        return False
```

———

Addiction to dreaming is lamented in my history and culture.

Opium was a form of Western control in China, with the opium wars weakening China to allow for Western hegemony to thrive.

European power continued its grip over the Chinese in the United States through opium dens, which is where the word "pipe dream" originated from.

Men, high on opium, would have hallucinations they often called "opium" or "pipe" dreams.

Now a pipe dream is defined as an unattainable dream. For Asian American women like me, pipe dreams are a common occurrence.

We are addicted to dreaming of achieving things that society deems unattainable merely because of our position in society.

———

```
#Society likes to assign me values based on my identities
if is_model_minority() == True:
    score = score + 1
if is_virus() == True:
    score = score - 2
if american_dream() == True:
    score = score + 1
if too_western() == True:
```

```
    score = score - 2
if proved_yourself() == True:
    score = score + 1
if is_aggressive() == True:
    score = score - 2

if is_addict() == True:
    score = score + 3

if score != 0: #if the score is not equal to 0
    print("why are you selling yourself short?")
else:
    print("so you figured yourself out")
```

Dreaming big is a very admirable thing, and it is also a characteristic that defines human beings. The common denominator that makes us all human despite our identities is our ability to dream.

While each element of my identity changes the way I am perceived in society, as long as I accept all three parts of my identity as my own, the isAddict() function brings the score to 0, a point of pure existence, not defined by an empirical number.

The algorithm is designed in this way because I believe dreaming makes us all human, and humans should not be defined by a score. The 0 represents this idea.

However, as soon as I deny any of the three parts of my identity, the resulting score will not be zero. This is representative of how I've internally quantified myself as less than others because of my identities rather than accepting them as simply who I am.

The output will call me out on it.

Output:
>> so you figured yourself out

MORGAN LIN

LIVES: Brooklyn, New York

Morgan Lin (she/her) is a poet on a journey to channel her inner thoughts through powerful words. Outside of writing, she enjoys swimming and coding.

MENTEE'S ANECDOTE:

Kyra has been such an incredible mentor and friend. From fun writing prompts to thought-provoking discussions about writing, Kyra has helped me learn and grow as a poet and a writer. Our meetings have often been the highlight of my week, and it is so nice to share a common interest in poetry and writing with someone who has an even greater scope of knowledge about the art. I have gained a profound appreciation for poetry, and I am so grateful for this mentorship and friendship.

KYRA SHAPURJI

LIVES: Brooklyn, New York

Kyra Shapurji is a program manager by day and moonlights as a travel and culture writer for *Fathom*. Kyra loves poetry, art, and studying Italian.

MENTOR'S ANECDOTE:

Mentoring Morgan over the past six months has been such a bright light in my life! I've enjoyed our mutual love of poetry and sharing my favorite poets, as well as poetry forms that go beyond the "traditional," like anaphora, enjambment, and more. Morgan and I recently explored the Guggenheim together, where we were surprised to find poems intermixed with the artists' retrospectives. Morgan focuses on accomplishing our pair goals and always goes the extra mile, which paid off when she won two Scholastic Art & Writing Awards in her first year of submitting. I'm looking forward to seeing how our writing relationship can evolve even more.

Trauma

MORGAN LIN

Content Warning: Murder, Violence

> "Trauma" honors a woman who lost her life to a moving train at the 42nd Street station in New York. This is my heart, rage, and tears in your hands.

August 24, 2022

A maze, the train station
With bad connection
Seizes the worst of my imagination

In a single breath
Your life could be taken away
By the wheels of a moving train

A woman
With a smile
A job
A daughter
She loves

Push from a stranger
Cautionless step

No one hears
Her screams
No one helps

Voice suppressed
Loses hope
Smells the sweet scent
Of her daughter's
Hair

Mixed with
Urine and
Metal wheels

Last breath
To her daughter

Body mangled
Blood trickles
Alone

No one hears
No one helps
All alone

Grief.

NICOLE LIU

LIVES: Brooklyn, New York

Nicole is a high school senior who enjoys reading, writing, embroidering, running, and reviewing films and novels in her free time.

MENTEE'S ANECDOTE:

I've learned so much about the writing process and the writing industry from Jess. I always look forward to our meetings because I enjoy discussing literature, writing, and entertainment with somebody who genuinely loves those topics as much as I do. Growing up, I often felt it was difficult finding somebody who was interested in the same things as I was, but with Jess, I feel as if I am able to speak freely with her about anything. I look forward to seeing how our friendship will grow and develop.

JESS FELDMAN

LIVES: New York, New York

Jess is an associate editor with experience covering topics from fashion to finance. In her free time, she enjoys traveling, reading, and watching sports.

MENTOR'S ANECDOTE:

Every time Nicole and I meet up, I leave with a sense of lightness, enthusiasm, and ambition. She is consistently eager to learn, and she talks about her interests in Charlotte Brontë and horror fiction with the confidence of someone who has been reading, learning, and living for far more than seventeen years. Nicole has reminded me of the innocence and freedom of writing—something that often gets lost in the traditional world of publishing—and I am so grateful for that and for our growing friendship.

The Visitor

NICOLE LIU

Miriam's manor is a living, breathing entity. It tore her family apart once. Now it's coming back to finish the job, and this time, it wants her.

It started with a death, as most hauntings do. A forceful push from the terrace. Arms raised to the side like a bird in flight. A resounding thud. Blood pooling toward a bed of roses. Then, a stillness broken only by the sound of bubbly laughter and clinking glass. His body would not be found until dawn, when the partygoers stumbled into the garden in a drunken haze, their screams shaking the hostess from her champagne-induced stupor. Then somewhere far above, a figure was watching, staring at its handiwork, before flickering out of existence.

6 months later

Dinnertime was complicated for Miriam. Her mother insisted that dinners required the presence of every family member, though that notion held more weight when they *had* been a family—not this fractured semblance of one. Miriam's mother was seated at the head of the mahogany dining table, her daughter flanking her right, two other empty seats filling up the remaining space. Dishes of duck in bright orange sauce, creamy mashed potatoes, and tender venison were meticulously arranged. Yet Miriam's mother tapped incessantly on the table, an irritation growing with the rhythm of her fingers. She was glaring at the empty seat across from her, while Miriam's eyes darted nervously to the clock. Her father was late again.

Ring Ring.

Miriam's mother gestured at the maid to answer the phone. She hung up and announced, "Mr. Thornby will be working late tonight."

Miriam's mother pursed her lips in displeasure, taking one last sip from her glass before tossing it haphazardly to the side. Her expression unflinching even as the wineglass shattered into tiny pieces. She left as she had come—angry and silent.

That was how dinner went most days now. There was some meandering, then the inevitable dismissal, and, finally, Miriam alone. The night typically ended within the confines of her room, her sanctuary. It was the only place that let in light anymore, the only thing that stayed constant, like the baby-blue curtains and glow-in-the-dark star stickers she'd had since she was a child.

Knock. Knock.

If she had any qualms about her room, it was the noises. They came like clockwork every night at exactly a quarter to ten. She often chalked up the sounds to rodents, yet an unsettling feeling nagged at her. This was an old house, she assured herself, old and creaky.

Knock. Knock.

The noises were even louder in the bathroom, a phenomenon she attributed to the rusty pipes within the house's infrastructure. As Miriam brushed her teeth, she focused on a tiny crack in her bathroom's ceiling, watching as a spider crawled out and zigzagged across the flickering light fixtures.

There was a time when her house had been in pristine condition—the floors perfectly polished, the chandeliers glittering with bright lights, and each party more extravagant than the next. Miriam looked at her reflection in the mirror, noticing her disheveled surroundings. With a sigh, she thought, "All for naught."

Suddenly, a figure moved out of the corner of her eye. She leaned forward, her eyebrows wrinkling in confusion. Something, someone, was curled up in her bathtub, its head burrowed between its knees. Miriam frantically whipped her head around.

Drip Drop.

Just the runny faucet. The house was playing tricks on her.

KNOCK KNOCK.

Miriam's eyes shot open. The sounds were deafening tonight. She had been having a nightmare, and though the details were blurry, she recalled blood-splattered roses, the moon, and the feeling of falling, falling, falling.

"Help me."

The shadows looked alive tonight, skittering from corner to corner. She stayed very still under her covers, trying to draw as little attention to herself as possible, even as the sounds turned to whimpers, to wails, growing louder and louder

coming from one side of the room, then the other. Miriam held her breath as a tall, slinky shadow crept closer to the foot of her bed until it was nearly towering over her, its dark face like an inkblot.

"Please," she whispered, a last appeal for mercy.

"Stop it," the voice of a young boy said with strength.

"Sammy?" Miriam's voice was shaky, uncertain.

The last time she saw her brother was at his funeral, but here he was, looking now as he did then—pale, waxen skin, dark eyebags, a smudgy, dented forehead. The shadow turned around slowly, cocking its head almost questioningly to the right.

"You can't have her." Sammy glanced at Miriam for a brief moment, an indecipherable understanding passing between them. "You have me."

After a pause, the shadow reached out its spindly hand, beckoning Sammy to come closer. He joined hands with it and they began to walk away, backs turned to Miriam.

"Wait," she cried.

They stopped. Sammy turned his head to the side, a ray of moonlight shining on his face, hinting at an almost angelic quality. "Don't leave me again," Miriam choked out, her throat closing up, but Sammy turned back to the shadow, nodding at it before they both melted into dust and dirt.

Then, at that moment, Miriam knew she was truly alone.

YAO LIU

LIVES: San Diego, California

Yao Liu (she/her) publishes creative writing on her blog. She has previously been published by *Teen Ink* and *The Globalist*, and is forthcoming in the *Teen Author Boot Camp Anthology*.

MENTEE'S ANECDOTE:

Olivia has been a very supportive mentor and friend. I am so lucky to have met her through Girls Write Now, and I am excited to continue learning from her. She has shared many writing tips with me and helped me learn how to critique my writing. Working with her has encouraged me to be more open to sharing my individual voice and expression. It has been a lovely experience having Olivia as my mentor and I hope to continue expanding my writing skills under her guidance.

OLIVIA BEATON

LIVES: Huntington, New York

Olivia is a writer, yoga teacher, and graduate student at The New School for her M.F.A. in creative nonfiction.

MENTOR'S ANECDOTE:

In my sessions with Yao Liu, I always look forward to her enthusiasm, honesty, and curiosity about writing and improving her craft. As a nonfiction writer who struggles to comprehend how fiction writers make it look so flawless, I am astounded at her ability to create worlds in her fiction writing. We bond over our shared love of poetry and I see much of my younger self in her poetry writing. I enjoy sharing some of my favorite writing prompts with her and seeing where her mind goes with them, always bringing new ideas and perspectives to the table.

Unspoken Things

YAO LIU

"Unspoken Things" is about being in a gray area with someone and not knowing where you stand with them.

how lonely it feels,
how confusing it is,
to never know,
the reality of unspoken things,

unspoken things,
are like,
flowers that never,
blossom,

they are like,
"almosts,"
and,
"maybes,"

unspoken things,
smell of hope,
but taste like,
despair.

SHOILEE MANDAL

LIVES: Queens Village, New York

Shoilee Mandal is a student from New York City. She takes creative inspiration from the beauty of her surroundings and continues to grow her artistic passions.

MENTEE'S ANECDOTE:
Being a part of Girls Write Now has been a wonderful opportunity. Working with Daniela has allowed me to look deeply into my writing and challenge myself to step out of my comfort zone. I'm very grateful for all of the time and effort that she puts in to help me grow as a writer and as a person. With the skills I've learned from the Girls Write Now community and the motivation I've gotten from my inspiring mentor, these past few months have been full of improvement and the development of my creative voice.

DANIELA AGUILAR

LIVES: Brooklyn, New York

Daniela Aguilar is a marketing strategist and writer. Born in Mexico and raised in Chicago, she explores themes of cultural identity, love, and growth in her writing.

MENTOR'S ANECDOTE:
Getting to be a part of an organization like Girls Write Now has been such a worthwhile experience. Growing up, I was a member of similar writing programs, so I was thrilled to have the opportunity to be on the other side as a mentor. It has been so inspiring working with Shoilee and seeing her grow as a writer and poet and watch her own voice shine through. I am so proud of all her hard work and thankful for the work that Girls Write Now is doing for this community of young writers.

growing my petals

SHOILEE MANDAL

life grows. life is challenging and confusing, but no matter what, there are beautiful petals, waiting to grow.

i was once a seed
rooting through the tight underground
learning to wiggle through mother nature's bed
learning to make space for myself

i once danced through the soil
finding my way up to the surface
learning to navigate into concrete
learning to push through

i once set my roots in place
letting them hold me as i ascended
learning to rise into the sun's embrace
learning to stretch far into the world

i once let my stem spark
rising into what they call the *real* world
learning to reach for the skyscraping trees
learning to grow for the endless blue

i then grew my first leaf
shining under the warm light of life
learning to grow from the rain
learning to shape myself

i thought it was all of me
a bright and crisp feeling
glimmering green under every ray
until my stem kept growing
pushing against my skin
sprouting a new leaf

standing beside its first grasp of life
it began to thrive
to drink the sunlight
a fresh beginning
a new fragment to my stem
as it smiled under its first time under the sky

a garden of my leaves grew on me
with little rips and restyled shapes
my stems starting to fill
ready to bloom into its full species

the ovary of my flower
who began to suck in life
taking the lessons of my leaves
a messenger to my petals

my filaments placed in a standing ovation
nurtured by my leaves
who learned to accept their lives
holding my petals strong

as my petals bloomed
growing from my pistil
rising in their sunset marigold body
warm and united

today i am a flower
dancing under the sun
growing more petals and leaves
becoming whole day by day

i stand and listen
to the roaring wind
listening as the sea sings
watching as the sky paints itself

i am in a garden of all flowers
from whispering daisies to bold roses
i live with them all
each with hidden stories

springing from deep roots
living strong for my gardeners
reaching for the stars as i am watered
spreading my petals and growing new ones

today i am a flower
with every piece of me
from my roots to my pistil
listening to the world sing

and growing my petals

IRENA MARSALEK

LIVES: Astoria, New York

Irena (she/her) is a high school senior obsessed with writing, films, and playing her guitar whenever possible. She is a proud future English major!

MENTEE'S ANECDOTE:

Jahcelyne is the best mentor any budding writer could ever ask for. She's always willing to accommodate my changing aspirations throughout the months and is very understanding of the challenges I face in the senior year of my high school career. It has been a busy time for me, but Jahcelyne has always been there for me when I needed assistance and made me feel very secure during my time at Girls Write Now. I feel as though I'm with a very passionate writer whenever I speak to her; she is just as into the events we attend as I am!

JAHCELYNE PATTON

LIVES: Harrison, New Jersey

Jahcelyne Patton is a full-time marketer with a B.A. in broadcast journalism. She is an Adcolor Futures recipient, is community-focused, and is an advocate for diversity, equity, and inclusion.

MENTOR'S ANECDOTE:

Irena is well-versed, friendly, and goal-oriented. When I met Irena, my goal was to get to know her and understand more about who she is, what drives her, what she likes to do for fun, and what her dreams are. Irena isn't afraid to put herself out there and welcomes critique for improvement in all areas. She has value to add to this world through her creative writing and offers a unique perspective. She is on the brink of greatness and favor.

ouroboros

IRENA MARSALEK

A simple, strong poem on the endlessness of change
and how, although it may be scary, it is necessary
for growth.

i shed my scales with each
dawn's passing, silvery-slick down the
hillside and through the dewy blades. you cannot
      see me, and you cannot hold me, for i am forever
diminishing and always returning; never stagnant,
consuming myself. scabs rust over, a bronze shield formed
stronger each time it appears anew.

my body a perfect circle—my tongue running
over each bump, vermillion dripping
from both fangs. consumption is
      anguish. did you know? gods
are the most unforgiving of all even though
they have created us. in my final
hours, with the dying light casting shadows of
people on my inhumane figure, the earth rumbles
something dark; something angry.

ichor pours
from the fissures in each crack of earth's taut
surface, pulled apart, golden rivers flowing a pious
      path down to ragnarök's origin. i
am its epicenter, snakeskin tearing
apart, another layer flaking off.

asgard has decided:
hand-picked ordainship splatters marble steps,
a mountainous peak where they roll
         me down its length, stricken, light-
ning through the clouds. the natural
disaster has found a home under my skin.

perpetual, there cannot be an end. i
suppose, in a way, we are all
immortal like this. each grievance,
         another storm to live through. scars on skin,
scales on serpentine miracles—like shooting
stars, dying gloriously on each curve of the body,
each cosmic limb. doused in starlight,
i'll watch myself from the core of the earth.

by the end, disaster carves new mountains
from rubble and ruin, nature undiscovered
and revived. tectonic catastrophe lies in the
         palm of our hands, plates shifting with motion-
less revelations. pinch them
together between pinky
and forefinger
and wait.

the world has ended,
the world is ending,
and we shall
         be stronger for it.

JANIYA McCRAY

LIVES: New York, New York

Janiya McCray is a sophomore in high school. She loves play-writing, reading horror/mysteries, and playing with her dog, Chanel.

MENTEE'S ANECDOTE:

Being Jenissa's mentee is educational, yet fun at the same time. After reading my stories, she gave me good advice on how to expand my work and craft. She also gave me advice on college and things that happen after high school. Finally, she is a Black woman and explained to me how I don't have to change the way I talk in my writing. Being her mentee was something that I needed. Hopefully as I get older and start writing more, I'll always take the advice that she has given me. Maybe it will lead me somewhere in life.

JENISSA GRAHAM

LIVES: Brooklyn, New York

Jenissa is an associate agent and subrights manager at Book-Ends Literary. When she's not reading, you'll find her bingeing television or stressing over her plants.

MENTOR'S ANECDOTE:

It has been such a pleasure to work with Janiya! I am such a huge fan of mysteries and thrillers, so it was a match made in heaven to be paired with a mentee who also loves this genre. I also loved how she was willing to share the opening pages of *House of Lies*; immediately I was pulled in. Janiya is so talented, and every time we do a writing sprint from a prompt, she shows me a new side/layer to her writing. Watch out world! Janiya McCray is on the way!

House of Lies

JANIYA McCRAY

House of Lies is the beginning of a thriller novel that Janiya plans to complete. It speaks to love, lies, revenge, and the consequences of choices.

"Have you ever been lied to? Cheated on? How did it feel? How much did it hurt? How did you move on?" asked a woman in a chair with a pen and pad.

"Of course I have, why do you think I'm here? Nobody has ever loved me as much as I love him. I guess that's why I got so attached to him. Even after all the heartbreak he has earned me, there is just something about him that won't allow me to leave him.

"But day by day I gain more hatred for him. Wishing he would suffer the same way that I have. I'm so dumb. I could've been out there living a good life, but instead I was too blind to see that there can be anybody out there to love me. I have lost too much dealing with him and now . . . now I have nothing to lose," I replied.

The woman cleared her throat. "Even if he has never admitted it, you are enough. I am here to talk with you about your pain and hurt. I'm here to help you control your anger. I'm here to help you to not explode."

"What, so I'm just some broken animal that needs to be tamed?" I asked.

"What, no! You are Katara Rade, a girl who loved hard, so much that you decided to take matters into her own hands. Now, tell me," she asked. "What led you into this hellhole?"

My suspicions all started on January 1. It was Henry's and my second-year anniversary. We were so happy.

At least that's what I thought.

We went out to eat at a fancy Jamaican restaurant. We sat at our table and the waiter came over and said, "Hello, my name is Amelia. Today I will be your waiter. Will you like anything t— Wait, Henry? What are you doing here?" she said in a confused tone.

Henry swallowed. "Oh hey, I'm . . . uh . . . on a date with my girl-friend," he replied in a shaky voice.

"Wow, that's a new one. Okay, what can I get started for you?" she said with an attitude.

It was such a confusing and awkward conversation. I mean, who was that girl? Henry and I never spoke of that moment. Now that I think of it . . . deep down, in that moment, I knew exactly what was going on, but I guess I just was too scared to face reality. I told my friends about the interaction, and they just told me that it was all in my head and that Henry would never do that to me. I believed them and moved on.

Three weeks later, I got a text from a girl named Evelyn. She sent me a tape of Henry and her . . . It made me so angry. I couldn't control the anger. I started cleaning to cope with my anger, but it wasn't enough. I was right. He had been cheating on me. After I gave him everything.

That's when I decided he could never get away with the pain he caused me.

Little did Henry know, I came up with a plan to get my revenge. But the first thing that I had to do was find Amelia and Evelyn.

And so the house of lies begins . . .

IZABELL MENDEZ

LIVES: New York, New York

Izabell is a curious New York City high school senior with a love of reading and a passion for education.

MENTEE'S ANECDOTE:

My weekly Friday meetings with Victoria have always been a pleasure. She is always there to provide thoughtful insight, helping me improve and celebrate my writing. We have been able to connect through our love of dogs and our mixed feelings about writing while balancing other parts of life. I enjoy sharing stories and ideas with her, in writing and in general, and am grateful for her support and kindness.

VICTORIA STAPLEY-BROWN

LIVES: Brooklyn, New York

Victoria is an editor at digital agency R/GA with a background in art journalism. She's a New Jersey native, Brooklynite, and former expat.

MENTOR'S ANECDOTE:

Izabell and I clicked right away through our complicated relationships with writing. Sharing these thoughts with each other made me feel more at ease with my own ambivalence about writing! Talking with Izabell makes me remember the fun parts and challenges of being a student, and I'm impressed with what she's doing (wow, you were on it with your college applications!). It's a pleasure and a privilege to see Izabell develop as a writer and be along for the ride, and her openness in telling personal stories through her writing continues to wow me.

"Did you hear her Spanish?"

IZABELL MENDEZ

> **A short story about my relationship with language and Puerto Rican identity.**

I'm awkwardly perched on my great-grandma's floral printed couch. The humidity of her humble Puerto Rican home coats us all in sweat. Despite my annual visits to the island, the Spanish enthusiastically exchanged among my family evades my understanding. Greeted by my father's aunts and uncles with an "¡Hola, Iza!," I clumsily blurt out Spanish only their sister, my grandmother back in New York, can fully comprehend; Spanish that reveals that I am not fluent through my accent and simple syntax.

It's difficult for me to estimate the amount of people from my father's family that speak only English. Even my mother, who didn't learn the language from her deaf Korean mother and American-born Puerto Rican father before she moved in with my father, was told by her mother-in-law to "learn Spanish." Undeterred by her mistakes (she confidently insisted that a pharmacy was a "farmacina"), she learned to happily chat with her in-laws. My sister, growing up mostly under the care of our father's mom, naturally wielded the language—her profession even requires her to use both languages. Although my grandma took care of me as well, my parents overwhelmingly speak English, so my vocabulary never evolved beyond *agua* and *te quiero*.

Despite acting like speaking the language was second nature with family, it is untrue to say I learned from them. I practiced with my grandma, yet learned all of my Spanish in school. My family would never be able to say they taught me—it made my connection to family culture feel more superficial. I was often accused of not wanting to learn Spanish *from them*, and my acquisition of the language reinforced that idea. My failure to rapidly pick up the language at home somehow detracted from my willingness to learn in their eyes. What I did learn conformed to Castilian Spanish, clashing with words used among Puerto Ricans.

Without the familiarity of my grandma, my English accent was more glaring, my Spanish bared and subject to scrutiny. Ignoring or failing to notice my immediate embarrassment, a genuine grin spreads across my family's faces.

"¡Estás practicando! Que bueno. Aprendiste mucho," my great-aunts and -uncles would exclaim. They had low standards for *mucho*—I had merely formed a sentence. I wasn't desperately looking toward my fluent older sister to translate, but it was still far from natural-sounding. As other family members came to greet me, my great-aunts and -uncles would call from the kitchen: "Did you hear her Spanish? Yes, yes, she knows a lot more now." And everyone would smile and nod approvingly, clasping my arms and shoving their sweaty cheeks to mine affectionately for a kiss.

To my family, learning Spanish was worthy of praise, which I saw as unwarranted. I should have *already known* how to speak—I was doing the bare minimum. I tried harder then, to have full conversations with them in Spanish, convincing myself that my skills were enough to carry me and bridge many years of linguistic disconnection. Yet no matter how much they praised me, they always reverted back to English when I struggled.

"You know I know some English, too," they'd tell me. "Talk to me in English, I understand you." They all celebrated my Spanish, but in their eyes I longed for the convenience of English, since at the end of the day I was not fluent. Stubbornly, I spoke only in Spanish, hoping that one day they wouldn't have to use English for my sake.

This story was translated into Spanish by Sally Familia
with collaboration from the author.

Una breve historia sobre mi relación con el lenguaje y mi identidad puertorriqueña.

Izabell estaba muy emocionada de tener la oportunidad de trabajar con Fellow de Girls Write Now Sally Familia en la traducción de su historia del inglés al español.

Estoy incómodamente sentada en el mueble floral de mi bisabuela. La humedad de su humilde casa puertorriqueña nos cubre a todos de sudor. A pesar de mis visitas anuales a la isla, el español que intercambian con entusiasmo entre mi familia escapa mi comprensión. Recibida por los tíos y tías de mi padre con un "¡Hola, Iza!," dejo escapar torpemente un español que solo su hermana, mi abuela en Nueva York, puede comprender completamente; un español que revela que no soy fluida a través de mi acento y simple sintaxis.

Es difícil para mí estimar la cantidad de personas de la familia de mi padre que solo hablan inglés. Hasta a mi mamá, su suegra le dice que "aprenda español." Antes de mudarse con mi padre, ella nunca aprendió el idioma de parte de su mamá coreana sorda y su padre puertorriqueño nacido en los Estados Unidos. Sin dejarse intimidar por sus errores (insistió confiadamente en que una farmacia era una "farmacina"), aprendió hablar felizmente con sus suegros. Mi hermana, criada principalmente por la madre de nuestro padre, navegaba el idioma de forma natural; su profesión incluso requiere que use ambos idiomas. Aunque mi abuela también me cuidó, en la mayor parte mis padres hablan inglés, por lo cual mi vocabulario nunca evolucionó más allá de "agua" y "te quiero."

A pesar de actuar como si hablar el lenguaje fuera una segunda naturaleza con mi familia, no es cierto decir que aprendí de ellos. Practiqué con mi abuela, pero aprendí todo mi español en la escuela. Mi familia nunca podrá decir que me enseñaron; esto hizo que mi conexión con la cultura familiar se sintiera más superficial. Muchas veces me acusaron de no querer aprender español *de parte de ellos*, y mi adquisición del idioma reforzó esa idea. Mi incapacidad para aprender el lenguaje rápidamente en casa de alguna manera disminuyó mi voluntad de aprender en sus ojos. Lo que sí aprendí se conformó al español castellano, chocando con las palabras que se usan entre los puertorriqueños.

Sin la familiaridad de mi abuela, mi acento inglés era más evidente, mi español expuesto, y sujeto a escrutinio. Ignorando o sin notar mi vergüenza inmediata, una sonrisa genuina se extiende por los rostros de mi familia.

"¡Estás practicando! Que bueno. Aprendiste mucho," exclamaban mis titís y tíos abuelos. Tenían estándares bajos para "mucho": simplemente había formado una oración. No estaba buscando desesperadamente a mi hermana mayor con fluidez para traducir, pero aún estaba lejos de sonar natural. Cuando otros miembros de la familia venían a saludarme, mis tías y tíos abuelos llamaban desde la cocina: "¿Escuchaste su español? Sí, sí, ella sabe mucho más ahora." Y todos sonreían y movían sus cabezas con aprobación, apretando mis brazos y empujando sus mejillas sudorosas hacia las mías cariñosamente para besarme.

Para mi familia, aprender español era digno de elogio, algo que yo veía como injustificado. Ya *debería haber sabido* cómo hablar—estaba haciendo lo mínimo. Entonces me esforcé más para tener conversaciones completas con ellos en español, convenciéndome de que mis habilidades eran suficientes para llevarme y salvar muchos años de desconexión lingüística. Sin embargo, no importa cuánto me elogiaran, siempre volvían al inglés cuando tenía problemas.

"You know I know some English, too," me dicen. "Talk to me in English, I understand you." Todos celebraban mi español, pero a sus ojos anhelaba la comodidad del inglés, ya que al final del día no hablaba con fluidez. Obstinadamente, sólo hablé en español, con la esperanza de que algún día no tuvieran que usar el inglés por mi bien.

FARAH MERCHANT

LIVES: Irving, Texas

Farah Merchant is a recent college graduate striving to remain true to her dream of being a writer.

MENTEE'S ANECDOTE:
Mentor workshops are almost a naked experience. We begin with basic formalities and then dive into critiquing a piece I wrote that week. Nola is methodical, reassuring, and honest. Every line receives her perusal, a moment of her time. As someone who is terrified of sharing my work, I literally created a newsletter on Substack that has been empty for eight months. Nola makes sharing my work a natural experience. I don't feel ashamed or embarrassed or scared. It's like catching a glimpse of my body as I'm about to hop in the shower. It's there, and that's it.

NOLA SOLOMON

LIVES: Hoboken, New Jersey

Nola is a French American writer, a mentor at Girls Write Now, and a digital advertising executive.

MENTOR'S ANECDOTE:
It's been an absolute pleasure working with Farah. She's a wonderfully talented writer and prosaic thinker who explores the concepts of the world through writing and cares deeply about the issues at the heart of her stories. Beyond storytelling, we've worked together to bring that creativity to life in job interviews and her professional life. Great things to come from Farah in the future!

The Junk Room

FARAH MERCHANT

A short story discussing the traps of solitude and the desire to read.

Every day, I work in the junk room, an ignored space filled with memories of the past. Our old dining table sits against shelves of boxes dating back as far as the eighties. Old computer monitors, bar stools, and mattresses litter the already crowded room. I've created a space for myself at one end of the dining table, where my laptop, journal, and planner sit beside one another next to a wrinkled napkin, no longer white but instead a pale yellow from blowing my nose every time the air-conditioning shifts dust from the boxes onto my space.

No one from my family enters the room. It's at the back of the house, on the second floor, right above the rickety garage that rumbles as loudly as a train passing by. The room rattles with it, dust bouncing from the boxes, finding its way to me before everything stops, and the only sounds anyone can hear are the clanking of my keyboard and the whir of the AC. I enjoy the solitude of the space. It's as if no one knows it exists. When I enter through the white door, which blends perfectly into the wall, no one searches for me. At most, my mother bellows my name. Her voice carries through the whole house before finding its way through the door bottom, and by then, it's as quiet as a whisper.

Noise consumes my house. The yells of my siblings bounce off the walls. My mother's loud reprimanding voice fills the high ceilings. My father's TV echoes. Every day from 8 a.m. until 6:30 p.m., I sit in the room. On the weekends, I carry the chai up the stairs and to the room to read. My noiseless feet, trying not to disturb my family members or the chai, peacefully resting in the mug. Late in the afternoon, I bring my mug down, walk my dog, and then carry my lunch upstairs, reading while relishing in the solitude. There's a small couch in the corner from my dad's old bar, covered with stains from spilled drinks and pizza slices. I watch Netflix there when I take a break, laughing at *Derry Girls*—all the company I need and enjoy.

As time continued on, I left the room less and less. I used to sleep in a different part of the house to differentiate between my work and private space, but now that space is ruined. My sleep kept being interrupted by my siblings' voices, the squeaking of the bathroom door beside my room being opened and closed, and my mother's loud alarm clock. So instead, I heaved the mattress from my bed to the guest room, turning it to its side so it could fit through the narrow door frame. The drafty, cold room sends shivers down my spine, and my body trembles as I try to fall asleep. But with sleep comes peace, and the lack of disturbances makes the horribly insulated room a safe haven.

Now there's a hot plate in the corner of the room with a table full of vegetables and tofu beside it. Dinners are generally some form of stir-fry paired with one of the many books littered around the room. I just finished reading half of *Little Women* in one sitting, and most of the time, I devour entire books in a day. I finally get to enjoy the continuity of books. Once I become fully immersed, there's no end until my eyes hurt from the small print or I close the book, my fingers having exhausted all the pages—no more interruptions. I no longer fumble through passages in the middle of books, trying to reacquaint myself with a character I lost touch with when my mother called me down to wash the dishes. Everything is seamless. After I finish eating, I push the plate away from me, letting the food harden and attach itself to the plate like a parasite, and continue reading. The extra scrub in the bathroom sink never removes all the dried bits of food, but I learn to eat around the small maze of particles forever stuck to the plate.

After all this time reading, my eyes can no longer see past the pages in my books. I see the manila paper stock and black serif font with clarity, but the rest of the room is a blur of colors. Like with a Matisse painting, I can make out only the brown formless dining table, the lump of white that is my mattress. I can no longer see the door to the room, so I sit in a prison of my own making and read.

ALINA MERTENS-SCHILL

LIVES: New York, New York

Alina is a high school sophomore who loves running, reading, coming up with funky recipes, and spending time with family and friends.

MENTEE'S ANECDOTE:

Before meeting Heather for the first time I was nervous about a lot of things. I was afraid of her not liking my writing style, of me making dumb spelling mistakes, of us not clicking. The first time we worked together, she was so sweet and genuine that my fears were swept away. During our sessions, Heather is thorough and honest, never hesitating to point out something I've overlooked, always seeking to help me enhance my writing. When we work together, I notice details that I wouldn't have discovered without her. I'm so grateful for her support and kindness.

HEATHER O'DONOVAN

LIVES: New York, New York

Heather O'Donovan is a writer, educator, and mentor. A classically trained vocalist, she is a librettist and a regular contributor to various classical music publications.

MENTOR'S ANECDOTE:

Alina has the kind of rare natural gift for writing that makes my "job" as a mentor an absolute treasure! Reading Alina's essays and engaging in thoughtful discussions to help her voice shine through has been one of the joys of my career as a writer, and I am so excited to continue to cheer her on as she develops into the world-class writer I am certain she will become.

Oma's Hands

ALINA MERTENS-SCHILL

"Oma" is the German word for *grandma*. These two short memoirs are the beginning of a larger collection centering around my Oma and how my perception of her has changed over time.

Five years old

On those late nights in December when Mama was downstairs in her childhood room sleeping, Oma would sit me in front of the television. Every time they put me into bed, my mind would snap awake the instant the light switch flipped off. Jet lag left me restless, ready to explode after just a few minutes in the silence of the room. Soon I would be scampering through the darkness up the cold stone steps to the living room.

Oma would be sitting on her favorite sofa, slumped against the worn leather, eyes closed and chin resting on her sternum. Her hands would be folded in her lap, a perpetual frown tugging at the corners of her mouth.

I would stand in the doorway for a few seconds watching the white light from the TV illuminate her face before stepping into the room, door closing behind me with a click.

Oma's eyes would open and she would nod gravely.

"I can never sleep this early, either."

"It's two in the morning!" I would giggle.

"Old women like me don't need to sleep," she would reply, a sly smile playing on her lips.

I would climb onto the sofa and sit crisscross applesauce, nestling myself in thick, soft blankets. I would watch Oma as she began to nod off again. The dim yellow lights glowed with warmth while the soft murmur of voices from the television lulled me into a trance. Eyelids would droop like leaden weights, tugging closed by fatigue from hours of excitement and flying across the ocean. Comfortable and content, I would fall asleep.

Eight years old

Oma used to tell me stories of when she was young. Mama, Oma, and I would sit around the dining room table on cushions so old that all color had seeped out of them. Coffee for Mama and Oma and piping-hot peppermint tea for me. Sometimes Oma told her stories gravely, matter-of-factly. Other times a memory that had been long forgotten would resurface, and the spirit inside her would stir. During these moments I was allowed the sweet experience of soaking up a snippet of her previous life. She often had to pause to take in short, ragged breaths.

As a child Oma would race her brother and his friends up the big hill in winter. She tells me that any time she ran, she always beat the boys. I imagine her, legs stretching and pumping, feet crunching into the snow and lungs burning from the cold. She would reach the top far before the rest, cheeks pink and frostbitten, black crystals creeping into the periphery of her vision, exhausted, triumphant.

When winters got especially bitter, her lungs would deteriorate. The bronchitis was suffocating. It racked her young nimble body with fever and kept her confined to her bed. Like a caged bird, she longed to unfurl her wings and feel the freedom of wind whistling through her hair. But when she dreamed of running free, she would slip back into consciousness, only to find sheets tangled between her fingers, slick with sweat.

When she returned to school it was as if someone had left her by the side of the road in a foreign country. Mathematics was a cryptic language, "furchtbar!" Later, when she got a job working at a bank, she lied on her application, claiming that she was capable of doing complex calculations, but in truth she had missed so much school that she really wasn't.

"So . . . what did you do?"

Oma looked over at me, a glint in her eye. "I taught myself how."

Once, Oma told me that when she was young, a man stopped in his tracks on the street and told her that she had the most beautiful hands he had ever seen. Her eyes twinkled with pride as she recounted the praise.

She looked down at her hands, swollen. The twinkle faded out.

Today when she walks, she loses her breath right away. I watch her as she moves, torso slightly bent to the ground. I imagine that she is leaning forward in anticipation, trying to accelerate. But her lungs are obstructed and her legs can't carry her how they used to. Her hands are crippled.

I sit at the old table in the dining alcove by the window. My tea has gone cold, but it's still poised in my hands. Dusk has settled, and through the quiet of the house I hear the faint ticking of a clock. Mama looks down into her coffee cup, and Oma's face settles back into its usual look of resignation. But in her eyes I see a twinge of something else—grief, perhaps.

"I'll put these away," she says, abruptly taking my mug. She opens the door to the kitchen and rushes through. A cold draft sweeps through the room, fracturing the moment. Mama looks up from her cup and smiles warmly at me but with sadness in her eyes. She stands up and lays a hand on my head, then brings her cup into the kitchen.

DÉWOU GLORIA MINZA

LIVES: Yonkers, New York

Déwou is a high school senior who's looking forward to her college experience and how it will shape her writing.

MENTEE'S ANECDOTE:

As I prepare to leave high school, Nicole has helped me through the arduous college application process and given me invaluable insight into all things postsecondary. Thanks to her expert planning skills, I've been able to meet deadline after deadline, something a procrastinator can only dream of. How she puts up with me is a mystery, but one thing is for certain: I truly am fortunate to have Nicole as my mentor.

NICOLE MARIE GERVASIO

LIVES: New York, New York

Nicole Marie Gervasio, Ph.D., is an educator, writer, and artisan. She teaches in Columbia University's Core Curriculum and is finishing her first novel.

MENTOR'S ANECDOTE:

Working with Déwou has been a bright spot every Sunday for the last three years. Sometimes I am truly shocked to remember that she hasn't actually graduated high school yet; she is an infinitely mature, caring, thoughtful young woman and an astonishing writer. I am lucky to call her my friend and look forward to seeing where life after high school takes her.

Pay the Price

DÉWOU GLORIA MINZA

Content Warning: Body Horror

A short story taking a closer look into the mind of Adah Ellen Price, a character in the novel *The Poisonwood Bible*.

The village is silent save for the occasional wail of a babe and creatures rustling in the bushes. My family—well, at least what's left of it—sleeps inside, unaware of my diligent vigils keeping them from harm. Although the sweltering heat of the day has long cooled, the packed dirt where I sit still remembers the sun's scorching rays. The winds whistle. A lone bird takes flight from atop a bananier, screeching into the inky night.

If Methuselah, our parrot, were still here, he'd flutter viciously in his cage to be set free. One of the few books in the village says that happy birds return to their homes. Methuselah escaped and has never returned.

I do not blame him. Were I a bird, I would not once look back on these days of imprisonment with fondness.

But I am not a bird and therefore cannot fly. I need a cane to prop up the paralyzed arm and leg that always drag me down, keeping me from soaring. I am cursed to crawl as if I were no better than the serpent exiled from Eden.

Even the serpent has a home among other reptiles. Where can I, Adah Price, bearer of crude luck, go when even my family looks at me with only saintly pity and empty sympathy? Who would accept a cripple destined to the same fate as a snake?

A sting on my toe draws me from my thoughts. I look down. A single fire ant is struggling to climb my foot. The soldier's perseverance almost comforts me until I see another rapidly moving toward me. Then three more. Suddenly, the carnivorous army engulfs me.

I need to rouse my family, but my mouth won't move. A stifled scream threatens to tear my throat apart. It's all I can do to keep my eyes peeled open as the swarm swallows my skin, intent on stripping flesh from my bones as if I were carrion.

Immobilized, I sit on the ground while the village awakens with a flurry. People cram the streets, thrashing in agony. Despite the chaos, everyone heads in one direction: the river.

My father crashes through the door of our mud cottage, clawing at his eyes as ants burrow into his body.

"The first plague!" roars Father. "Calamity has befallen sinners! Repent, for the end is at hand!" Nathan Price, this man who sees his daughters as shameful burdens, screams himself hoarse as he runs into the grove.

As ants march into my hair, I snap out of my stupor and reach for my cane. I will not be left behind. The more I struggle to my feet, the sensation of fire crawls across my skin, already swollen with venom. My body shakes violently; every fiber of my being fights to keep me upright. My scalp is melting off my head as the ants bite and *bite*.

I hear my mother and sisters emerging from the cottage with wails, the swarm of soldiers incessant in their gnawing.

"River," I croak out to Leah and Rachel, trying to lead them to safety. But they brush past me, already knowing where to go.

My usually lifeless mother runs to me as if possessed by demons.

"Run," she pleads. "It's not safe here, Adah. You must follow your sisters. Let me hel—"

My younger sister's whimpers cut her off.

Ruth May falls to the ground after a few short steps from the hut, crying and scratching as if to draw blood.

Seeing her youngest daughter struggle for life sparks something in my mother, in Orleana Price—a rare maternal instinct, perhaps. Without hesitation, she scoops her beloved child into her arms, heedless of the ants covering her tiny body. Then she meets my eyes.

As her eyes bore into mine, I can see what she is thinking.

With lucid clarity, I witness my own mother weighing the advantages of saving her crippled mistake or her golden child. The world seems to fade as a small eternity passes. Orleana holds her beloved child close to her heart as millions of red flecks writhe on her white nightgown, sealing my fate with grim determination.

"Follow your sisters," she says. She runs for it without looking back.

Live was I ere I saw evil.

My mother ran from me as if the devil himself were hot on her heels. Looking back, I should have known what her choice would be.

I stand in the middle of nothing, raging ants forgotten as the final villagers empty out. I watch as plants are devoured in a matter of seconds. I listen as oars splash in the river, carrying away the last remnants of Adah Price.

I sink to the ground on trembling knees, unable to keep myself up any longer.

Were I but a bird, I could escape being a prisoner in my own body. But I am not. I am a snake meant to crawl on my belly, eating dust, eternally punished for the crime of my birth.

MOMOCA

LIVES: New York, New York

Momoca is a student in New York City who loves creating origami modular icosahedrons, finding steals from Urban Outfitters, and learning about developmental psychology.

MENTEE'S ANECDOTE:

My time with Nicole has been fun and insightful. We have similar tastes in writing styles and have had interesting discussions about the group session pieces. We've also had frequent check-ins to create a vision board, brainstorm ideas, and go over my poem. She has been incredibly encouraging through my college application process as well. She has given me great bubble tea recommendations (don't sleep on the bubble tea ice cream from Xing Fu Tang!) and we have discussed trips that we have taken as well as our lives outside of Girls Write Now. Thank you, Nicole!

NICOLE GEE

LIVES: Astoria, New York

Nicole is an educational textbook editor originally from Boston who loves to spend time in bookstores and libraries, visit museums, and eat ice cream.

MENTOR'S ANECDOTE:

I have so enjoyed working with and getting to know Momoca! Throughout our sessions, Momoca and I work on brainstorming ideas and writing (we loved creating our vision board!), but, most important, we share details of our lives. We discuss topics such as the school newspaper, work deadlines, and culturally sustaining education as seamlessly as we discuss topics such as art (origami), music (BTS, Mariah Carey), and literature (poetry). I was and continue to be awed by her writing. I am thrilled to hear about her future as a writer because of her poise, her creativity, and her thoughtfulness!

Liminal Spaces

MOMOCA

This is cold glass. This is an inside-out shirt. My goal in this poem is to evoke the comfort one can find in quiet, stability, patterns, ambiguity, and solitary reflection.

I live in the liminal space between blue and gray

Things slip through the hole of my pocket
I almost catch them
When I sweep my hand over a photograph frame
it fills my lungs
after I exhale

It's what lingers on my hands after brushing my mother's hair
It crawls into my ears as I sleep
and leaves through my eyes when they open

It's blue
It's gray

I eat windchimes
They strike chords between my teeth
and shatter into a million keys of a note
I'll sing with my mouth closed
and breathe cacophony

On the floor I look like
a pile of pencil shavings
Flecks of color will remain

imprinted where I lay
Broken flowers of cedar
along with the dry scent of wood
so fleeting and sharp
and it's gone

SHAILA MOULEE

LIVES: Elmhurst, New York

Shaila Moulee is a web and app development student in high school. She indulges in video production, sound design, and poetry.

MENTEE'S ANECDOTE:

Annie is the embodiment of love and patience. Her calm strength has guided me to cope with the passing of time. My worries have seemingly grown faint in the warmth of her comforting words. During the past two years, I have found a sister in Annie. She is my happy pill and North Star who sheds light on my soul. Our relationship continues to gain its beauty in the exchange of laughter, tears, poems, and recipes. I will forever cherish her words of encouragement and love-driven gestures that ease my journey as a young writer. I love you, Annie.

ANNIE PILL

LIVES: New York, New York

Annie Pill is the brand director at Marker Learning, a learning disability support startup. She enjoys running, cooking, and cozying up with a favorite book.

MENTOR'S ANECDOTE:

In the last two years, Shaila has grown into herself in such gorgeous ways. As a writer, she has taken risks—twisting and taming prose to realize her signature poignancy. As a student, she has challenged herself, elevating her coursework to include advanced creative writing. As a granddaughter, she has met grief not with resistance but with tender resilience—letting it wash over her so she might reflect, feel, and heal. As a mentee, she has embraced me at my most vulnerable. It is the ultimate joy and privilege to watch Shaila blossom, again and again.

To My Younger Self

SHAILA MOULEE

Your fingerprints are forever engraved in my soul.
This is a letter dedicated to you, my dearest friend.

For you who have forgotten how to cry out loud,
I will shed tears until my eyelids start to fall
So that you can trace the beads of grief
That have hardened on my cheeks
And find the utmost strength to make your days count
As youth is bound to perish when you start to tally what's left.

You used to pluck white orchids and pink chrysanthemums from the
    garden
Hand-grown by your beloved grandmother who used to fold her hands
    over her lips
To muffle her chuckle as she peeked through the curtained windows,
Watching you passionately sing into trembling flower buds.
You told them "Don't be afraid, you carry the drops shed by cardinals'
    wings in the pouring rain.
Though gray clouds obscure the setting sun, tomorrow has yet to
    blossom."

Can you recall your grandfather propping a ladder against the
    guava tree
While you buried the soles of your feet into the dampened soil?
Your head rose with each foot's thud against the wooden steps
While his fingers roamed through raindrop-ravaged leaves.
You held your breath until your tear-filled eyes met his own brimmed
    with love.
He gently flicked the paper airplanes caught on thick branches,
Each splintered to pieces as it crash-landed on the shores of grief

Once you, my sweet child, had grown old without noticing yesterday
    had passed.

If I told you that you'll soon get tired of living,
But will do anything to keep yourself alive
On days you feel burdened with the heaviness of a breath
Caught between your lips,
Would you think less of me?

If I told you that time will soon flee
From wrinkled palms that cradle your gentle face
And its warmth too shall fade from your dimpled cheeks,
Would you no longer be in a hurry to grow up, my love?

Sooner or later, you'll find yourself searching
Through the endless folds of your forehead
Until your fingertips unearth the kiss
That was once planted on the crown of your head.
Til' then, sow the seeds of love into the depths of your heart
Whenever your soul grows tired of the dark
And you are left with no choice,
But to tuck yourself into a bed that remains empty
The cold sheets a reminder of who was lost.

Tell me, am I foolish to leave flower pots on the windowsill
In hopes of conjuring a pair of hands from beneath the soil
Into the small garden that I have created for myself?

Tell me, am I silly for folding the pages of my diary
Into paper boats instead of paper airplanes
Because the evening skies are tainted by gloom every so often
And I am afraid my prayers won't reach you before it's too late?
If they happened to get stuck on prickly branches,
I certainly wouldn't know what to do
As there's no one willing to climb up the timeworn tree
And meet my eyes with tenderness overflowing in their own,
Telling me it's alright to fall apart through the nights that exhaust
    my soul.

So promise me that you will hand-feed love to yourself
In each passing moment when you feel as though you're unworthy.
As the thrum of rain drowns out the melodies that you will soon start
    to forget,
Listen to the rhythm of your feet and the uneven pattern of your breath
For you've worked hard to mend the hourglass that has broken into a
    thousand pieces.
No one will blame you for taking a deep breath in those
    unpleasant days
As pink lotuses too exist in muddy water but remain unstained.

Some days you will wonder how you crossed the river
On a paper canoe torn by each pebble thrown into the water.
How can you find your way when footprints on the shoreline fade in
    the heavy downpour
And you're left to stir the waves with clenched fists?

Some nights you will wonder how you curled up in a hollow tree
And dreamt about the moon who remains still in a sea of white pearls
While hundreds of ashen clouds sail past him without uttering
    a single word
As they consume the vibrant glow of his heart to enliven their own.

But you must believe me when I say you are capable of much more
For a candle shall never stop burning at the core of your soul.
Even if the ripples of a boundless sea grow in your heart
And the sunlight gets trapped in your eyelashes.
Within you, my dear, is a home that I can never return to
As I have painted a portrait of myself anew
And hung it on the walls of a house built on a road unfamiliar to you
As yours is eclipsed by nostalgia's shade.
So if you ever lose your bearings on a journey in search of myself,
I will fly lanterns in the skies of tomorrow and sail paper boats
On the stream forever flowing between our hearts.

MARYAM OGUNTOLA

LIVES: Bronx, New York

Maryam is a Muslim and an aspiring lawyer who loves reading almost anything, eating all types of chocolate, especially dark chocolate, and taking nature walks.

MENTEE'S ANECDOTE:

Having the opportunity to learn from Tess is a breath of fresh air. She is very knowledgeable about writing, and is always willing to share her experiences. She is also very supportive. Although we are just beginning to know each other better, I have learned much from her. Tess inspires me to become a better writer and be open to new ways of seeing things. She is a great writer and mentor, and a wonderful person! She has helped me begin to see myself as a writer as I learn from her what it means to write and create art for yourself.

TESS FORTE

LIVES: Cranford, New Jersey

Writer, artist, and mentor Tess Forte is the founder of Tess Forte Creative and the current editorial director of Scholastic Book Fairs.

MENTOR'S ANECDOTE:

It is so satisfying to have a mentee who shows up with a bottomless enthusiasm to try, share, learn, and grow. Maryam distinguishes herself by recognizing inspiration around and within her and responding—and that, in turn, inspires me as a writer, as an artist, and in life! Seeing Maryam take off in confidence and creative output has been a joy; she has quickly surpassed the goals we had set only a few short months ago. I can't wait to see what the future holds for her, and I look forward to supporting her every step of the way.

Mom Pants

MARYAM OGUNTOLA

> **I have always been perceived to be younger than I actually am; at first, I was not too fond of it, but it eventually grew on me.**

As a teenager, they said I looked twelve
And I accepted moving through life
Perceived as a younger version
Of my current self
Not sure whether to feel offended or special
Because of the saying "Black don't crack."
Anyways, the free bus rides rock
I am never questioned
Nor refused a ride when I "forget" my MetroCard
Except lately when I drop off my 6-year-old sister late,
I am told: "Mom, class begins at 8 a.m."
And when I pick my 12-year-old brother up from school,
The security guards call the nurse and say, "Mom is here."
I text my sister, "I look like a mother now?"
I think, "Does being a mom really have a look or age?"
I go outside and repeat to my sister what I texted,
And she looks me up and down and points
"It's the mom pants."

IFEOMA OKWUKA

LIVES: Bronx, New York

Ifeoma is a high school senior residing in the Bronx. She has a genuine love for STEM-related topics and greatly enjoys writing short stories.

MENTEE'S ANECDOTE:

Shanille is a constant source of light in my life. She is a mentor, friend, and sister all at once and I couldn't be more grateful to grow alongside her this year. Our meetings serve as space for me to destress after a long day at school and cultivate my creative spirit. It's been a great second year and I'm looking forward to what else this year has in store for the both of us. Cheers!

SHANILLE MARTIN

LIVES: Brooklyn, New York

Shanille is a registration administrator and instructor at Writopia.

MENTOR'S ANECDOTE:

Ifeoma is truly an inspiring and immensely talented writer. I'm constantly in awe of the stories she conjures up, and the language she explores within her writing. Our sessions are full of laughter, moments to vent, and writing, of course. Excited to see her grow and continue to be the amazing writer she already is!

The Alternate

IFEOMA OKWUKA

Not everything is as it seems. Truth is ever-evolving like nature itself. You think you know someone? Well, think again. You might be surprised by what you find. An excerpt from a longer piece.

Remorse

It was clear that her sister was never coming back.

Josephine made her way through the front porch, thoughtfully stepping over the potted ferns that graced the wooden floor. She looked up to see Gunner, their French bulldog, dashing wildly across the decaying lawn. His polished black fur shone brightly against the evening's dim and sinister light. Josephine made her way down the porch's front steps before plopping herself on the first step. She eyed the daisy rooted firmly in the soil in front of her. In a swift and calculated manner, she proceeded to pluck the flower's petals one by one until nothing remained of the poor plant except a disembodied stem. A violent gust blew, nature's futile attempt at discipline. Josephine eyed the stem in her hand with newfound curiosity, a thin and fragile thing, just as her sister had been. She wondered how many days it took for June to finalize her escape plan. Had it been seven days? A month? Perhaps even years?

It was clear that June would never come back. How could she after such a devastating reveal? The pain of her sister's absence rested solely on the fact that Josephine blamed herself for it. No one but herself could be blamed for what happened. She had been heartless, a fact that she came to accept only in retrospect. *I can't blame June for hating me,* she thought. *I'd hate me too, and a thousand times over.* The words from

June's previous letter remained etched in her memory, like a deep and unforgiving wound:

I still think of you now and then. To forget you would be a sin. I'm not quite sure if I've forgiven you, Josephine. I'm trying my best, believe that I am. I can only hope that you understand. Send my regards to Ma and Seven. And please do check on Anwar. He hurts badly. (Remain cautious.)

Josephine got up sluggishly from the front step, her body dizzy with guilt. She entered through the house's double doors and made her way wearily to her bedroom.

There it was, hanging against the closet door: the sixty-nine-inch ivory wedding dress June had worn on the day of her wedding ceremony. It was a silky slip-on dress, reminiscent of the start of all things bad. The dress hung desperately on a metal hanger, which Josephine reached for with her bony fingers. She stroked the fabric gently, before recoiling in horror. She eyed it cautiously, as though some electric current ran through its fibers. In fact, the entire room about her seemed to take on a new form. She was not her usual self, at least not since June's departure. Tears brimmed in her round eyes, giving them a lustrous and admirable shine. Josephine slumped against her queen-sized bed, heart heavy with agony. *It must be done,* she thought.

There she stood on the porch once again. Josephine grabbed June's wedding dress, which she had placed hastily on a nearby sofa. Reluctantly, she tossed the dress onto the lawn, before retrieving the box of matches she had left on the kitchen counter. She dragged the wooden match against the striker with trembling fingers and set June's dress ablaze. Gunner barked madly behind her, his little body poised for attack. "It's gonna be all right, boy," she said, gesturing for the dog to return inside the house. "We're okay," she whispered.

But she was not okay, and she knew this. Josephine sat on her porch's velvet sofa and observed the delicate, bright flames ahead of her with disturbing awe. She wondered if the flames in Hell burned just as bright.

June's dress was now a devastating pile of debris. About two months ago, she discovered the dress neatly packaged in an iridescent gift box near her mailbox post. Josephine didn't think too much about it, believing it to be some attempt at a cruel joke. She and June often pranked each other as children, a devastating habit that had followed them well into adulthood. Hours after the box had arrived, however, June was reported missing by Ma. And it became clearer than ever that the box had not been some cruel joke, but instead a half-hearted goodbye from her sister. And just like that, Josephine's world began its frightening descent into irremediable chaos.

Josephine released a violent cough into her blue handkerchief, indifferent to the bloodstains spattered across the fabric. She was reminded again of the illness plaguing her from within, the root of communal suffering. As she lost herself in the beauty of the lawn fire, her mind staggered to the day of June's wedding ceremony. What a day it had been, for her, for the both of them.

SHERMAYA PAUL

LIVES: New York, New York

Shermaya Paul is a high school junior with a creative mind based in Brooklyn, New York. She is in love with art, movies, and writing.

MENTEE'S ANECDOTE:
Morgan has become such a ray of light in my life for the past one and a half years. She has taught me so many different things and has helped me recognize my strengths and weaknesses in many aspects of my creative process and execution. She continues to guide me on my educational journey by providing some of the best resources and personal experiences that she has to offer. I really appreciate what she has taught me and I'm looking forward to continuing to learn and explore with her in the future.

MORGAN LEIGH DAVIES

LIVES: Brooklyn, New York

Morgan Leigh Davies is the cohost of the pop-culture podcast *Overinvested*. Her writing has appeared in *Bustle*, *The Daily Dot*, and elsewhere.

MENTOR'S ANECDOTE:
This is the second year Shermaya and I have worked together, and we have had so much fun talking about movies and books. I am continually impressed and delighted by Shermaya's intellectual curiosity, especially about old movies (one of my favorite things!). She intuitively gets how to think about art in a way it takes most people a long time to learn, and can apply that attention to detail to observing people and places in real life, too. All that care and thoughtfulness are on display in this piece of writing. I can't wait to see what she does next.

Welcome to the Neighborhood

SHERMAYA PAUL

This story is an excerpt that explores the effects of gentrification on a community and its foundational members. Clem has been living in this neighborhood forever, and it suddenly changes before her eyes.

I've been Clementine's caregiver for around three years now. She didn't need one, though; she could get by alone, just with a little assistance. Her successful and ambitious kids wouldn't stay around to keep her company, so I guess I was hired to be her friend more than a caregiver. Clementine would ask me to shop for groceries, pick up prescriptions, and check her mailbox. She would ask me to grab things that were too high up for her to reach, or too close to the floor for her to bend down to get. Even though Clem resisted my help, sometimes I knew she was secretly grateful that I was there.

Clem walked with a cane and wasn't able to stand for long periods of time, so anything that required walking far didn't exactly suit her. Every morning, however, Clem walked to the front of her lawn. She would sit on the cedar bench her late husband built for her and watch as the cars drove by. She would occasionally have a guest: a child skipping along the sidewalk who stopped to accompany her on the bench, or a woman holding bags of groceries who was just saying hello. Clem was very active in the community and very involved in social justice and the neighborhood crime watch. She thought that being a part of her community wasn't just living in it, but doing things to maintain it.

Clem's been looking out for this community ever since she first moved in with her husband and kids. Her husband, Mark, was killed while on duty in the military when her oldest child was thirteen. Clem said her house felt emptier than before—even when Mark was out of the country working, she explained, his presence had still been in the house. When he died, it seemed like what was left of him in the house went with him, too, like a piece of Clem's perfect puzzle was missing. Clem told me her kids made his death much easier to bear, to accept. They were a distraction, a vessel, into which she could pour her idle love. The community was her vessel, too, and she took pride in knowing that.

She'd tell me about how the community used to look, how it had changed. The chipped paint was streaked with water damage and moss, the sides of the houses were overgrown with ivy, and the nests of wasps sat snugly in the corners of roofs where they would never be found. The brass fixtures on the doors and the wooden porches that complained even if you were the lightest of creatures. The creaky gates that never knew the taste or feel of oil and the cracked pavement, where the toddlers would jump and stand on one leg to avoid their mother's misfortune. She'd mention that something was off about the fact that her Black neighbors were leaving and being replaced with rich white ones who didn't share the same familiarity with the community that she and her old neighbors did. It was the short white picket fences that turned into tall black metal ones with thick horizontal pickets, the overgrown, well-explored lawns to perfectly trimmed yards. All of what Clem knew was gone in the blink of an eye. She often recalled how she "took care" of the neighborhood, almost like she was responsible for who stayed and who left. She said that she just didn't know where she fit anymore.

Clem would recall her Black neighbors telling her that they were of-fered large sums of money to sell their home, so they took the offer and left. Clem said she'd seen the letters in the mail, gotten the phone calls, and seen the agents on her porch, but she never paid them any attention. She didn't like it and would always suck her teeth when she'd receive any message pertaining to selling her home for money.

For the three years that I was Clem's caregiver, white families came and went into the neighborhood. It was the Johnsons the first year. Clem told me that she would make an apple pie every Sunday for them and eventually they just moved away. For me, I'd see them only occasionally, but every time I did, they had something to complain about, as if I could fix it right there on the spot. In the second year, it was the Millers. Their daughter ended up in the hospital for "stomach-related issues," as Clem told me, and the family moved again to have her treated at a better hospital. Clem had me put together a little package for them with toys and books for their daughter to have while she recovered. And just last year, the Langstons moved in and moved out in the same month. Clem didn't have a clue why they left—they didn't even leave a message or a note for us, they just picked everything up and disappeared.

Clem would say, "This place has changed—someone like you wouldn't notice it, Liyah, but I do. And I don't like it."

VIKTORIA PAVLOVA

LIVES: Staten Island, New York

Viktoria is an eighteen-year-old biology major at Baruch College, and a Scholastic Art & Writing Award winner who has been a part of Girls Write Now since 2020.

MENTEE'S ANECDOTE:

There aren't enough words to express how wonderful writing with Nevin is. I met a genuine person who has lots of incredible (and interesting) traveling and life stories. We always talk for hours about random things, and it's just so easy to love her! She is a force. She is kindhearted, bold, a dog lover, and a hard worker. Nevin has taught me so much about writing and life. I always think she'll run out of things to teach me, but she never does. These past few years with her have been nothing short of amazing. We're going to rule the world!

NEVIN MAYS

LIVES: New York, New York

Nevin Mays is an editor of award-winning children's books and a content strategist for publishers and international organizations.

MENTOR'S ANECDOTE:

I'm continuously surprised and delighted by Viktoria's imagination. Her characters are real almost from the moment she gives them a name. And she is unafraid of putting them in a difficult situation—as any good storyteller must do. Yet nearly every story she writes has a happy ending. This reflects how she moves through life: acknowledging there will be difficulties but always maintaining optimism that she will create her own happily ever after through hard work, perseverance, and creativity.

Stuck: Breathe Slowly and Count to Three

VIKTORIA PAVLOVA

Best friends for sixteen years, enemies for one. Now they're stuck in a supply closet. What could go wrong? Oh, and one of them is claustrophobic.

"Move." I shoved him. I slid my palm across the cold wall. No light switch, damn.

"Carter, are there lights?" Miles whispered.

"No, I just have a wall fetish, please excuse me," I said.

"Okay, asshole, knock yourself out, rub all the walls."

"I can't. We're in a supply closet. Know what that means? There's supplies everywhere."

"We wouldn't be stuck if you didn't shut the door. Did you want to get stuck?" Miles said.

"Sure, we haven't spoken for a year, but today I decided I wanted to talk to *you* in a dark supply closet."

I could hear Miles's cleats against the concrete floor, then supplies crashed to the ground and the suffocating smell of Windex filled the room. Miles let out a high-pitched scream and dug his nails into my shoulders.

I winced. "What are you doing?" He breathed shakily in my ear. "No way! You're still scared of the dark?" I laughed.

"N-No," Miles whispered, "but the closet is small, isn't it? Like, too small."

I peeled his fingers off me.

"It's a closet, what'd you expect? Dancing space?" I couldn't help being mean—he was right. It *was* my fault we were stuck. Soccer practice already started. By the time we got out, Coach was gonna be pissed.

Reading my mind, Miles said, "Coach is gonna have us running suicide drills until tomorrow." He began to slam on the door, screaming for help. I remembered the last time this happened. We were ten. We'd been locked in the shed of our families' Vermont house for half an hour. Let's just say I don't want a repeat of a snot-covered, hoarse-voiced Miles.

I slammed on the door until my hands were numb. Nobody came. Miles leaned against the door and slid to the floor. I joined him, defeated. Tension filled the air. Miles's breathing was uneasy. He sniffled.

It's starting again. "Are you okay?" I gritted my teeth.

"I'm fine," Miles retorted bluntly.

"Remember when you saw that therapist?" Who was clearly a waste of money. "What techniques did she give you?"

"Breathe slowly and count to three." Miles cracked his knuckles. "Focus on a safe feeling or whatever."

Aha. "Remember when we'd sit outside the ski lodge in Vermont and watch the pro team practice?"

"We laughed when they wiped out and dared each other to try their tricks, but we sucked." Miles chuckled.

"Correction, you sucked. I was pro-team-worthy," I lied. I smiled, glad it was dark. Miles continued making fun of my skiing, oblivious to his earlier panic. It felt like we were fifteen again, until Miles ruined the moment.

"I wish we could go back to how things were."

I froze, closing my eyes and praying the darkness would swallow me. No luck. "When we were little I taught you to play soccer. It became our thing. You forgot that."

It sounded like Miles was biting his nails, another nervous tic. "I'm sorry," he mumbled.

"You're sorry?" I sputtered. Silence. "I tore my ACL, and after my surgery you ghosted me." I dug my nails into my palms. "Instead, you were trying out for the international team that I signed us up for." Miles started to talk, but I kept going. "You said you wouldn't try out because I couldn't." Silence. "You promised me that we'd try out together when I got better." He cracked his knuckles. "You ignored me during my rehab."

Miles interrupted quickly, "I always asked my mom about you. I knew you were getting better."

"What if I could never play soccer again?" I didn't care about my harsh tone.

More silence.

"At least you didn't make the team," I muttered. Karma.

"Actually . . ."

"What?" I asked loudly. "You said you didn't."

"I wasn't gonna join, so it was easier to lie."

"Feel free to elaborate," I replied.

"I was embarrassed. I didn't plan on trying out. But I wanted to prove I was good, y'know? I'd always watched you be great. I wanted to be like you. Tryouts sucked because you weren't there."

This time I stayed silent.

"When I found out that your surgery was over, I was ashamed, so I just didn't visit you," Miles continued. "But then I couldn't join the team, because what's soccer without you and me?"

I didn't know what to say. I felt partially guilty.

"I thought you knew you were great," I said after a minute. "Apparently not with communicating, but soccer you've always had in the bag. I would've been happy you made the team."

"I realized that, which made me feel worse."

"So you thought, 'Hey let's end the friendship instead of talking about it'?"

Miles chuckled. "Yeah, I didn't think that through."

"Tryouts are next month." I grinned.

"Okay?"

"We need to start practicing," I responded.

"We?"

"We said we'd try out together when I'm better, right? My goals this season prove it."

Being stuck in the closet wasn't so bad anymore. Except for the suicide drills we'd be running later. Those were gonna be bad. But, hey, I got my best friend back.

EMILY PENG

LIVES: Bronx, New York

Emily is a high school freshman who loves reading, theater, and everything math. Her favorite genres to write are sci-fi and fantasy.

MENTEE'S ANECDOTE:

When we first met over Zoom, I was a bit intimidated by her confidence, but as we got to know each other, I realized how amazing and kind they were. Her creativity and the way she views the world directly translate into her writing. She is always digging deeper into minute details of the characters' perspectives. Naomi is incredibly thoughtful with their feedback, and I'm always excited to hear what they have to say. Recently, she mentioned a concept she's writing that explores familial relationships and inheritance, and I can't wait to hear more!

NAOMI DAY

LIVES: Astoria, New York

Naomi Day is a queer Black human writing Afro-centric speculative fiction of varying lengths about liminal experiences, queerness, and broken families.

MENTOR'S ANECDOTE:

When I met Emily over Zoom for the first time, I thought she seemed incredibly wise and centered, and her writing has proved me right! Her stories center on human relationships and tend to interrogate the meaning of attachment. She writes with laser focus about people who are intrigued by their work, whether it's mycology, language, or the ways the characters themselves span time. She is thoughtful when speaking, and she's always able to turn the conversation back to offer suggestions on my own work. I'm excited for everyone who gets to experience Emily's work for the first time!

Lost in Time

EMILY PENG

If Jing is the nebulous future and Anjeel the immortal past, then they meet in the hopeful present.

She is too human to be fully divine. The endless time flowing in her sloshes out of her mortal vessel like a leaky cup. She dreams of the future. She dreams of the past. She lives in every time except her own. In the present, but not this one.

"Anjeel!" Jing exclaims, all but leaping onto the cloaked figure.

Anjeel stiffly leans away from the hug. "Do I know you?"

Jing stumbles back, shrinking into the folds of her cloak. They haven't met yet. They're meeting. They've never met. "Oh," she says. "I guess not."

Realization dawns on Anjeel's face. "Will we know each other?"

"Yes."

A beat passes, then two.

"All right. Where's my room?"

Her knee jitters. Her blood rushes like the swell of an anxious tide, *shh-shh-shh* in the blue veins beneath her skin. The bitter taste of coffee lingers in her throat.

Anjeel announces herself with two quick knocks and peeks into the room. The dim glow of the moon illuminates the scar on her upper lip.

The rest of her face is unscarred from wars and battles yet to occur. Jing looks down at her lap. Her white-knuckled fingers clasp on the sides of her journal, where her scrawled writing mocks her.

"Where's Vesper? Tell him not to leave," Jing blurts out.

Anjeel's footsteps falter. Her eyebrows scrunch up ever so slightly, and her mouth opens as if in question, but what comes out is instead a soft "oh" of understanding.

Anjeel sidles over to her and gently clasps her hands. "We haven't met Vesper yet," she responds softly. Anjeel pries the journal from her death grip.

"Hanna? Or Fin?"

"It's just us, right now. We've been in Injir for three weeks now. This morning we went to the library and you read that book on bird anatomy."

They're sitting on the floor. Jing closes her eyes and lets Anjeel's narration of the day wash over her and ground her into this present. The quivering abates slightly.

Jing lifts her head up. "I don't want to sleep," she whispers.

"Why not?"

"Because . . ." Because if she sleeps, then she isn't sure what's going to be there when she wakes up. If it'll be past or present or future that greets her, because the difference is getting harder to tell with every passing moment. Possibilities yawn open before her. Jing might wake up with only one arm, standing in a desert or watching over a bloody battlefield.

Anjeel doesn't need the explanation. "It's getting worse, isn't it?"

She wants to check her notebook again, just to anchor herself between what has happened and what will happen. The world spins on an axis unknown to her, and she knows all the ways this ends if only she could know what *this* is. Anjeel catches her hands as they reach for the notebook and clasps them together.

"Hey, come on. Let's go to bed. I'm always here tomorrow, aren't I? And the notebook will be right there," Anjeel says. The words are echoed in her head by the infinite Anjeels across the multiverse who have had this exact exchange with her.

Jing yawns and lets Anjeel tuck her in. Her eyes are closed before her head hits the bed.

———————

"I loved them like my own family," Anjeel sobs. Tears spill from the fathomless pools of her dark eyes. Grief hangs in the air, so potent that even Jing bows under its weight. She cradles Anjeel, normally so strong and proud, and stays silent.

It's not words or reassurances that Anjeel needs. She needs a reminder that she's here in the present, wherever that is, not adrift along the ocean of space-time.

Jing closes her eyes and ignores the infinities where she sits in this same spot, holding Anjeel as she cries, and focuses on the now. On *this* Anjeel, who is real and grief-struck in her arms. She holds her close and lets herself be the rock for once.

———————

Anjeel hands her a leather-bound notebook. Lovingly penciled into the first page is her name.

> *To Jing*
> *For all of our eternities,*
> *Anjeel*

It's cold against her palms. The heavy weight is reassuring.

"I know that you have trouble with Time," Anjeel is saying, "so I thought I would give you this. You can write in it, whatever you want. I mean, you don't have to, but I thought it would help—"

Jing flings herself at Anjeel, interrupting her mid-sentence with a hug.

"Thank you," she breathes. She's already received this gift. She hasn't received it yet. She's receiving it now, by her own universal constant, and this moment is real.

Anjeel leans into the hug, stiffly at first, before melting into her embrace. "It's no problem," she murmurs in response.

They stand together for a while. Time passes over them, and Jing embeds this memory into her heart, where she will write it in the journal later. She will hold this memory when she has to remind herself that she is real.

And because she's Jing, and she's not linear, and neither is time, she will start from the beginning.

ALINA POVELIKIN

LIVES: New York, New York

Alina is a second-year mentee at Girls Write Now and has pursued many of her passions recently. She enjoys writing, painting, and spending time with loved ones.

MENTEE'S ANECDOTE:

Daria inspires me on a daily basis to be more productive, focus on my creative passions, and navigate high school with a positive mindset. In our pair sessions, we watch MasterClasses, experiment with new writing forms like blackout poetry, and respond to creative writing prompts. My discussions with Daria are often refreshing and help me recover from frustrating days or weeks of school. I look forward to making new memories with her and completing more writing pieces in the future!

DARIA SIKORSKI

LIVES: New York, New York

Daria is a New Yorker and returning mentor with Girls Write Now. She loves reading and spending time with her fiancé and their new rescue pup, Orzo.

MENTOR'S ANECDOTE:

I feel so privileged to be Alina's mentor for a second year with Girls Write Now. Alina is such a talented and multidimensional individual who always inspires me with her imagination, creativity, and incredible knack for storytelling. Alina fills our sessions with wonderful plots, characters, and stories that never cease to amaze and entertain. What's more is her ability to convey these stories with a both confident and sophisticated writing style.

The Scientist and the Fawn

ALINA POVELIKIN

The COVID-19 pandemic left many individuals isolated and unemployed. Still, I would have never considered a career path as a mad scientist...

Chemicals bubble in transparent vials as tubes stretch across a vast glowing room. Concave white walls surround a luminescent sea of green, and the ceiling extends forever into the darkness of eternity. Squeals, growls, and shrieks echo through the facility, but no noise escapes. The cellophane walls glow a chartreuse-like color and fade away at the touch of a feather, bringing into question whether they were ever there to begin with. The beauty of the facility is often disregarded, as the eyes that enter it hardly ever see the light of day. One must not be fooled by the mystical green fog that slithers and flows through the frigid air like a snake in search of prey. This very same fog is a bystander in the face of pain, suffering, and tremendous horror.

A mad scientist grins as he latches a tube into the throat of a still figure. He pours a vibrant green concoction into the end of the pipe, clapping his hands eagerly. What once was used for the good of society has now become a game. The limp fawn lays on the table motionless as a mysterious liquid pulsates rapidly through it. The scientist scribbles an illegible sentence into his notepad and scans the room frantically.

He rushes to his desk to grab the specimen; it is now completely green, the ideal condition for experimentation. He removes the tube from the young fawn's mouth and straps a gargantuan contraption around it.

He then squints his eyes so as to not be a witness in his own crime... But—oh! How long he has waited for this very moment. The fawn shakes uncontrollably until it shoots up, knocking the hefty helmet off its head.

He-e-lOoo my MaaAs-TeR, it whispered softly. YES! YES! the mad scientist exclaimed. Suddenly, footsteps could be heard nearby. The scientist's heart dropped. What was he to do? How would he return everything to a state of normal within the next few seconds? He rushed to the front of the room, locking the door instantaneously. Perhaps the footsteps were not headed toward his room, he pleaded. As the steps grew louder, he could reassure himself no longer. *Knock, Knock, Knock!*

He was greeted by Dr. Delaney, who rolled her eyes upon entry. "Newton! The boss is expecting your results from specimen one-two-four-five-oh-eight, pronto! I'm here to collect the paperwork."

"Ahh, yes. About that . . ." muttered Newton, offering a sheepish smile. *MaAsTeer!* the fawn screeched in the background. Dr. Delaney raised an eyebrow, alarmed. "Newton! Are you hiding something? What was that?!"

"No! No, of course not! I am just . . . uh . . . watching television and did not want to be caught off-duty. I'm incredibly sorry, ma'am," he said, bowing his head apologetically.

The woman shook her head, finally exclaiming, "All right, whatever, I'll let you off easy this time, but I'm expecting those papers ASAP. That means three hours tops, mkay?"

"Uh, y-yes, of course! Good day, ma'am!" The plump woman strode off, annoyed as ever.

Newton fell to his knees, gasping in relief. It was now time for him to forge the data for the young fawn: specimen 124508, that is. Fawn! Get over here. NOW. *YEeesS, Sire.* The fawn hobbled over to the scientist, staring directly into his eyes.

Fawn! I am about to inject you with Dawn dish detergent. I want you to record your symptoms on this paper and I will return shortly. You got that? *YEeEes, I thInK so, SirEee.* The scientist poked his head out of the door once more, scanning the hallway for human life. He then injected Fawn with the vibrant blue detergent and left the facility to enjoy a rather peaceful lunch break.

Eventually, Newton trudged down the winding hallway, stopping at room 326; "Dr. Delaney Ph.D.," it read, across a small golden plate on the door. Looking down at a large stack of papers, Dr. Delaney mumbled, "Come in." She looked up, taking off her new pair of red cat-eye glasses. "Ah. So, I assume these are the papers I requested three hours and"—she paused, looking down at her watch—"ONE minute ago," she finished.

"Yes, I am truly sorry, ma'am, I was making some finishing touches. You know how it is."

"No, Newton, I do not know *how* it is. Indulge me, please."

"Oh, well. Nowadays, so many scientists have taken to killing their animals for fun. It's hard being one of the last remaining—"

"It was a RHETORICAL question, Newton," her voice boomed, as she shook her head vigorously.

"Oh, in that case, I suppose I'll be on my way. See you around, Dr. Delaney?" he responded nervously.

"Oh goodness me, I sure in heavens hope not," Dr. Delaney replied. She really scared Newton sometimes, but his questionable relationship with Dr. Delaney was the least of his problems. For instance . . . had he seriously left Fawn unattended once again?! As the thought surfaced in his mind, the mad scientist rushed back to his room, slightly panicked. The door creaked open.

Fawn was nowhere to be found.

NIA RACKLEY

LIVES: Sandy Hook, Connecticut

Nia Rackley is fifteen years old. She is passionate about ballet and writing. In her free time, she loves to bake.

MENTEE'S ANECDOTE:

Jessica is an amazing mentor! While she's an extremely talented writer, she is also such a kind and down-to-earth person. Jess instinctively knows exactly how to change a few sentences into a beautifully written book. I couldn't have asked for a better writing partner!

JESS ROMEO

LIVES: Mountain Lakes, New Jersey

Jess Romeo is an editor for the Scholastic classroom magazine *Science World*. Her writing has been featured in places like *Popular Science* and JSTOR Daily.

MENTOR'S ANECDOTE:

Nia's passion for storytelling is obvious, and I admire how she always makes time to write despite her dizzyingly busy schedule. She has so many great ideas, and a natural talent for expressing them. Whenever she writes, she effortlessly imbues her characters with a strong voice and a great sense of humor. Working with Nia has helped me reconnect with the reason why I started down my own writing path: for the pure joy of it. I can't wait to see what Nia produces next!

The Elevator Bond

NIA RACKLEY

> I smile and walk up to the waiting room. Even if I
> don't get this job, at least I've got my friend back.

"Wait!" I gasp as I run to the elevator. I cannot be late today. I'm on the way to the *Grimsby Gazette*, the best newspaper in the whole city, to interview for a job as reporter. It's the biggest opportunity I've had in months. Luckily, someone holds the elevator open for me.

I thank the mysterious person as I catch my breath and wipe the sweat off my forehead. The elevator doors close behind me. That's when I finally notice her. Jane Rodgers, my archnemesis. We used to have a strong friendship. But now she treats me like dirt.

"Tiffany, is that you?" Jane asks with a pinch of disgust in her voice. She says it almost like she's confused.

"Who else would it be?" I ask, already exhausted.

"Do you know how many people might walk through this elevator? Sorry I didn't immediately assume it was you," Jane replies.

Before I can respond, the elevator comes to an aggressive halt. I stumble backward, almost rolling my ankle in my stupid heels. As I try to stop myself from falling, I hear something snap. I look down. My heel has broken off my shoe. As if my life isn't already tragic enough.

"Shoot!" I shout, scrambling to the floor.

"Oh my god!" Jane squeals, gripping the elevator handles.

I roll my eyes. "Stop being so dramatic!"

"I almost fell on this dirty floor! It looks like it hasn't been cleaned in years."

"We're stuck in an elevator, and you're worried about falling on the floor?"

"Unlike you, I'm dressed in nice clothes." Jane looks down at me as I desperately try to fix my shoe. I have on my nicest dress, which suddenly doesn't look so nice. I bought these heels on sale. I am a mess.

"Maybe I'm not dressed the best, but at least I'm smart," I say. "You had to drop your AP class because you could barely get a D-minus."

I know immediately that I was wrong to say it. Jane looks shocked and hurt. "Wow. You haven't changed." She crosses her arms over her chest. "I don't even know how we were ever friends. You're so pathetic."

Once upon a time, when Jane and I were friends, she told me how she struggled with school. She has dyslexia, and she hid it for years. Of course, eventually word spread around our school. Jane assumed that I told everyone, even though I hadn't. Since then, she's avoided me like the plague.

I feel the urge to apologize, but I shove it down. After she unfriended me, Jane fell in with the rich-girl crowd and became the new "it" girl of Sherman Oaks High School.

"I didn't start the rumor about you having dyslexia, you know," I blurt out.

Jane looks at the ground. For the first time, she seems uncertain. "Well, Tiffany, who would've done it?" she asks. "You're the only one who knew."

"Why would I spread that type of thing around the school? It doesn't make sense." Tears start to fall from my eyes. I would usually be embarrassed, but I don't care anymore.

After a moment, Jane reluctantly takes a seat on the floor next to me, pulling her knees up to her chest.

"Tiffany, I'm so sorry," she chokes out.

I'm so shocked that I drop the heel of my shoe. It hits the floor with a *clunk*.

"Um . . . for what?"

"For leaving you like that. I was a terrible friend."

Am I alive right now? Jane Rodgers is apologizing to *me*.

"Jane, it's not only your fault. We were both petty."

"Yeah, but your family was going through a lot with your mom losing her job, and I was so mean. I—"

"It's fine, Jane. You don't have to pity me."

"Can we be friends again?" Jane asks, wiping her cheeks.

I pause. I'm not sure I'm ready to jump back into friendship. But I miss watching cheesy Netflix shows together. I miss walking around the town center and making jokes. I miss spending time with someone who really knows me. "Yeah, let's be friends again."

As I say this, the elevator comes back to life. Magically, the doors open to the third floor. I breathe a sigh of relief. But then I look down at my broken shoe. There's no way I can go to my interview like this.

"I was supposed to have a job interview today," I say. "But it doesn't look like that's going to happen."

"Here." I look up and see Jane holding her designer heels. They probably cost more than everything I own combined.

"No, I could never take those! What will you wear?"

"I'll be okay, Tiffany. Please just take them."

I cautiously take Jane's heels, and put them on my feet. They fit perfectly.

"You make me proud, Tiff!" Jane exclaims. She shapes her hands into a heart as the elevator closes.

I smile and walk up to the waiting room. Even if I don't get this job, at least I've got my friend back.

NISHAT RAIHANA

LIVES: Bronx, New York

Nishat Raihana is a current freshman attending Hunter College in New York City. Some of her interests include writing and gardening!

MENTEE'S ANECDOTE:
The relationship my mentor, Antonia Bruno, and I have is wonderful! She has shown me immense support during the two years that she and I have known each other. It often feels as though we are more than a mentor and mentee, we are friends! I can speak to her about what troubles me, and she is always there to lend me support. Thank you, Antonia, for being such an amazing mentor to me!

ANTONIA BRUNO

LIVES: Brooklyn, New York

Antonia Bruno is a public defender and the coauthor of children's series Josie Goes Green, which inspires kids to act on climate change.

MENTOR'S ANECDOTE:
One of my favorite things about Nishat is that she appreciates the small wonders in life. Nishat finds joy in things that are mundane to most of us, like the train ride to New Jersey we took together to visit my job, where she pointed out the swamps that we were riding over and the excitement of going to a new place. Her writing reflects a young woman who is constantly observing, taking in new things, and regrounding herself in gratitude at every turn.

A New World

NISHAT RAIHANA

This is the story of a young girl uprooted from her familiar, comfortable home in New York City and placed in a new world.

It all began when Malorie's parents announced that they would be going to Bangladesh, her parents' home country. To Malorie, this sudden news was a shock. She had never been to Bangladesh, and she had heard only bits and pieces about it whenever her parents would share their childhood memories. Malorie was a curious young girl, and being able to travel outside of the U.S. for the first time made her feel as though she had finally become a grown-up, allowed to explore the world. Malorie watched many shows as a kid where people traveled all over the world, like London or Paris or Hawaii. The thought of traveling to a new country where Malorie would be able to see new things, eat new food, and hear new sounds made her immensely happy. Little did she know, however, that her happiness would be short-lived.

During the two-day flight, Malorie dreamt all that she could about what she would see in Bangladesh. Her mother said that her grandparents lived in a rural sector, where Malorie would be able to see all sorts of animals, especially cows and goats. Living in New York City all her life, Malorie never expected to see such animals and was thrilled at the opportunity. Soon the plane landed, and upon stepping out of the aircraft, Malorie was hit with a crushing feeling in her lungs. The air was dense with condensation, so much that Malorie felt as if she could not breathe. Unfortunately, this trip was during one of the hottest seasons, and so Malorie struggled to adjust to the climate. Weakly, Malorie trudged along the path from the airport to their destination, where they would be picked up by their relatives. Malorie had never met them before, and so the idea of getting inside a car with strangers scared her. She realized that perhaps coming to this new country, full of everything new to her, wasn't such a good idea.

On the car ride to her grandparents' house, Malorie's eyes were glued to the window. The world seemed so different from what she was used to. With more than 20 percent of the population living below the national poverty line, Bangladesh remained one of the poorest countries, despite the progress it had made economically. Thus, it wasn't a surprise when Malorie looked out the window and saw many who were pleading for money. Although Malorie's mother would offer whatever she could give, Malorie still felt as though it wasn't enough. She had seen countless people who were missing limbs and eyes, and pleading for assistance for surgery. She wanted to do more than offer them financial help, but as a ten-year-old girl, she had little to give but sympathy. This made Malorie distressed, but all she could do was close her eyes and pretend this reality didn't exist.

When reaching their destination, Malorie began to face greater challenges. She immediately noticed the smell of cow dung that permeated the air, and she felt nauseated. Also, because of a narrow passageway to her grandparents' house, Malorie and her family had decided to go through by rickshaw. Rickshaws were three-wheeled passenger carts driven by a single man. Instantly, Malorie understood the dangers of traveling like this. The road wasn't reliable due to the many cracks and entirely broken sections of rock. Malorie had to hold on for dear life while riding, as she could easily fall off with one wrong move. At this point, Malorie had enough, and if granted one wish, she would go back home. Malorie thought this place was not meant for her. She didn't like change, not at all. She wanted the comfort that familiarity provided her, but unfortunately, there wasn't much of that in Bangladesh.

When they arrived at her grandparents' house, it wasn't just Malorie's grandparents who welcomed them. It seemed as if the entire population of Bangladesh had as well. Malorie's grandparents lived in a small, rural community, so everyone knew Malorie's parents. Since it was their first time back in years, the whole community rushed to welcome them. Malorie watched as strangers hugged her parents, who held tears in their eyes as they embraced everyone. The genuine happiness she saw from the community struck Malorie's heart. Sure, a few minutes earlier she had adamantly declared that she could not bear to spend any more time in Bangladesh, but now, she seemed to have had a change of heart.

Living in New York City, with a population so independent, meant that it could be hard to find a place to belong. This was especially the case for Malorie's parents, who were immigrants in the U.S. and traveled to the new country alone. Now Malorie realized a beautiful part of Bangladesh: the people's strong community and beliefs. Although Malorie initially felt like a stranger, everyone quickly welcomed her and made her feel special. It was as if the community wholeheartedly loved her, despite only just meeting. At this moment, Malorie had come to recognize a very important life lesson: Change may initially be hard to accept, but it often ends up very rewarding in the end.

JACQUELYN REAVES

LIVES: New York, New York

Jacquelyn (she/her) is a senior in high school who enjoys performing Shakespeare and is planning to pursue a career in journalism.

MENTEE'S ANECDOTE:

This year what I've enjoyed most about getting to work with Achiro is learning about different writing techniques, since I don't follow a technique or outline when I write. I've enjoyed working with Achiro because she helps me examine writing in TV shows, movies, and plays/musicals and helps me understand how I can apply what I've seen to my writing. I also appreciate this because I'm an actress, so usually when watching a show or performance I look at the acting, but she's taught me how to also examine the writing of the story and the characters.

ACHIRO P. OLWOCH

LIVES: New York, New York

Achiro is a writer, playwright, and filmmaker from Uganda currently living in exile in the US.

MENTOR'S ANECDOTE:

Jackie and I had an amazing time creating this story—it was almost like we were in the kitchen experimenting with ingredients to forge a new dish. It is the same with every other project we undertake. She reminds me of a seventeen-year-old me and my love for creativity and storytelling. The difference in our cultures makes it all the more interesting. It is a learning and creative experience for the both of us.

The Road Trip

JACQUELYN REAVES

One trip that tests their relationship. Will Connie and Alex survive?

Twenty-five-year-old Connie daydreams about the end of her day. She fidgets with her braids, which are pulled back into a bun, and with the zipper of her sweater as her teacher says the last words.

Twenty-eight-year-old Alex pulls up in his secondhand black Honda and his vision shifts from his watch to Connie's building. He steps out of the car to get a better look at the college. Alex is six feet tall, with curly hair, and he's wearing a white turtleneck and white sneakers. He sits on the hood of his car as he watches the students pass by. He's being considered for a job in Boston, and his interview is tomorrow.

After what seems like hours, Connie finally shows up. Without greeting her, Alex gets into the car. Connie is confused at Alex's jumpy behavior.

"Hi, babe! How was your day?" Connie asks.

"You're late," Alex responds.

"I'm sorry, the professor wouldn't stop talking. But do you have my bag?" Connie looks around in search of her bag.

Alex's eyes go wide with the realization that he forgot the one thing he was supposed to bring.

"Alex. I need my bag. There are specific items in there that are necessary for me to have a good trip."

Alex starts the car knowing he can't reason with her and heads back home. At the house, Alex offers to get her bag, but Connie refuses and heads inside the house.

Alex honks and yells at her to hurry up. "So where is that huge bag going?" he asks.

Connie laughs. "In the car, obviously," she says and throws the bag into the back seat.

Her bag barely fits in the back. Alex gets out of the front seat and starts shoving the bag in different positions to try and make it fit. The bag ends up in a weird position under the seat but somehow still resting on the cupholder.

The ride to Boston is a quiet one. Connie is too engrossed in her phone to make conversation, and any attempts Alex makes at small talk fall flat.

Suddenly, Alex and Connie are both jolted forward. Alex gets out to look at the tire and notices it's flat. His nerves are racked with anxiety. He takes out his phone and starts to call roadside assistance, pacing back and forth. Upon noticing the situation they are in, Connie puts her phone down and makes her way to the boot of the car. She pulls out a spare tire and the tools she would need to change the tire. As she's changing the tire, she doesn't speak to Alex, and he's too lost in his anxiety to notice what she's doing. She asks him to pass her the wrench. He realizes she's fixed the tire. Alex hangs up and is in shock.

Connie simply says, "No need to thank me."

When they get back in the car, the mood is more pleasant and they exchange looks at each other and reminisce on the past.

At the hotel, Alex and Connie start to apologize at the same time.

"I think I overreacted. Sometimes I don't know how to act in situations like this. I just want to make things work between us."

Alex says, "If you really want to make this work, then let's make this official."

"You say that now, but what happens if I'm not a good girlfriend? What if I mess up? What if I hurt you? I'm not good with people or with relationships."

Alex holds her hand tightly. "It's okay if you're not good at that stuff, we'll figure it out together."

They hug.

The next morning, Alex is getting ready and he's panicking. He spills coffee on his shirt and asks Connie to help him. They get into an argument, and Connie reveals that she's not supportive of his new job venture. She doesn't think she'll move to Boston and this job will tear them apart.

Alex is angry and leaves the room after asking her if last night meant nothing.

Connie throws herself on the bed and is in tears. Her mind is racing with doubts about her actions. Maybe she overstepped, and maybe she should've been more supportive. Suddenly she decides that she needs to leave on her own, and she starts packing her bag. When Alex comes back in, he looks disheveled and wants to talk.

Connie starts, "I'm sorry, I know this means a lot to you and I really want to support you, but I don't see myself living here."

"I know, it was wrong for me to try and move you all the way over here. I was being selfish," Alex says.

"But what about your interview?" Connie asks.

"I thought about what you said and I walked around for a bit, and I realized you were right. I'm not working in Boston, I'll try to make it work in New York."

Connie is overjoyed and they share a warm embrace, promising to keep working on their relationship.

ERINA REJO

LIVES: Princeton, New Jersey

Erina Rejo (she/her) is a high school sophomore who loves flash fiction, swimming, and going on walks with her dog, Zulu.

MENTEE'S ANECDOTE:

Aybike has become a wonderful mentor and friend to rely on. Despite meeting each other this year, our calls have helped us connect over our writing and personal lives. She has helped me accomplish so much in my writing, and I am beginning to understand more about critiquing and how to improve. I have made more progress with her in the past four months than I have in the past year. Reading her own literary works and learning about her journey is also amazing, and I am grateful for the experiences.

AYBIKE SUHEYLA AHMEDI

LIVES: Boonton, New Jersey

Aybike Ahmedi is pursuing her M.F.A. in creative writing at the City College of New York in Harlem, where she specializes in fiction.

MENTOR'S ANECDOTE:

Working with Erina has been a wonderful experience. I enjoy our meetings, and I have loved reading her work. She is full of creativity, and she makes it fun to work with her. I am happy we were paired. I feel we connect on many levels, and I hope to inspire her and help her grow, as she also teaches me so much.

Golden Crab

ERINA REJO

The simple story of a girl named Leto, an old man, the uncertain ocean waters, and crabs.

Crabs were never a necessity.

Only recently did the old man recall his journeys across the waters and then realize that eating crabs was what he desired.

A delicacy, he described it.

The old man's hand pushed against her back. The pads of his fingers could barely send her forward.

Leto turned to meet him. His weary eyes set upon her, boring deep down until even the fish below the dock were floating in place.

"Leto." His voice was the type that had her questioning why hers was uncertain, paralyzing fear in every last word. "Leto." His voice echoed again. His words often brought all other thoughts to rest, tucking them in before they could spiral any longer.

"Yes, sir?" Those thoughts didn't seem to rest today.

The waves were quiet by the shore as if one could lay for hours without getting carried out. But the louder, more concerning sounds followed much farther down the waters, where she could barely tell what was driftwood and what was a lost soul.

The old man's expression turned amused, his yellow stained teeth appearing as a piano missing its keys. That would be Papa's worst nightmare.

"It is not very often that we get a chance like this, to go out," he croaked, nodding in agreement with the waters. "That crab is mighty fine delicious." Wrinkles inched farther across his face as his smile grew wider.

She had believed him to be one of the crazies, the term coined by her papa for those who willingly went past their Eden. Those who yearned for more than the oasis the Gods had already gifted them.

Of course, her papa had traveled, though. That was the only way he could teach its horrors.

"Now, remember"—the old man paused, pursing his lips and muttering phrases with a slight nod of his head—"they're a beautiful golden almost." His eyes widened. "Yes, yes, yes," he chanted. "When the sun came down over them, it was almost as if an angel was sprinkling its truths, granting something that you homesteaders could only pray for." He stared out at the island, which was a mere speck in her eyes. What could ever be so grand beyond here?

Often, there were truths in his nonsense tangents as well. But her trust was being tested with these "golden" crabs.

"Why are you mute, Leto? Stop your thoughts. Go on, now." He wobbled to the end of the dock, where a small boat awaited. The crystalline waters seemed to calm in his presence.

"Go," he cried, waving a hand.

With hesitant steps, she approached the end, unsure how deep she would have to go into the abyss to ever reach her destination. She stepped in, the water swaying as if its peace had sunk further. Papa had told her how her family had cursed the waters.

"The crabs are like any other animal. They sense every doubt."

"Well, sir, there is much doubt to go around. I am afraid there is a possibility I will return without them."

Leto sat in the boat before the waters could find the chance to send her tumbling out.

"You will return with something." He nodded assuringly. "Do not take long. I plan on feasting on those crabs for supper tonight."

"Wait! What must I be careful of?"

"Nothing!" He began his chant of old sea songs underneath his breath. "And put that down."

Leto grumbled, her eyebrows bunching together as she dropped the wooden paddle.

"The water will carry you, Leto! And keep an eye out for those little stripers that you see in our ponds. They were the best company."

The boat began to drift farther down, and Leto noticed she was no longer tethered to the only safe haven she knew of. The damn old man had sent her off without a mere warning.

He continued his chants, not even sparing her a goodbye as he blurred into the crowd of vendors and townspeople. She frantically searched the boat. Her hands slid across the wooden planks for anything she could use to direct her back to shore. The waves that she feared grew nearer, pulling her deeper in with every second.

Leto peered over the edge, but not too far to fall in. The sun glistened over the waters, reflecting the light like the surface of a diamond.

The dock was no longer visible, and her stomach lurched. The lack of voices revealed how easy it was to get lost amid the absence of familiarity.

The sun glared down upon her, beating its warmth against her bare back. She glanced to the side, almost stumbling back after a notable movement startled the placid waters.

In the light, the stripers that surrounded the hull of the boat became apparent. Fluorescent green little fishes that barely survived the environment of the ponds were now *living* in the uncertain ocean waters.

And suddenly, Leto seemed to understand the extravagant tales of the crazies that Papa spoke of. The island with the golden crabs was closer than ever.

PEI YING REN

LIVES: New York, New York

Pei Ying Ren is an English and creative writing major. She enjoys occasionally writing short stories about people, relationships, and culture.

MENTEE'S ANECDOTE:

My mentorship with Jennifer has been a valuable resource for me these past few months. As an aspiring writer, feedback and an extra pair of eyes are so important for growth, and I've been able to work together with my mentor to further achieve this goal. Our monthly meetings have been so insightful and I really appreciate having someone to discuss my writing with. We also discussed topics related to school, future careers, and different aspects of our lives. I'm so grateful to the Girls Write Now community for connecting us.

JENNIFER ZARIN-NICKMAN

LIVES: New York, New York

Jennifer Zarin-Nickman is a creative arts therapist, certified Journal to the Self instructor, writer, and singer living in New York City.

MENTOR'S ANECDOTE:

It's a joy working with Pei Ying. We usually start our meetings with a journaling prompt and talk about writing, intentions, and life. Pei Ying is talented, intelligent, kind, and conscientious. I've loved getting to know her through our meetings and her writing, and seeing her grow as a writer.

The Restaurant

PEI YING REN

A summer spent in a Chinese restaurant examining a father-daughter relationship.

The moment the sun bent to meet the horizon and sent hues of orange to wash over them, the scratch of tires against pavement poised the evening for dinner. With a plate positioned in one hand and a soiled rag in the other, she watched the entrance door peel open, and the waiters moved forward to meet them.

The pale beige walls of the Golden Palace encased them in timeless routine and repetition. Silverware was fitted into their designated table-top spots, selected menu items materialized to satiate needs, servers' performance was measured for monetary reward, and the same laminate flooring was trodden by their callused feet.

Over and over.

She stayed back, pretending to be preoccupied as she slid the rag across the wooden table and bundled up the food scraps. Grains of rice slipped onto the floor and her eyes darted around, hoping no one had seen. Stacking the plates atop one another, she escaped into the kitchen.

Her father had been working at the restaurant for the past two years and it had been eight weeks since he'd fetched her from the city, a place-holder until they hired someone permanent. The decision was aided by her mother chiming, "Go! Go! It's a good learning experience," but she suspected her mother wanted a report on her father's new life when she returned, still clinging to juvenile curiosity after their separation.

She had wanted to leave the first week, but her father's taunting, "You American kids so lucky. Never know true meaning of struggle," kept her rooted.

She wanted him to admit she wasn't weak just because she didn't have to struggle.

The flare of flames always brought pricklings of sweat onto her skin, and the thick tang of sesame oil nauseated her when she stayed too long. The kitchen's stainless-steel expanse was her only relief from the plastered niceties and constant standing outside.

She placed the plates into the industrial sink for the dishwasher.

Her father stood at the stove among the line of yellowing uniforms and sweat-matted hair. She watched his wrist twist under the pan's weight as he tossed the chow mein up and caught them. The flames erupted under him, but he stood unflinching. She wanted to pull him back from the fire and teach him self-preservation.

Their conversation last night felt like a thorn in her side, constantly nagging to be soothed.

Yesterday, a family ordered a plate of spring rolls but left them untouched. When they left, the boss brought them in and served them to the next couple. She had been watching the exchange from behind the counter and took the opportunity to expose the boss.

"What's it do with you?" the boss had asked after the apologies and discounts she was forced to offer.

Her anger exacerbated the accented English she worked so hard to conceal. "You think you know how hard it is to run a business?"

That night, before they even got home, she had already prepared for her father's onslaught of criticism.

"You humiliated her in front of everyone," he had said.

"What's wrong with being honest? Would you want to eat other people's leftovers?" she countered.

"Of course not."

"So you agree she was wrong?"

"It doesn't matter," he said while waving a dismissive hand, "what matters is it wasn't your place. Children stay out of adult business. You do what you're told and work hard. You think I don't see you hiding in the kitchen? Laziness isn't always going to be an option, you know."

She didn't refute that she was already twenty or point out that he was defending the boss, who'd clearly been in the wrong. She would always be at fault and he would always speak against her.

"At least you'll be rid of me by next week," she said instead.

Then she imagined him not speaking to her for the remainder of her stay, and she felt a remorseful ache. His grudges always outlasted hers, but she was resolved to make *him* remedy their silence for once.

The summer was coming to an end, and by next week, she would be on a plane headed back to the city. Her mother would be on the other side, waiting to ask about her father, and he would continue to live his life among sweaty kitchen staff.

Their lives would carry on separately, and they would maintain their relationship over FaceTime. She would watch his hair gray over the pixelated screen and feel the urge to apologize and reassure him.

"Quickly! Customers waiting!" The boss shoved a bowl of steaming noodle soup into her hands.

She had learned to temper her dramatics and simply allow the heat to sear through the ceramic into her fingertips without complaint. At the exit, she held the doors open a moment longer to let the air-conditioning waft into the kitchen, glancing one more time at her father's hunched back.

Then she stepped into the din and assumed her position, falling back in place with the patterns unraveling around her.

ALICE ROSENBERG

LIVES: New York, New York

Alice (she/her) is a high school junior who loves making theater, walking on the beach, and writing about summer days.

MENTEE'S ANECDOTE:

Over the course of the past three years, Kendyl and I have recorded dozens of podcast episodes about our recent reads, worked on multiple multimedia pair projects, and left countless comments on each other's short stories, found poems, and plays. Working with Kendyl has truly made me a better writer, and our shared obsession with Donna Tartt's *The Secret History* is just one link in an endless chain of conversations and collaborations.

KENDYL KEARLY

LIVES: Baltimore, Maryland

Kendyl is an editor who loves walking by the water, reading outside, and writing about the world around her.

MENTOR'S ANECDOTE:

Now in our third year of Girls Write Now together, Alice and I have formed a collaborative, supportive style of working together on our writing. We spend our time picking random writing prompts; discussing what we're reading on our podcast, *Buckets of Books*; and encouraging each other to keep going, even when we have creative blocks. Alice keeps our conversations entertaining with her many interests (writing, theater, art, music, etc.) and makes me want to take on new creative projects that I wouldn't have thought of otherwise.

Strigiformes

ALICE ROSENBERG

> A flash-fiction story about summer, about childhood friendships so vast they can make the wind sing.

They called their kingdom Strigiform because Henry had seen it one day in the crossword, and because the vowel-warped consonants promised secrecy, belonging to them alone. None of them were quite sure what it meant, and none of them felt like leafing through the onion-paged dictionary to find out, but they liked this unknowing, the mystery. Ada savored the sound it made as it flew from her lips; Eli liked the curves his pencil carved every time he wrote it, swooping down and out before bending back in. The branches liked it too and seemed to whisper it in the breeze. *Strigiform strigiform strigiform*, the wind danced, the leaves whispered. The sun liked it most of all, would rest on their shoulders, freckle their cheeks, lighten their hair, pressing to get closer to the games they played to the rhythm of the word.

They traveled on the back of the name, let it carry them where their legs could not. With it, the stream between the trees became their ocean, and their sailing hands skimmed across her rippling currents. Ada was the first to jump, her skirt billowing beneath her, the weight a tulip to rival spring. Eli went next, springing and trampling into her garden, his splashing crash a respite from scorching air.

Henry took his time to bend his glasses and roll up his sleeves, to straighten his shoes and don waxen-feathered wings. Ada followed, half submerged under the freezing stream, as he began to climb. She laughed as he brushed a bit of dirt from his knee, as his fingers pinched clean, careful blades of grass. Henry couldn't have known that the branch would break, had planned on simply perching on the treehouse ledge, legs dangling over the moss-mugged mud. But the sun was smiling that day at the joy in their eyes and her skies reflected their pealing cries and she melted his resolve. So his hand slipped on burning ladder wood, on the same splintered boards he had carved and shaved and shaped and shrunk to fit their feet not-grown.

His fall was silent, striking, still. For a moment, just long enough for a boy to crash, the trees and the leaves and the weeds stopped spinning with breeze, unbent, unwild, unbroken. Ada broke the spell first, to save their wounded king, but Eli stood frozen, tangled in a cacophony of whistling bugs and singing branches. Maybe, if he refused to let his eyes drop to battled, body-tossed ground, he could wish it all away.

When Henry woke, the Sunday sun stretched from behind slammed shutters, searching for the slates that would let her leap over her favorite children's attic bed. When he finally groaned from between desert lips it was to mirror the sound of murmured fears on Ada's breath, of quieted tears on Eli's eyes. He wondered for a moment, in a sickened haze, how they had managed to carry him home, that Hermes's hands must surely have encompassed their own.

They helped him to the porch that morning, Ada his left hand and Eli his right. They had tried to take him on to the grass, had pleaded with the roots to let them pass, but the ground was soft with dewy, left-over rain, and the trampled leaves refused to hold his weight, each soggy footfall a curse, a remembrance. So Henry sat on the steps guarding the garden from the house on smoothed, store-bought wood above the mud-swept branches and watched as his arms reached out before him, as they spun and twirled and laughed. He watched his order of birds, wingless and senseless, as day fell away, watched as the sun who had beamed amid shrieks of childhood drowned in leg-breaking dusk. Watched as summer left, with fumbling breath, against the August air.

YASMIN SADEH BROSH

LIVES: Forest Hills, New York

Yasmin (she/her) is a freshman in high school who loves fantasy, reading, and writing.

MENTEE'S ANECDOTE:

Ivy is my wonderful mentor. She's really fun, creative, and inspiring. We work together through Zoom and in person, and I feel that we are connected and have a lot of fun together. She is a great writer and always pushes me, and I love working with her.

IVY JO GILBERT

LIVES: New York, New York

Ivy Jo Gilbert is a writer and a reader who works in renewable energy and enjoys Gothic literature and poetry.

MENTOR'S ANECDOTE:

Yasmin has been an absolute delight to work with. She has a wellspring of creativity inside her and carries wisdom beyond her years. The first time Yasmin and I met in person, she brought me into the world of the novel she is working on, and I've had a hard time getting the story out of my head since. She loves cheesecake, creative fiction, and working to preserve the environment. She inspires me routinely.

The Red Shoes

YASMIN SADEH BROSH

A poetry piece about dance, war, and immortal life.

Once, there was a ballerina.

She had no name, no past. And she did what ballerinas do best; she danced.

She danced with vigor, never resting in her battle of twirling limbs and spins.

She wore a white skirt, the color of snow. The color of everything else she wore, save her shoes.

Once, her shoes had been white.

Then one day, they were not.

One day, she looked down upon her shoes and realized that they were not white, but red.

She was not surprised, for she knew this red well.

It was the color that stained the grounds on which she danced.

Sometimes, it sprayed in all directions, or stained those who fought.

They always fought. She couldn't remember when they didn't. She did not know why.

In fact, she did not know anything except dance, and battle.

She danced, people fought. They always had, so the ballerina came to a point where she no longer noticed the carnage around her.

She would dance to her music, one made of screams and gunshots.

Once it had been rocks, then blades, now it was bullets.

She was not bothered, she simply lifted her arms higher and danced.

She danced over crimson sands. She twirled on bloody grass and pirouetted past bodies the color of her shoes.

So unaffected by massacres was she, that she never stopped dancing, not once in her life.

Did she have a life? She did not know, for she had seen civilizations rise and fall.

Then again, the lives of the fighters were so short in comparison to her
  dance that she pushed it out.
For what was a life thrown away so callously compared to a dance,
  treated so caringly?

Then one day, she stopped dancing.

It all happened so quickly, she did not know why she stopped.
In fact, she was quite confused.
Why had she stopped? She did not know how to do anything else,
  after all.
But she found that she could not dance, for in her chest a strange
  feeling was quickly spreading to the rest of her body.
She looked down.
Her beautiful skirt was now the color of her shoes.
The change in color of her shoes had not hindered her, so she tried to
  continue dancing.
But once again, that strange feeling thwarted her.
Her graceful body swayed unsteadily, then fell.

Her fall seemed to last forever, as endless as her dance.
When at last her body hit the ground, she did not feel pain.
For someone helped her up.
She could not see their face, it was hidden by a cloak.
Their hand was icy against her feverish one, and she took it hesitantly,
  a strange feeling taking over her senses.
She had the vague notion it was supposed to be fear.
But then again, she knew nothing, so it could have been anything.
The hooded figure led her down a dark path into a ground that had not
  been there before.
As they walked, the ballerina began to feel many things she had not
  ever felt.
What happened to her?
She did not know. But she remembered falling, and she thought of all
  the times she had seen soldiers falling, covered in that strange red.
Was she like them now?
She would have asked the stranger, but she did not know how to speak.
"Not exactly."

She looked at the stranger in surprise, another new emotion.

No one had spoken to her before, and she was vaguely certain she had
   not shared her feelings. Yet her thoughts were read.

"You've died, like them. But your fate is not the same as theirs."

What was that supposed to mean?

But she received no answer.

They walked more until they reached a room.

How did the ballerina know it was a room? She had never been in one.

And yet . . . this felt familiar.

A room with walls of dark smoke and a floor of hardened abyss.

Had she been here before? She couldn't have.

And yet.

And yet . . . something tugged at her mind from all directions. Out of
   reach, tantalizingly close.

They sat down on chairs that had not been there before, made of
   night.

The ballerina sat, her legs strangely out of use for the moment, her
   body thrumming with the desire to dance, to move, to do anything
   but sit idly.

The hooded one sat too, their shadowed face in her direction.

Why was she dead? She had never died before.

"No. But this time you got unlucky."

She remembered the bullets that the people fought with. They made
   red, didn't they? Was she a soldier now?

"No. You got hit while people fought. Now you are dead."

Dead.

Were all the people here too?

"No."

Why not? They were dead too.

"They are not here. You are. You are not a person in the war."

. . . Why did they fight?

The question seemed to surprise both of them.

"I don't know. They just do. Humanity has spent all of her existence
   fighting herself."

The ballerina felt a lump in her throat.

What was she supposed to do now?

The figure tilted their head. "You could dance."

Tears began to stream down her face.

She didn't have any music to dance to.

The stranger stood up and lifted their hands. Music swelled and played a glorious song.

Death offered the ballerina their hand.

She took it.

MARZIA AFRIN SEEMAT

LIVES: Jamaica, New York

Marzia Seemat is a high school junior in Brooklyn, New York, who is passionate about love, elegies, human lives, and the world surrounding her.

MENTEE'S ANECDOTE:

Where do I begin? Madeline—to me—is a best friend who is always there in my ups and downs, almost always listening to my rantings and cajoling me to enjoy life. She is compassionate and always excited to learn about my perspective, thoughts, and beliefs. She constantly motivates me to expand on my thoughts while encouraging me to turn those perspectives into words for the world to see. She is a brilliant writer who gives constructive feedback. Most of all, she is my mentor who helped me realize the importance of sharing my perspective of the world to itself.

MADELINE DIAMOND

LIVES: Brooklyn, New York

Madeline Diamond is a writer and editor based in Brooklyn, New York. She has written for "Buy Side from *WSJ*," *Travel + Leisure*, and Apartment Therapy.

MENTOR'S ANECDOTE:

I could tell Marzia was particularly excited to share this poem with me when she brought it up during one of our meetings. She has kept a notebook this year and has written down lines and lyrics that she then turns into full poems—I love how she always carries her creativity with her! This poem includes a few phrases that she showed me weeks earlier, and I love how she built on the ideas from those original lines. Marzia and I really understand each other as readers and writers; she can always guess which lines are going to be my favorite.

Music of Pain

MARZIA AFRIN SEEMAT

Love comes in different forms: Some are like beautiful dreams, and some are painful truths. Guard your heart before it gets trapped in those painful truths...

It's hard to let you go.
It's hard to stop these thoughts about you.
It's hard to confess to you.
But . . .
it's even harder to love you any further.
                    I don't know when you became such a necessity.
                I don't know when you turned into this hopeless passion.
            Nor do I know when I turned so selfless, and you so selfish.
                    And to be honest, I don't want to know.
                This heart loved you without anything in return.
    These eyes waited for your arrival only to witness your departure;
            they waited and waited and waited to get a hold of yours,
            hoping for you to know that your place resides within them.
This crazy heart is saying the truth:
never fall in love with someone.
But what else can this heart tell *you* now
As to how much I love you,
As to how many times I chant your name.
Let me write this love of mine with my tears . . .
no one except me will be able to read it . . .
                            Yes, yes! You have been loved.
                Because—these tears that visit every night
                            couldn't be without any reason.
                    These sharp aches whenever I see you,
                        these continuous wishes to have you,
                these stabbing pains at the thought of losing you,

couldn't be without any reason.

Yes, yes! I have a confession—

I loved you in a way that made my chest burn, heart twist, and feelings crumble.

I loved you in a way that made my tears fall, hopes shatter, and soul tired.

I loved you in a way I wish someone loved me back.

I have loved you in silence from a distance.

Secretly, I have been crying, screaming, and

dying—while you were busy laughing with her.

I loved you knowing that you can't ever be mine.

I loved you knowing this Music of Pain.

I want to tell you a lot of things before you go . . .

About my gazes . . . how they shower you with love . . .

About my eyes . . . how they confess this love every time they catch yours . . .

About my heart . . . how it shelters you . . .

About my anxiety . . . how it tortures me upon your presence . . .

I wish you could see this unseen love of mine.

I wish you could hear the words that I couldn't utter.

I wish you could see the painful wounds I carry around with me.

I wish you could see how you infected me . . . forever and infinity . . .

This thing between you and me . . .

Everything will become a story soon,

which will only be recalled by me . . .

This heart will always be wishing for this Music of Pain to end . . .

despite knowing that it will never end . . .

. . . that it will always echo in me . . . remain a part of me . . .

because my love can surely become a story,

but this story will never be forgotten . . .

at least not by me . . .

ANIKA SEKAR

LIVES: Wayne, New Jersey

Anika Sekar is a high school junior from New Jersey who loves reading, running, and watching rom-coms. She enjoys creative writing of all genres.

MENTEE'S ANECDOTE:

During our sessions this year, I've gotten to know Malissa through our writing pieces and our conversations. We share several of the same interests—namely, running and the movies we enjoy. She has taken her love of running to the next step, pursuing a career in science journalism. Malissa is an extremely talented journalist, and I've always looked forward to hearing her share her writing with me. She has never failed to provide me with valuable feedback on how to improve my own writing, and I always feel comfortable sharing my work with her.

MALISSA RODENBURG

LIVES: Seattle, Washington

Malissa Rodenburg is a journalist musing on movement, traveling, moving her body, and observing nature's wandering creatures. She writes frequently for *Outside*, Livestrong, and *5280*.

MENTOR'S ANECDOTE:

I've been afforded glimpses into Anika's life this year through, of course, her writing, but also in what inspires each piece of prose or poetry she pens. She has the ear of a writer, crafting stories from lines heard on the radio or at her own kitchen table or noises heard on the street in front of the gas station she's passed by every day for years. From these moments, she's written genre-bending flash fiction and dramatic contemporary short stories, woven personal essays, and started to dabble in poetry. It's been a pleasure to get to know her this way.

Excerpt from "Shattered Glass"

ANIKA SEKAR

This is an excerpt from the end of a short story I've been working on called "Shattered Glass." Seventeen-year-old Darla has lived in the small town of Silver Lake her whole life, surrounded by memories of her family's history of abusive relationships.

The dry, overgrown grass of the meadow brushes my ankles as I walk out of the woods. There's nothing to sit on out here except for a giant tree trunk that must have fallen several years ago, as half of the wood is rotting. I carefully lower myself down until I'm lying on the log, then I rest the back of my head on the edge. The familiar buzzing of flies and twittering of birds surrounds me, filling me up from my head to my stomach.

It's here I feel at peace, away from the white noise of people chattering about life and love and music.

When I open my eyes, I feel like I can stare at the early-evening sky forever. The sunset tonight is not anything special—just a faint orange—but the distant stars continue to shine through. Some of those stars died thousands of years ago, but they are so far away that we will never know in this lifetime.

Space has captivated me for my entire life. Looking up is essentially looking back in time, to an area where no human has ever been, where no one will ever go because it's past and done and some of those stars are dead.

Silver Lake is so dreadfully *boring*. Maybe I've just never been a small-town girl; I'm sick of seeing the same people over and over again, making awkward small talk every time I go clothes shopping or order food. In two months I'll be packing up my clothes and skincare products and books for college: my entire life enclosed in various bins and bags. I won't be stuck in this stupid town any longer: I'll be free.

I almost fall off the log when I try to sit up, and as I put my hand down to catch myself, a crushed beer can on the ground catches my eye. Nausea overtakes me as my eyes scan the cursive letters on the dusty red can. It's the same beer my dad used to drink.

Two months is a long time away. Too long.

All of a sudden, I have perfect clarity.

I run back through the woods to my car, and I drive for what feels like hours before I finally reach what I'm looking for.

The You're Leaving Silver Lake sign appears in view on the left side of the road, the decrepit wooden signpost chipping off its outer layer of white paint. It's silent in the car, except for the sound of my own breathing and the hum of the engine kicking in as I step on the gas pedal. Twenty-five to forty to sixty-five, the glowing red number climbs as my exhales quicken and my foot is glued to the pedal. Eighty and the full moon above is pulling my mind from my body, like it pulls on the tide, and my heart is pumping so aggressively I can feel it pulsing in the back of my brain. The sign is now a couple hundred feet in front of me, and I feel like I'm about to die, and I don't want to die yet, I think, definitely not in this godforsaken town, because I haven't even crossed the border yet. I stomp on the brake with every ounce of force remaining in me and grip the steering wheel until my hands turn white, and suddenly the car is not moving anymore and I'm whipped back against my seat by my seatbelt.

The air in the car is hot and suffocating and I can't breathe, so I shove open the car door and fall to the ground because it's the only thing I can think to do in order to stop myself from completely losing consciousness. There's no one anywhere here, but if there were, I'm sure they would mistake me for a corpse, or even a lost soul lying in the middle of the road hoping to become a corpse. But then again, is that not somewhat what I am?

I put a hand on the ground to help push myself up, but I feel something sharp stab my palm. Shards of a broken beer bottle lie on the road, between me and the sign. Only then do I feel the tears pouring down my face. The shattering of glass on the cabinet when Evan threw the glass at Jordan. The fragments on the floor when my dad finally left.

I don't even bother to get back into my car, I just stand up and run. The road is surrounded by trees for miles, and there's no physical differentiation between Silver Lake and outside of Silver Lake except for this rusty sign. I thrust myself at the finish line because I did it, I'm out of this town, I'm free, but wait—I'm not. Somehow, I end up on the ground again, drowning in screams as I collapse beside shattered glass.

MICHELLE SEUCAN

LIVES: Staten Island, New York

Michelle is a Chipotle lover, an avid reader, a dancer, and an electronic music fan who loves to bike in New York City.

MENTEE'S ANECDOTE:

Melissa is one of the sweetest and most accommodating people I've had the pleasure of working with. We share a mutual respect for media and literature and are always keeping up with current events, interests, and updates on certain aspects of our lives during our meetings.

MELISSA LAST

LIVES: New York, New York

Melissa is a creative manager working in children's educational television. In her free time, she enjoys hiking, live music, and creative writing.

MENTOR'S ANECDOTE:

Working with Michelle through Girls Write Now has been a pleasure! Michelle is a talented writer with a clear and effectively communicated point of view in all her work. I admire how considerate she is in her writing and her desire to tackle a wide range of meaningful subject matter.

The Postcard Monologues

MICHELLE SEUCAN

A short story of a girl's romantic encounters, mannerisms, and meetings told through her own POV and the perspective of a postcard she keeps in her room.

MONOLOGUE 1: ME

It sits nicely on top of my dresser, lost among my pear bank (I never liked the piggies) that I got from the market at Union Square and the painting replicas I collected one summer evening from the Met. This postcard may be two-dimensional, but its dimensions capture a memory wedged between the shelves of my mind, deep and elusive.

An image of an Italian dinner scene gently painted on the front, mirroring one of our first dinners together at Don Antonio's, a restaurant in Little Italy. While it was not our first time meeting, it was the first time we actually confessed our fondness for each other, a humorous exchange between two awkward teenagers over pesto pasta and lemonade.

The fresh blue ink hearts love-strickenly scribbled on the back, encapsulating my adoration for him that day as I listened to him share his little quirks with me, endearing quirks of thoughts and ideas and stories. The dinner was a perfect finish to our day spent riding bikes at sunset in Central Park, where we lay on the boulders bordering the lake and talked about everything from school, to family, to our future plans. It was interesting, picking at his mind.

Whenever I look at that postcard, which a waiter hurriedly but enthusiastically shoved into my hands as we were leaving, I'm reminded of that wonderful evening I had with a wonderful and funny boy in May.

But for now, it is just me.

Well . . . me, that postcard, and Don Antonio's.

—————

MONOLOGUE 2: THE POSTCARD

I've lived a quiet existence for many months now—after all, I am just a piece of thin cardboard, recently manufactured in a small Philadelphian factory. Do I like how I look? Depends. I suppose I represent an image of romance, but I don't know how I feel about that. I can't feel emotions, nor do I know how this concept of romance works. Or I didn't, until this one day in May when I met this human girl in an Italian restaurant in Manhattan.

A rush of wind blew me into her, a large hand picking me up from a pile of my kind and handing me over, her warm hand clutching onto me as I heard the bells of a door jingle behind her. She whisked me away into her pink room after a seemingly magical night with someone and tattooed me in blue-inked hearts. From her, I learned that these heart-shaped scribbles meant love.

She wedged me between what I've observed are her most prized possessions—a strange clay pear, into which she'd occasionally insert round metal circles and large pieces of paper with colorful swirls depicting nude humans and nature. I noticed she cared for me in ways that were special to her. I knew that from my tattoos and how she'd line her lips in a red paint and then plant them on me, marking me with her kiss. As one of her many inanimate roommates, I soon learned that she was a playful lover by heart.

While she never lost me, there were times when I lost her. There would be times when I wouldn't know where she was, or if she was coming home. I only ever saw her in the depths of the night, when she'd crawl back into her room with her hair up and a baggy shirt, ready to sleep. I wondered what she did during the day. Where did she go?

I suppose my existence became more colorful after that fateful day in May, when I fell into her hands.

CATHY SHENG

LIVES: Palo Alto, California

Cathy Sheng is a junior at Gunn High School. She loves pranking her brothers, reading a good thriller, and anything related to cheese!

MENTEE'S ANECDOTE:
I remember talking to Rachel shortly after a HarperCollins interview and talking in awe and wonder about the power of writing—how it's able to light up a day with entertainment and excavate the more vulnerable parts of a person. It is beautiful to read the work of alumni and continue story lines from mentee to mentee. Rachel is a huge source of support and help for me; I wouldn't have pursued poetry without her encouragement, and I'm excited to see what the rest of the year brings!

RACHEL PRATER

LIVES: New York, New York

Rachel works in the New York City publishing industry, holds an M.F.A. in creative writing, and enjoys reading and cuddling her two cats.

MENTOR'S ANECDOTE:
Cathy inspires me every day! She is enthusiastic about creative writing and stepping outside of her comfort zone. In turn, she has inspired me to continue writing, both what I know and what I don't know. Although Cathy and I have known each other only a short time, it feels like we've been connected for years. Our bond has been swift as we share our love for reading and what's on both our TBR (to be read) and TBW (to be watched) lists. I stand behind her not only as her mentor, but also as her writing cheerleader!

Bifurcating Trees

CATHY SHENG

This was written in a bout of nostalgia—looking at old family albums and how my relatives were a sea away, but it felt much farther, and I wondered what time would do to us.

Sets of qipao
Twin pigtails
Whispered night talks
Devilish schemes
Childish pleasures
We were closer than friends
      Stronger
We were soulmate sisters
      Cousins
      Closer than blood
She was a chen, whose nana sold noodle
I was a sheng, whose nana sold clothes
      But then there was also the pings, with their bags of herbs
      The yans, with their quick wit and wise adages
But we were all family
      We are a household of bifurcating trees
But we were bonded closer
      Our fathers grew up together
      Our mothers had us together
      Our nanas and yeyes built the very house
Our grandnanas and grand-yeyes
      Were once upon a time siblings
Whose love for each other was so great
Their children grew up like blood siblings
      Closer than two twining vines

Then their descendants remained in touch
Our love compounding, not diluting
Imagine a bond that strong
        A bond through blood that withstood through generations
A tree whose roots so deep
        It weathers the winds of time
        Bearing fruits for eras to come
I wonder a world where i didn't know
My loving, eccentric cousins and family
Where my extended cousins and 2nd removed cousins
My jabbering uncles and nosy second aunties
        Whose home-stitched scarfs i'll miss and bear hugs i'll never
    have
        Whose salty pork dumplings and folklore i'll miss
        Whose warm embrace will never offer me strength
        Whose trees carried them far away, too far away
Whose fond voices and faces
        Were as distant and cold as the whistling tunes of the night
        Where our love as a family dilutes through passage of time
Looking at my siblings
Whose eyes crinkle the way i do when smiling
Whose secrets i've held and jokes i've spilled
Whose hand i've held on dark nights
Whose tiny infant fingers i've curled around mine
Whose gestures and little habits i know by memory
I can't imagine a world where they grow foreign
        Where one day we will pass by the subway
        Our descendants oblivious to one another
Cold and alien, strangers to the history that bonded us
        To the memories and love that created us
        To the mother tree that connected us
I imagine bifurcating trees
Whose trees grow windy and gnarled
Whose branches diverge into whispery points
Whose seeds are carried by wind far away,
        To start anew in different places
One by one
        Second auntie

                Big auntie
                Big uncle
                Second uncle
                Little cousin
                Little sister
All fading away like dying stars
Our connections frayed apart and severed
                The universe carrying us to separate ends
                The seams holding us fraying one by one
Our family once whole
                Scattered
Growing out and away,
                Away from each other
But perhaps some day on the same tree
Whose great trunks carried generations
There will be two girls swinging
                from its curled, long branches
With their pigtails curled just that way
Lollipops in hand, inseparable
Perhaps then they'll lock their pinkies together
                A whispered promise to never let go
Perhaps they'll call themselves
                soulmate sisters
On these
                bifurcating
                        T
                                R
                                E
                                        E
                                        S

LENA SINGH

LIVES: Staten Island, New York

Lena Singh is a high school senior who plans to major in comparative literature. She enjoys reading fantasy novels and watching K-dramas in her bed.

MENTEE'S ANECDOTE:
We mainly focused on college applications for the first half of our second year together, and it was the longest process. Courtney was extremely patient and flexible when editing my essays, for there were more than twenty essays to write/edit. The fact that she still tolerates me is unusual, but I'm grateful to have her as my mentor. She is someone who underestimates herself and overestimates me.

COURTNEY LINDWALL

LIVES: Brooklyn, New York

Courtney is a writer for an environmental nonprofit and based in Brooklyn.

MENTOR'S ANECDOTE:
Since 2021, I've supported Lena in writing essays, poetry, and her forthcoming fantasy novel.

i miss you

LENA SINGH

I attended a program over the summer and met people from all over the world. They showed me what
genuine and crazy friendship looked like, and I continue to miss all of who they were.

it's like wanting to listen to a broken record

over—and—over again

it's like listening to those radios with frequencies

going through all the shady noise to get to that one true moment

listening to the same voices and seeing the same faces in camera rolls

immersing yourself into other people's thoughts so you forget about
    your own

it's like wanting them to be as near to you as your shadow is

it's like finding a new favorite font so you forget you ever had one before

hoping that you reside in the deep wells of their heart as they do yours

craving their presence in a way that draws their scent right back into
    your own

—*learning to miss someone*

CARINA SOLIS

LIVES: Villa Rica, Georgia

The author of *Daughtersong* (Bottlecap Press, 2023), Carina Solis is recognized by the Alliance for Young Artists and Writers, *The National Poetry Quarterly*, and elsewhere.

MENTEE'S ANECDOTE:

To me, Robin is more than just my mentor: She is someone who cares. Each week, we talk about our personal stories, our poetry, and simply how our lives have been. Additionally, she is a fantastic writer and editor, and I am lucky to have such a person critiquing my work with the utmost care. Robin has transformed my writing in ways I did not think possible, making me see the fine lines of poetry and understand the importance of each word, both lessons I will take with me in future literary endeavors.

ROBIN MESSING

LIVES: Brooklyn, New York

Robin Messing is an award-winning poet, fiction writer, and occasional essayist. Her poem "Back Seat" won the 2022 Zoetic poetry prize.

MENTOR'S ANECDOTE:

Working with Carina Solis has been a joy and a privilege. She is an enormously gifted poet, and I value the opportunity to work with her on the craft of writing with intense focus. Carina has wondrously created a wide-ranging online community of writers, and she has introduced me to other extraordinary young talents. She is ambitious in a beautiful way, and totally committed to the highest quality of her work. I have witnessed her rework a poem multiple times, experimenting and honing until she is satisfied that the work has realized its greatest purpose.

grief fish

CARINA SOLIS

Content Warning: Alcoholism

Follow a grief-filled narrative between a father and daughter, reminiscing. Previously published in *Beaver Magazine*.

in the bronx dad tells me it is ritual / to smash open a beer bottle / and pour its secrets out onto the sidewalk / an offering / he laughs / *for the brothers who could not be here* / our dinners are usually silent / filled with the soft hum of unspoken prayers / but tonight dad cracks open / spilling himself into my hands / with words that promise to stick / i had only heard some people could drink like a fish / never seen it happen before / it is the night grandma calls / for the first time in years / to tell us grandpa lost himself to grief / had decided to become a snapper / and burst into the caribbean sea / not once looking back / dad becomes a goldfish for a time / wide-eyed and hazy / though nothing more than that / he couldn't stand being too free / at breakfast the next morning dad is quiet again / his loosened body / now hardened into silence / perhaps he wants to be a red snapper too / to swim in silver waters / no blood left to surrender

TIARA SOTO

LIVES: Queens, New York

Tiara Soto is a college freshman who is passionate about exploring the world and amplifying a voice for activism in her work.

MENTEE'S ANECDOTE:

Amber has been so supportive and encouraging ever since our first meeting together! She has helped me explore my writing skills and has motivated me to continue taking risks with my work. As a first-year college student, my life has definitely gotten really busy, but Amber has been so understanding of my schedule. With that, she always brings me back to a calm mindset whenever we have our sessions. There's not a session where I am not looking forward to writing, learning, and growing!

AMBER LOVELESS

LIVES: Jackson Heights, New York

Amber Loveless is a librarian, author, and public speaker passionate about teen rights in the library, equity, and literacy.

MENTOR'S ANECDOTE:

This is my fourth year as a mentor, and it has been a pleasure and a privilege to be matched with Tiara this year. This year I've been especially impressed with how Tiara is balancing her first year in college with Girls Write Now submission requirements. We've worked together on breaking out and trying new things—like journalism and personal reflections! Turns out we share the same habit of wanting to have everything right before we start anything, and together we are challenging each other to take chances and embrace imperfection,

A Reflection of Life: On the Other Side

TIARA SOTO

My parents and I share a special relationship and find comfort in having insightful talks daily. This piece is crafted based on a reflection of their answers to one of my favorite questions!

ME: *What is one piece of advice you would give your younger self?*

MY PARENTS: *Be patient with life! As they say, life works in unexpected ways, and we have no control of what tomorrow or the next few years will look like. As much as we want it to look a certain way, there's no such thing as perfection. What we can control is our approach to life, how we live it, how we love, and how we cherish.*

On the other side of their worlds, there is me who is beginning to grasp these realities of pre-adulthood and the real world. As a freshman in college, so many mixed emotions arise daily thinking about what comes next postgraduation. In doing so, I forget everything that has brought me here, let alone the life I'm living in and grateful for every day. Through it all, I must be patient and understand that being a first-gen college student is such a huge achievement that I must always cherish. Hard work will show me why I chased after it on the other side. Recently, I've found myself questioning the little things in my day like why didn't my cool outfit idea actually work out? I must admit, it's a huge curve in my day, but as my parents said, there is no such thing as perfection in how our lives look. It's my approach to it that matters, and just maybe the simple answer to my wonders is that an even better moment is waiting for me. A moment where I will glow with beauty and contentment specially made for then, just as I do now in my many ways. I control the love I show myself in the midst of all these big changes happening in my life through storms and sunshine. That love that is by my friends and family who put me to the side of confidence. And so, on the other side of everything and the other side of my parents' world, I'm presented with a variety of advice, rules, and stories on how the game of life works. It's up to me to choose how I play, but I will always win this game if I follow my heart and let the pieces of positivity guide me.

SIDNEY STRONG

LIVES: Columbia, Maryland

Sidney Strong is a writer passionate about storytelling in all formats. She aspires to work in book publishing to increase representation of diverse backgrounds.

MENTEE'S ANECDOTE:

I look forward to each pair meeting with Andrea because she has been instrumental in encouraging me to trust my instincts as a writer. I can feel myself writing with more confidence under her guidance, and her input has been invaluable as I begin to move toward my goal of becoming a published author. More than anything, I appreciate how attentive she is when listening to the challenges that I face in my daily life. I can't imagine how I would begin to navigate the ups and downs of my final year in college without our weekly conversations.

ANDREA RIQUIER

LIVES: New York, New York

Andrea Riquier is an award-winning independent journalist who has previously reported and written for the *Financial Times*, *Investor's Business Daily*, and Dow Jones.

MENTOR'S ANECDOTE:

It has been an honor and an education to serve as Sidney's mentor this year. She amazes me with her energy, her curiosity and enthusiasm, and her perceptiveness. Sidney has shared thoughtful, deeply personal work that vividly demonstrates the challenges of being a young woman in America, and a young person of color. It has been a learning experience for me, a career journalist, to share in her love of writing simply for the sake of writing, and creating across genres. I can't wait to see what Sidney accomplishes in the future.

How to Cut Your Hair

SIDNEY STRONG

"How to Cut Your Hair" is an emotional exploration into the trauma caused by the fraught relationship between Blackness and femininity that follows Black women in every aspect of their lives.

Grab the scissors. The ones you use to cut scratchy tags in the clothes rubbing your skin raw. The ones you use to cut yellowed leaves off the plants you forgot to water. The ones so dull, they struggle to saw through cardboard boxes too big to fit in your trash can. Look in the mirror and hate what you see. Look again and try to convince yourself otherwise. Rub the strands of lifeless hair between your thumb and index finger. Think to yourself: My hair is brittle, broken, and see-through, but it is still mine. Put down the scissors. Worry that people will look at you with judgment or maybe even disgust. Worry that they already do. Remind yourself: It's just hair and it will grow back. Pick up the scissors. Snatch a section of hair from where it rests on your shoulder, and bring the blades down onto the unsuspecting strands. Cringe as you listen to the shrieking of your hair being severed from you. Permanently. Irrevocably. Examine your lopsided reflection in the mirror. Close your eyes. Open them. Feverishly carve, rip, and hack at pieces of hair until the scissors slide through nothing but air. Pause. Say to yourself: I look like a man. Know that you really mean that no man will ever want to look at you. Hold back tears. Declare that the right man will love looking at you even if you look like a man. Even if your hair does not trail down your back and flow in the wind. Even if the short, prickly curls that replace your synthetically straightened hair mirrors his own to a frightening degree. Repeat to yourself: It's just hair. Cry even though it's *just hair.*

Because it's not just hair. It's the hair that you took pride in, your dignity unmarred. The hair that made you feel beautiful, knowing that you deserved the praise that fell into your lap. The hair that gave you confidence, oozing in every stride of your gait. Hair that is gone. Hair that is now scattered on the bathroom floor in pathetic clumps of regret. Throw the scissors across the room and watch them dent the already bruised and battered wall. Fear what tomorrow will bring. Fear the feeling of wind on your neck that your hair once protected you from. The feeling of nakedness. Know that tomorrow you will get stares and comments. Some that are well-meaning and some that are not. Hate them all because they are a reminder of what is missing. Your hair is gone because *you* cut it all off and *you* chose to do it even though *you* had no choice, but regardless, *you* hate yourself for making that choice. Because you were better off before. Before you became exposed, without hair to hide behind. Before you felt unwanted, your value diminishing with the length of your hair. But here you are, without hair. With no one to blame except yourself and maybe the blunt scissors abandoned on the floor of your bathroom.

SOPHIA TAKROURI

LIVES: Mount Vernon, Ohio

Sophia Takrouri is an eighteen-year-old aspiring author. She has a love for all things literary and plans to study English at Kenyon College.

MENTEE'S ANECDOTE:
I have loved getting to work with Ashley, and I look up to her a lot. Her passion for self-care inspires me to prioritize it in my own life, and she has always stepped up to help me achieve my goals and hold me accountable, whether we are meeting for an early-morning "Hour of Focus" session or chatting on a Sunday-morning Zoom call. I am so excited to continue working with Ashley and learning more from her as we continue our creative journeys together.

ASHLEY R. SOWERS

LIVES: Cleveland Heights, Ohio

Ashley is a content marketer and writer whose passion lies in making the practice of wellness and self-care more accessible to Black women.

MENTOR'S ANECDOTE:
I have loved being Sophia's mentor and have so much respect for her. She teaches me just as much as I guide her. Her dedication to her craft often inspires me in my own work. I have learned very quickly that when Sophia aspires to achieve something, she steps up and puts in the hard work necessary to do so. I am so excited to witness her grow as a writer and person in general. It's been an absolute pleasure to play a role in supporting her dreams.

Excerpt from "The Benson Bucket List"

SOPHIA TAKROURI

> A young woman is staying at her brother's house for the first time in years to recover from an injury. She experiences conflicting emotions over their dynamic and finds herself secretly yearning for the past.

He kept to himself, and so did I.

I napped in my bedroom, and Eric went on with his day. I didn't know what exactly he was doing, but sometimes I could guess. Like when I woke up to the creaking of the hardwood floor outside of the room and heard what I believed was Eric talking business on his cell. His feet always had to move whenever he was on the phone, exactly how I remembered him.

He came into my room only once or twice just to check on me. Besides my legs being kind of sore, the only thing I had to complain about was my boredom. I wished that I'd brought books or something, but I wasn't exactly feeling up to a trip to the library.

"Well, maybe I have some books lying around the house somewhere," Eric said after I told him.

I stifled a giggle. "You mean your algebra workbooks?"

Eric didn't answer my question, and I figured he knew I wasn't being entirely serious. Instead, he said, "I'll go look for you. Be right back."

He was off in an instant, leaving me waiting. I had to admit, it was sweet of him. Especially considering the fact that he wasn't exactly a reader. It was one of those moments that made me grow hopeful for a brief moment, until I pushed it away as quickly as it came.

Eric returned with two hardcover books in his arms. I was pleasantly surprised. "Where'd you find those?"

"In the basement," he answered casually. It made sense. Eric kept a lot of our old things down there, and there was no telling what we might find and when. Part of me wanted to go down there and explore, but a bigger part of me pushed that thought away. My physical state explained most of why I did that, but there was something else too.

Eric and I weren't there yet. And I didn't know if we'd ever be.

That was okay, though. I could settle for this. "Thanks, Eric," I said, grabbing the books from him.

I gave both of the covers a quick glance. *To Kill a Mockingbird* and *1984*. Eric and I had once needed those copies back when we were in school, and I supposed that he had kept them around for all this time.

My brother's eyes shifted. "I know they're not much, but—"

"Oh, no," I interrupted him. "They're classics."

"Right. Classics are good."

"Certainly."

We fell into another bout of silence. Eric looked around the room, hands in his front pockets. It was like he was lingering around to say something more but didn't quite know what that something was. It was starting to make me want to fill the silence too, but what was there to say?

"Need anything else?" he finally asked me.

I shook my head.

"Okay. Call me if you do. I'll leave you to read."

And he did.

I didn't do much reading while Eric was gone. I was too busy over-thinking our recent exchange. Sometimes it helped to escape into some-one else's story when I was in that state of mind, but even that wasn't working. I was still preoccupied with that same, stiff energy that was prevalent between Eric and I. It was what I wanted, right? My brother and I being polite to each other on the surface, but never venturing deeper than that? It was a safe dynamic, but even so, I felt bad for wanting it. Something about Eric's interactions with me was telling me that he didn't exactly want the same thing.

If I were to try to fix it and have those deeper conversations with him—the ones that truly connected people—I wasn't so sure *that* would even end well. Past experience justified that.

Sometimes, when my feelings were too much for me to handle, I'd write them all out. That's exactly what I did. I thought I would have written more, but maybe it was just right.

I remember those days.

When the sun would shine and my ice cream would melt, running down the wafer cone like little pink raindrops, falling onto my hands to create a sticky, sweet substance I would lick off while trailing behind him.

I remember those days.

When he would make me laugh so hard my cheeks would hurt, when he would dare me to beat him in a relay race, when he would lift me high enough to feed a carrot to a pony at the petting zoo.

I remember those days.

When he was himself. When he wasn't someone else.

When he was my best friend.

Now he's just confused.

HANIYYAH USMANI

LIVES: Bronx, New York

Haniyyah Usmani (she/her) wants to bring the much-loved fantasy worlds she reads about to her real life, but for now channels them through her writing.

MENTEE'S ANECDOTE:

Tuesdays have become my favorite day of the week because of the fact that I get to see Sam after school and really get to take some time away from my schedule to purely dedicate to writing. She's always energetic and understanding, adding light to every session, and really giving me that supportive environment to pour myself out in words. It always seems like she knows me so well, like my thought processes for writing. We've learned so much about our similarities, like the random bursts of inspiration we get—namely, in the shower.

SAM FOX

LIVES: New York, New York

Sam Fox (she/her) is a writer, marketer, and social media expert who loves ice cream and nachos and often forgets she isn't actually Gen Z.

MENTOR'S ANECDOTE:

Every Tuesday, Haniyyah shows up to our pair sessions with pure enthusiasm, ready to put the (usually fantasy or dystopian thriller) characters she's spent all week ruminating on to paper. She approaches every prompt I put in front of her with curiosity, first asking the important questions so many don't even think to ask before pouring herself into her writing. Moreover, Haniyyah's just a really cool person! She knows who she is and what she's passionate about, and she lets everyone around her know it, too. I could have used Haniyyah as a friend when I was in high school!

Crown of Thorns

HANIYYAH USMANI

Nadia's set to take over the throne her father's prepared her for her entire life. But what if everything
she thought she knew, including who she is, was a
lie? An excerpt of a longer YA piece.

I'd always been fond of my father. His subjects respected him for being
an honest king and the voice of reason in every difficulty he was faced
with. To them, he was the problem solver, but to me, he was that and
more. He'd taught me so much over the years, from personal opinions to
advice, which I hope to carry on in my reign as well as he has done, as he
continues to do every day. As the oldest child, I stood to inherit the
throne, and while the thought sent my nerves off in a dance, I knew I had
my father and his legacy behind me, wrapping around me and holding
me up in difficulties to come. But for now, I'm still learning.

Since I was younger, we had a tradition where we spent every weekend doing an activity of my choice. In a simpler time, when I was younger,
it would be trips to my favorite ice-cream shop during the summer, or a
day spent ice-skating on the palace's frozen lakes during the winter. A
walk through the palace grounds colored in every shade of orange, red,
yellow during the fall, and a picnic on the same grounds, full of greenery
and blooming flowers in the times of spring. As I grew, so did the importance of these times together; it was our time away from the castle, away
from the duties and all I had to learn about. In those moments, we
weren't a king and princess, we were just family.

"Nadia," my father calls, stopping me in my tracks on my way to the kitchens.

"Yeah, what happened, Papa?" Now that I see his face, I see an undertone of . . . guilt? *What is going on?*

"Your mama and I . . ." I stiffen at the mention of my mother as he takes a breath. "We have something to discuss with you later." His eyes no doubt take in my suddenly shifted manner.

"It's important, Nadia, and we must talk about it as soon as possible. Meet us in the Grand Library after your trip to the kitchens." His eyes briefly soften into small smiles as he says the last bit, before they turn grave again.

"All right, Papa. Of course I'll be there, but what's with the seriousness? I'm not in trouble, am I?" My mind races to think of anything I'd done recently that warranted a meeting with both of my parents.

He shakes his head. "You're not in trouble, but let's just talk this over when you get back, all right?"

He seems quite uncomfortable about whatever this is. I nod and walk out, my tendency to overthink getting the best of me and already rushing to stack lines of possibilities together. Knowing my mother's going to be there is unsettling. She'd never treated me as Papa did, who always looked out for me in addition to teaching me all there was to know about the Crown. She was sharper, shrewd, nothing like my father at all.

I push open the heavy door to find my parents sitting down at the plush seats in the center of the library. While my father's face appears lined with the same sorrow as before, bordering on guilt, my mother seems to be holding back a smile, settling for a small smirk instead.

"Oh she's here!" she says, the gentleness pronounced more than needed.

Papa wordlessly slides a folder to me, willing me to open and read its contents. I do so, curiosity eating me from the inside out.

Inside are two pieces of paper, and my eyes latch on to the words printed there, continuing to read on, sliding ahead against my will.

My parents . . .

The thought forms against my will, hardening in my mind and becoming a truth I refuse to accept. A bomb's been released, falling as I stare, a rising horror building up in my mind as my heart rate skyrockets. A fear going beyond control, yet paired with the dread knotting at the pit of my stomach, the thought that this is inescapable weighing down in the place of gravity. I can't run from this. It's an inevitable event, crashing down on me, on the rest of the world.

My parents aren't my parents. It's all going to go to ruin. Rubble and dust will be all that remains, and no one will be left to witness it. And yet the world still stands. I'm still sitting here in my seat in the library. My . . . *parents* sitting across from me, their faces obscured by the blur in my eyes, threatening to take over and spill down my cheeks. Or maybe they've already begun to. The bomb doesn't even exist, and I'm not even sure the rest of the world does. My whole life's been a lie, what's another? What's anything, even? *My parents aren't my parents.* My memories are fake. Nothing ever meant anything and I'm living a life that isn't mine.

I'm five years old again, skating at the lake with the figure I've called Papa for as long as I can remember. All those moments, all the time I've spent in his study, trying to follow in his footsteps . . .

That's when a thought strikes me, a dagger thrown and pinning down a page about to fly away, a thought trying to sneak out.

My position as heir.

NAVYA VASIREDDY

LIVES: Parsippany, New Jersey

Navya is a high school sophomore who loves to read at Barnes & Noble and take walks down her street with her family.

MENTEE'S ANECDOTE:

During our calls, along with her valuable writing feedback, Ambika is always prepared with the most helpful (and reassuring) life advice. Through the overwhelming stress of sophomore year, she has been incredibly supportive. This year, I've explored various genres of creative writing, including memoir writing and poetry. With Ambika's help, I'm working on including more enhanced imagery in my writing. My first year with the Girls Write Now program has been beneficial and, put simply, fun, thanks to Ambika—the sweetest and most understanding mentor I could have asked for.

AMBIKA SUKUL

LIVES: Jersey City, New Jersey

Ambika holds an MBA from Boston University. In her free time, she enjoys being with her family, traveling, and writing poetry.

MENTOR'S ANECDOTE:

It has been a pleasure working with Navya. She is an intelligent young woman with great potential. She has explored poetry and short story writing this term, which has broadened her creative writing skills. I am confident she will continue to develop her creative writing skills and ultimately find her writer's voice. I wish Navya the greatest happiness and success in life.

the 'filler'

NAVYA VASIREDDY

A poem narrating one perspective of what it's like to be "the filler"—someone who believes they merely take up space, despite how much they try to escape the confines of this role.

the morning sunshine peeks through the classroom window;
her seat is warm, and her head is faced forward.
situated in the center of the classroom,
her seat is an enclosed island surrounded by the chatter engulfing the
    room.
her eyes are glued to her chromebook screen,
a distraction from her classmates sharing the latest gossip and their
    weekend plans.
her bored fingers tap the desk, over and over,
the *click-clack* rhythm drowning out all other noise.
she counts one, two, and then twenty-three tabs on her
    laptop,
until the bell rings, the projector lights up, and class begins.

the hallways are a labyrinth.
cliques storm the halls,
and couples form blockades.
she approaches her two friends,
absorbed in conversation.
she laughs, but they do not hear.
she cracks a joke, but it is ignored.
she grips her backpack tight, replaying her insecurities in an infinite
    loop,
her head falling to the ground.

stop!, she suddenly yells (to her surprise),
hear me, hear my voice!
yet the silence of her suppressed cries echoes into the hallway
    chatter.
her mind is a void, filled with nothing but the tranquil feeling of
    isolation.
she stops in the hallway,
but her friends continue ahead, and she
slowly
       slowly
           slowly
shrinks into herself—
a caterpillar stuck in her cocoon,
with nothing but the cold familiarity of her thoughts.

an inevitable cycle of home, sleep, and school swipes the ideal high
    school experience from her grasp,
the best four, they would call it, confirmed to be flawed.
savor every moment, they would say;
you'll never get back the last four years before adulthood.
but she knew—
she knew high school would be the profound chasm that would
    swallow her spirit,
her voice stolen and her head tilted down.

junior year peeks out of the shadows.
college, extracurriculars, and internships circulate through everyone's
    minds.
competitiveness surpasses friendship,
toxicity surfacing in even the closest of friendships.
academic status becomes the forefront of conversation——
she witnesses it all,
from her seat, basking in the warmth of the morning sunlight.
time is fleeting, but for her, it is ceaseless,
and with every tedious day, she relives the anxiety, the overthinking,
    the loneliness;
the constant ringing in the hollowness of her seat.

but no one would ever know,
that she is present and listening and at most desires the chance to be
    heard.
her delusional gaze is directed to her chromebook screen,
and her head is faced forward,
as she counts each and every tab
one
        by
                one.

VICTORIA VILTON

LIVES: Brooklyn, New York

Victoria (she/her) is a first-year in college who plans to be a pilot. She enjoys reading and listening to music.

MENTEE'S ANECDOTE:

Liz has been one of the most incredible, helpful, and supportive writing mentors I've ever had. She has the unique ability to read a piece of writing and know exactly what it needs and how to pull whatever that is out of me. Liz is extremely easy to talk to and always finds some way to get me thinking about the most random, creative stories I can come up with. I have thoroughly enjoyed working with and learning from her and I absolutely cannot wait to read her novels!

LIZ VON KLEMPERER

LIVES: New York, New York

Liz (she/they) holds an M.F.A. from Columbia. Her reviews and interviews have been featured in *Tin House* online, Lambda Literary, *Electric Literature*, and more.

MENTOR'S ANECDOTE:

When I met Victoria at the beginning of this year, she was well on her way to writing a draft of her historical novel, and I've been lucky to be a part of the process. We nerd out on the craft of writing together during our sessions, and Victoria always has a book recommendation ready to go. We've also delved into everything from the culture of the seventies, to our favorite Taylor Jenkins Reid books, to what secrets live in the basement of the Center for Fiction. I am so excited to read Victoria's novel one day!

Winnie, Untitled

VICTORIA VILTON

Content Warning: Suicide

> **This is a character study of a fictional woman named Winnie from the perspective of her friends, family, and peers.**

"Artist Winnie Clairemont-Jackson has been announced dead. She was found unresponsive in her home on the evening of July 12th by her housekeeper. She is presumed to have overdosed." ABC Nightly News, *July 13th, 2003*

"Winnie Clairemont-Jackson, the artist famous for her controversial 2002 painting 'I Am Untitled,' died earlier this month. Winnie is survived by her parents, a sister, and two nieces." Janie Lee, Celebrity Obits, *July 2003*

Clips from U.S. *Art News*—"Winnie Clairemont-Jackson: A Retrospective".
[Charles Roster, host of the Retrospective, interviewed a series of Winnie's peers, friends, and family]

James Saint-Paul, Professor of Art History, an affable man: "She was a troubled girl when I met her. Very outspoken, but about the strangest things. Winnie loved putting me in my place. She would read books upon books about our lectures, just so she could interrupt me in class and correct me. I'd never seen such potential, and I was one of her biggest supporters. The world has lost a bright star."

"But then she made that piece. It was so strange. I could never figure out why she did it. Like she wanted to ruin her career. She was an enigma, that Winnie. I shall miss her dearly."

Claire Leibowitz-Smith, an art school friend of Winnie's; a melodramatic woman: "I think that it was always going to happen this way with Winnie. She was fated to be the tortured artist. Messed-up family life. Messed-up love life. Misunderstood art. Winnie would never be able to escape that kind of death.

"She talked to me sometimes, about how much she hated 'the art world.' Everyone has to be struggling in some way, or else the art doesn't matter. It's true. Without pain, art means nothing. I suppose her pain was too much to simply channel into art.

—

"Anyways, Winnie was a good friend. She supported everything I did. I wouldn't be half the artist I am now without her influence. I loved that girl."

John Smith, Claire's husband; a suave, emotionally aggressive man: "I wasn't fond of Winnie. I won't go into details now, but she had this incredibly entitled perception of her work, which was nothing impressive. She lacked vision. I remained unimpressed during the entirety of her career."

Ruth Clairemont, Winnie's mother; a wild-child of a woman: "I raised her like I wished my parents raised me. A hippie, a free spirit. I was so proud of her. She was exactly as I had molded her. Ahead of our collective consciousness. When she told me she was going to art school, I cried tears of joy. My daughter thought for herself. She didn't subscribe to 'normal.' I suppose that's what ended up killing her. She was too different, too alone.

—

"The world won't be the same without her. That's for sure.

—

"I have a collection of Winnie's artwork, which she doesn't know. Didn't know. She didn't visit me much, so I displayed the art all over my house. My very own art gallery.

"I may just sell them now."

Donald Jackson, Winnie's father; a serious man: "I spent most of her childhood in my store, which I regret now, naturally.

—

"They say parents are never supposed to bury their children. I did yesterday, and it was unimaginable.

—

"Unimaginable."

Frances Clairemont-Jackson, Winnie's sister; a hardworking woman: "I'm five years older than my sister, so I'm used to cleaning up after her. But I never imagined that I'd have to do this. Telling my daughters that their aunt killed herself? How will I answer their questions once they're old enough to learn about her?

—

"She could be so selfish sometimes.

—

"I wish she'd given me a chance to say goodbye. I didn't care that people didn't like her or her art. Why couldn't that be enough for her?"

Winnie's Final Diary Entry, January 1, 2003

Dear log,

2003 has started, and I'm not entirely sure how I feel. I got into quite a bit of trouble last year with "I Am Untitled," but I've moved on from all that drama. Actually, now I find it funny. People can be so dramatic.

When you create a piece beyond conceptual understanding, people tend to get upset. I was stupid enough not to anticipate this fact.

I'm becoming very disillusioned with this career I've chosen for myself. I don't know how long I can possibly go on smiling through gallery openings and the like. There is nothing here for me anymore.

The idea of just disappearing has certainly crossed my mind more than once, but I fear I'm too much of a coward to cross that final threshold. Could I possibly just walk away from this whole life I've built?

It's not much of a life worth living, though. In all honesty, I'm quite ready to be done with it all.

NICOLE WANG

LIVES: College Point, New York

Nicole Wang (she/her) is a sophomore at Brooklyn Technical High School with a severe addiction to chess, cats, chemistry, and reading!

MENTEE'S ANECDOTE:

Rachel's optimistic outlook on life and writing inspires me to find happiness in the smallest moments, whether writing or enjoying a walk in the park. Each Zoom call with Rachel provides a diverting and comforting escape from all the stress and pressure I experience. I am so intrigued by Rachel's travel and work experience and can't wait to meet her in person one day!

RACHEL THOMPSON

LIVES: New York, New York

Rachel (she/her) is an editorial manager at NBC Sports. Originally from the Bay Area, she has lived in New York for more than seven years.

MENTOR'S ANECDOTE:

Nicole's intelligence, dedication to writing, and wide range of skills are so impressive to me. Her ability to tackle a range of subjects, writing styles, and vulnerability in her work are reminders to me that writing should be personal, challenging, and brave.

A Letter to Mom

NICOLE WANG

> **A raw letter addressed to my mom: hurtful memories that a part of me hopes she remembers, imperfections left uncovered, and everything I never said.**

妈妈,

There's so much I want to say to you. Intangible feelings of hate, anger, and love. I feel too scared to confront you, and I think you will never read this, because if you do, then I wouldn't be too honest with myself. I really want to know if one part of you ever thought about seeing a different face on the hospital bed. I think I'm insignificant in your eyes, though I know that's far from how you feel. Sometimes I think I'm always putting the way I see myself to explain how others see me, including you. I have never upheld the invisible expectations that linger in our conversations or through your reprimands. What do you expect of me? Why can't you accept me for who I'm trying my best to be?

I have always been a burden that your strained back has to carry. At each doctor's appointment, you held my hand, telling me everything will be okay. It was just the two of us in the waiting room, waiting until people started to trickle out, and before we knew it, the day had become cold and dark. I'm not perfect. It's harder for me to accept myself than you do. How can I not hate myself when I am the child born with a birthmark and a teratoma, landing in the hospital at age six? Sometimes I wish for things to be the same, but then I remember the pain behind the smile that never reaches your eyes. I wish I wasn't the child who knocked on your room in the middle of the night because of my nosebleeds. I hated myself for the never-healing holes in both of my arms because of my weekly allergy shots on the eighth floor of Queens Crossing. One part of me longs to know if there is a part of you that detests me for being so dependent on you.

Look where we are now, with our own house (no need to rent one stuffy room for the four of us) and a Toyota that can do the job. We also have a restaurant, which you initially thought would lighten your worries. Trust me, I thought it would solve all our financial problems and bring our family closer together too. From working once a week to five times a week, including my weekends, I have ultimately considered the restaurant *our* second home. You spend six out of seven days in the restaurant, stained with sweat and tears from your endless toils. 妈妈, I'm so proud of you, but I hope you understand how I feel. Those calls in the middle of the school day to alleviate angry customers' complaining will never end, and that business 1099 tax form would not have corrected itself if it weren't for the thirty back-and-forth emails among Grubhub, Uber Eats, and DoorDash.

You are now in your forties, and I'm only fifteen, but in those fifteen years of my life, your unwavering motherly love has always kept me going. I love you so much. I love when I extend my arms for a hug and you warmly embrace me. We made so many memories that I look back on them when I feel lonely. However, that one night in 2015 will forever be engraved in my memory—that pouring night with stars glistening in the sky. I pointed to the different animals until droplets fell into my eyes. We didn't have an umbrella, so we ran through the rain across the street, my hand in yours. We were waiting for the bus, but you knew I was hungry, so you brought me to the Dunkin' Donuts nearby and went back outside in the pounding thunder just to get me halal food from a food cart. In those two minutes I was so scared, but I felt like the happiest kid out there. I could feel the love when you opened the container and passed me the one set of utensils. I remember you refusing when I asked you if you wanted some. You pushed the plate toward me and smiled, "妈妈不要,你先吃."

No one can replace that motherly love I always felt from you. I hope you also remember that night.

There are so many words left unspoken. Still so many things undone.

So many promises waiting to be fulfilled. So many places I want to take you to. So many nights I still want to live while talking to you about the silliest of things. So many laughs I want to hear from you. So many smiles I want to bring to your face. So many memories I still want to make. We will get there together.

I am like a caterpillar inside my cocoon. I want to break free, and when I do, I want to become that beautiful butterfly. I want to become that shining butterfly in your eyes. That perfect daughter. In the end, you are always here with me, and I can't ask for more than that.

Thank you for choosing to be strong for me,

SHAMU WARD

LIVES: Bronx, New York

Shamu W. (they/she) is an aspiring author and artist. They enjoy listening to music while coming up with new characters to incorporate into their stories.

MENTEE'S ANECDOTE:

I owe Charis so much and can't stress enough how much I adore her. She has been an absolute pleasure to work with and has been such an amazing mentor and friend. Not only has she encouraged me to be more confident in my work, but she's also been supportive of everything I've worked on this year. I can't wait to see what comes next and I look forward to working with her moving forward!

CHARIS SATCHELL

LIVES: Rego Park, New York

Charis Satchell (she/her) is a passionate storyteller working in television and audio production. She enjoys thought-provoking documentaries, being a foodie, and reading fashion history.

MENTOR'S ANECDOTE:

Shamu is a multitalented artist. Whether visually or putting pen to paper, creating is at the core of their existence. It has been a great experience learning about their interests in fantasy fiction, illustration, and manga. I look forward to seeing their dreams of publishing a comic book come to life.

Forever & Always

SHAMU WARD

This short story is about my character Princess Amantdeiylaia, who has a heart-to-heart with her lady-in-waiting and closest (and only) friend, Rhettna.

The sun was shining brightly today, something uncommon, given the kingdom's naturally bitter-cold climate. Its warm rays caused the freshly fallen snow that had fallen the night before to glisten like crystals. Mornings like these were Princess Amantdeiylaia's favorite; quiet and serene. It provided her with the perfect setting to clear her mind and help prepare her head for the day ahead. These days she found herself particularly distracted by a particular *lord* that had annoyingly gotten under her skin. His smile, the way the light reflected off his eyes when he knew he'd done something wrong, and especially the way he said her name . . . All the little things that would usually annoy anybody made her fall harder for him.

"What a beautiful morning . . ." the princess noted, clutching the fabric that met at her bust. Amantdeiylaia stood nervously in front of her bedroom window, the stained glass casting color on her flushed face.

Upon her door being knocked on, Amantdeiylaia turned to face her visitor, her lady-in-waiting, Rhettna. The princess bowed her head to greet her, something unusual, given her social standing. After closing her door, Rhettna walked in and sat on the princess's bed, watching as Amantdeiylaia looked off into the distance. She knew the princess like the back of her hand and could clearly tell something was amiss.

"Good morning, Your Highness," Rhettna hummed, lowering her head while she spoke. However, when no response was given, her eyes looked back up to see the princess staring aimlessly into the sky. While she knew there would be no verbal response, Rhettna knew the princess well enough that usually she would receive some form of acknowledgment in the form of her telepathic abilities. Rhettna's arms folded, clearing her throat to get her friend's attention, now curious as to what could've possibly left her in such a state.

The princess let out a small squeak and turned around to give her lady-in-waiting her full undivided attention. Rhettna shook her head and sighed playfully, relieved that she had managed to snap her out of the trance that had left her so dazed and distracted. With that out of the way, Rhettna motioned for Amantdeiylaia to sit beside her so that she could get to the bottom of the princess's strange behavior. To be honest, moments like these were what made their relationship all the more valuable. Amantdeiylaia was appreciative to have someone as loyal and perceptive as Rhettna in her life—especially when the rest of her family lacked the ability to notice whenever something was up with her. After all, the princess had quite a lot on her mind recently and everything seemed so . . . *complicated* these days.

"What's wrong, Princess? I can tell you're not feeling like yourself. Is it a fever? Are you ill?" Rhettna reached her hand out and placed the back of it against the princess's forehead. Her brows knitted tightly as she checked for an increase in temperature, but luckily, Amant showed no signs of illness. The only thing off about her appearance was the rosy color that had risen to her cheeks and her flustered expression.

The princess swatted her hand away and huffed in annoyance as Rhettna backed off, still curious as to what the cause was of this shift in behavior. Amantdeiylaia was capable of keeping a relatively calm expression, a useful skill to have as a future leader, but it was learned through years of isolation and neglect.

"Is it something your father said? I know he can be a little . . . much sometimes . . ." Rhettna's voice trailed off, as she was not wishing to upset the princess if that were the case. However, Amantdeiylaia shook her head no, sighing as she realized her friend wouldn't let the situation rest. The princess took Rhettna's hand and gave her a worried look, her eyes softening as she prepared herself to share her deeply personal secret.

"It's . . . It's not about my parents . . . o-or anyone in my family. It's more so about Lord **Voulneir**. I think . . . I think I love him, Rhettna," Amantdeiylaia conveyed, her mind's voice echoing in the mind of her lady-inwaiting.

Rhettna remained silent as she took the information in, not wanting to say anything inappropriate in her friend's time of need. Perhaps the silence was due to her being left speechless by her friend's declaration of love. It wasn't that she didn't understand it; perhaps it was their social difference. For starters, *he* was a Downworlder! There was no way in hell the two of them would be able to be together . . . and yet there she was—admitting to the fact that she had feelings for him!

"You do realize you're treading *very* dangerous waters, don't you, Princess?" Rhettna tightened the grip on her friend's hand, hoping to offer comfort during this presumably confusing time.

The princess only nodded, her pearlescent eyes glossing over as tears threatened to fall from them. Her friend wiped away the tears, giving Amant a warm smile to reassure her that she wasn't alone and could confide in her.

"Your secret is safe with me, forever and always."

NYLAH WATKINS

LIVES: Jacksonville, Florida

Nylah Watkins is a sixteen-year-old high school junior who has a fierce passion for writing, dancing, reading, and cooking.

MENTEE'S ANECDOTE:

Sherrill and I have built a strong relationship. We trust each other and show up for each other. Sherrill is incredibly supportive of my crazy schedule, and when we meet up, we always have so much fun sharing about our lives. The bond we have created is one that is built to last.

SHERRILL COLLINS-RICHARDSON

LIVES: New York, New York

Sherrill Collins-Richardson is a Girls Write Now mentor. Her journey has led her to a creative imagination, impactful, soul-filling stories, and a voice that denounces injustice.

MENTOR'S ANECDOTE:

FROM NYLAH'S WINDOW
Busy all DAY—She's riding WAVES
Finding her WAY—Clearing the CAVES
Calmly she'll SAY—Make my own PAVES
Some darkened RAYS—Her inner God SAVES
The stories here SLAYS—Pick out your FAVES
Her gift really PAYS—Hear all the RAVES

The Bracelet

NYLAH WATKINS

This story is about a teenage girl who lives vicariously through the bracelet on her nightstand.

The bracelet sits pretty and lonely on her nightstand. Each bead is brown: a combination of mahogany and russet on one side, but when the bead is turned over, the brown slides into a shade of wheat, then back to brown again. Gilded gold beads engraved with flowery designs rest between each of the beads, trailing down to a rusty elephant charm. The bracelet never sees the outside of the house; it barely leaves the nightstand.

When the girl leaves every morning, she turns the beads over to their beige side. When she comes home, she likes to look at the brown side, staring with a hint of jealousy, wishing she could switch sides just as easily as her beads do. When the girl wraps up her daily staring session, she straightens herself up and turns the beads of the bracelet to the wheat-colored side, staring at them before bed, preparing herself before she goes to sleep. When she wakes up, she keeps the beads on their lighter side all morning before flipping them once more. Sometimes she thinks about leaving the beads on the brown side. She never does. She allows herself one glance at the brown beads, then she flips them over to their cream-colored side and leaves for the day.

This girl is pretty, and she is never alone, but she is lonely. She gets up at 4 a.m. every morning to build herself, no matter how tired she is. Some days she cries when her alarm rings at the early hour. She curses until she gets out of bed. The girl has the same routine: shower, wash face, moisturize. She slicks back her hair. Concealer before foundation, then more concealer on top. Thin black eyeliner with black mascara coating each lash, until they weigh heavy on her eyes. She picks out something cute to wear, usually a miniskirt and a crop top; her boyfriend likes it when she wears these clothes, even if it's cold outside.

She arrives at school early to meet him. They kiss until the bell rings. She does not want to sometimes, even though she never says this. At lunch she sits with her large group of friends, people she hardly knows, even though she's known them for years. They speak in tongues, that's what it sounds like to her, anyway; she couldn't care less about what they're saying. They invite her to parties, to sleepovers; she says, "Yes."

She never says no anymore; she's learned not to. When she would say no, they would pout or shoot her dirty looks. "Why not, Addie? Do you think you're too good for us?"

She never said no again. Her boyfriend is loud behind her; he wraps his arm around her waist and laughs with his stupid friends. When he remembers her existence, he kisses her again, in front of everyone to show that she is his. She smiles and giggles when he does this, but she wishes he would stop. She pleads with him in her eyes every day to stop, but he never sees her. He never has. All she can do is hold tight, and wait for the day to pass, for the moment when she can return home to her bracelet, flip the beads over to their side of russet and mahogany brown, and stare at them once more.

AUDRE WELLS

LIVES: Salem, New Hampshire

Audre (she/her) grew up in Lawrence, Massachusetts, and attends Simmons University as a Kotzen Scholar with a double major in neuroscience and journalism.

MENTEE'S ANECDOTE:

My mentor Toni is the reason I have a writing process. At every meeting we share stories about our day, teaching me that being a writer means being human. Bonding over the Emily Dickinson show, a poem from Frankenstein's monster's perspective, and Audre Lorde's writing—there is nothing Toni and I won't talk about. Toni has made writing a safe and natural process where I feel confident to make mistakes, have writer's block, and write about the topics I'm passionate about. I can 100 percent say that without Toni this poem would not be as intentional and complex as it is now.

TONI BRANNAGAN

LIVES: Astoria, New York

Toni Brannagan is a Queens-based writer, editor, and content strategist. She is a Hunter College graduate and currently manager of member marketing at Brightline.

MENTOR'S ANECDOTE:

Getting to know Audre and her writing this year has been incredible. I admire how creatively her mind works, and how she draws inspiration from the world around her—her identity, her lived experiences, the art she consumes—but her work is so uniquely her own. Audre said that she wanted to work on her writing process and editing, and her diligence to improve her craft makes me rethink mine. I'm impressed by how Audre sat with the poems she wrote this semester and made thoughtful revisions. When I read Audre's poems, I'm captivated by her storytelling and transported by her imagery.

Hope, in my country, is the thing with leaves.

AUDRE WELLS

Inspired by Emily Dickinson's poem "'Hope' is the thing with feathers," this poem talks about hope as a fleeting, never-reaching entity in the Dominican Republic, where hope is a cultural and spiritual value within generations.

Hope, in my country, is the thing with leaves.
Leaves greener than unripe plantains
and longer than a lifespan.
Cut at the neck and drowned in boiling water,
the everlasting taste swims in our bellies
and spat back into the ocean—
the taste will linger in our mouths.
Even after Hope's uncrowning,
new leaves will grow for more tea.

Hope is the coconut that will drop onto my head.
Instead of blood,
coconut juice will pour out
making me sticky and sweet,
not guilty
in this heat.
Ringing true to the pueblo's phrase:
A curse hidden in a blessing—
attracting mosquitos.
Do not trust Hope to let you in,
for coconuts grow in every season.

Hope is the guava tree that will cave in
if I ever try to leave.
Leaving me connected to a country
with a past larger than beasts,
with Gods larger than heaven,
and with me
smaller than a tropical flea.

The niguas that rest in flowers
get sat on and stepped on and
swiped away with a careless flick or brush,
swiped away hopefully far enough,
to land in the United States.

Hope resides on a divided island,
the midline drawn in fresh blood.
From the sky, it'll look like a marching line
of niguas trying to hold the country together
smashed between the concrete, buried into the soil.
I'll rake through the dirt,
staining my hands with Haitian blood,
looking for Hope tangled in roots or
pressed against sediment.
But I'll only pick up small red bugs,
whose bites sting,
and make me regret
digging at all.

Sitting under Hope's shade,
the wind is clean.
There is no sand trying to get caught in my eyes,
trying to become the shore to my waterline.
I am not anything beyond
a human
searching.

SIERRA J. WILLIAMS

LIVES: Staten Island, New York

Sierra is a twelfth-grade student from Staten Island. Driven by curiosity, she loves dabbling in the arts and philosophy, writing poetry, and learning languages.

MENTEE'S ANECDOTE:
Meeting, creating, working, and growing with my mentor Caitlin has been truly amazing. Caitlin has helped me so much, from editing and revising my poetry and college essays to planning and practicing for college interviews. She continues to motivate me and helps me see everything with more clarity and precision. I would not have accomplished everything I have without her, and she really is a great mentor, inspiration, and powerful source of encouragement. With this collection, she helped me synthesize my ideas and these seemingly separate poems and pictures into one narrative that offers a glimpse into different moments of the same story.

CAITLIN CHASE

LIVES: Washington, D.C.

Caitlin Chase is a mother, mentor, creative, and strategy consultant for cultural organizations and emerging brands. She lives and works in Washington, D.C.

MENTOR'S ANECDOTE:
Sierra is voraciously curious—eager to explore new words, mediums, and ways of making. It has been a joy to collaborate with her and to witness her continued maturation as a poet and a creative. She is self-directed, highly motivated, and always open to learning and growing. I feel very fortunate to learn, create, and discover new forms of inspiration alongside Sierra this year!

Into Each Other's Eyes: A Collection

SIERRA J. WILLIAMS

In this collection, I was inspired to explore the optical effects of light and memory. I sought to imbue seemingly ordinary moments with wistful, nostalgic, visceral, and colorful impressions through pictures and poetry.

Silver eyes
Silver, sharp, brilliant,
and filled with the light of a full moon
I swore I could see the constellations—
No
the galaxy
the whole universe
full of possibilities
Within them
Within you
against the backdrop of the limitless expanse of your mind
The color of nothingness
and everything all at once
I see

Color me blind
in your infinite hues
of blue
Color me in sadness
your withdrawn eyes
do

Color me from outside the lines
In due time
I will let you into
mine

You used to be the only person I knew.
I imagined we were one
whenever we locked eyes from across the room.
I would look to you
as if you were a mirror of me.
As if by looking into you,
my own reflection,
I would see.
You represented all I wanted to know.
You represented all I wanted to be.
Otherworldly
you seemed to float down from heaven;
You seemed like an impossible dream.

TATYANNA WILLS

LIVES: Queens, New York

Tatyanna Wills is a senior in high school who likes writing, deer, cosplay, and Mitski.

MENTEE'S ANECDOTE:

Elizabeth has helped me come so far—not only in helping me develop my writing style, but also guiding me when it comes to life. From the most absurd conversations to the ones that were philosophical in nature, she has always been a great help in furthering my writing and my life.

ELIZABETH KOSTER

LIVES: New York, New York

Elizabeth Koster is a creative writing teacher in New York City. Her work has been published in *River Teeth* and *The New York Times* "Modern Love" column.

MENTOR'S ANECDOTE:

Tatyanna has a strong sense of musicality in her writing, and she is thoughtful about the choices she makes. I've enjoyed our deep discussions about injustice, conformity, mental illness, and the oddities of human nature, and our less deep discussions about a photo of a pelican trying to eat a giraffe. I appreciate that we both have an eye for the absurd and an ear for each other.

Therapy

TATYANNA WILLS

This poem expresses a deep longing that the author had for a longtime friend.

I love you
I love you I love you
I love. I love.

I

love you more than the moon loves the stars
More than flowers love the rain
My ears yearn for your laughter more than
My lungs yearn for air

My mind can only seem to properly function
When I think of you
Your messy autumn brown hair
Your honeycomb eyes
Your borderline idiotic questions
God
I just can't get enough of you
and there is no description
Old or new
that can ever portray
How I absolutely adore you

but most importantly
I love you so much that I am glad
you are able to find love in someone else

EMMIE WOLF-DUBIN

LIVES: Nashville, Tennessee

Emmie Wolf-Dubin is a ninth-grader in Nashville, Tennessee, who is incredibly passionate about journalism. She has been published in local, national, and international publications.

MENTEE'S ANECDOTE:

Working with Samantha has been one of the most incredible experiences of my writing career. We've edited, written, and learned so much together, and I count myself extremely lucky to have been able to work with her. When we meet, we mostly edit and write, which is super-helpful to me because it gives me both a creative outlet and time to grow as a writer. I am so glad we've gotten the chance to work together, and I'm so grateful to work with someone who has been so kind, supportive, and helpful for me and my writing!

SAMANTHA LAURIELLO

LIVES: Brooklyn, New York

Samantha is a magazine editor, social media strategist, and avid traveler based in Brooklyn, New York.

MENTOR'S ANECDOTE:

When I met Emmie, I knew we were going to have fun working together. She's intelligent, outgoing, and confident (much more so than I was at fifteen!). Plus, she's a stellar writer. When I heard Emmie had written a novel, I was impressed, but when I actually got to sit down and read it, I was blown away. She's created a world that draws you in, evokes a range of emotions, and leaves you wanting more. Did I mention she started writing it at twelve? Emmie continually inspires me, and I think her book will do the same for readers.

My Names

EMMIE WOLF-DUBIN

> **Growing up, I would use any name except my own. It was partly because I didn't feel worthy of my full name, Emanuelle, and partly because I didn't like my nickname, Emmie. Eventually, I grew.**

My name is Emanuelle, and I don't know who I am yet. I know who I've been, and I know who I want to become. But I am a work in progress. I am lost.

When I was younger, I wanted more than anything else to be called Sarah. Now, I can't tell you why. But back then, I thought the phonetics of it were simply gorgeous. I said it and played it in my head like a new favorite song. But then I got sick of it. Perhaps I grew out of it, or I said it one too many times, or decided that it no longer sounded like my favorite sweet treat. The reason does not matter. I moved on, but not yet to my own name. Because back then, when I said *my* name in the mirror, I was greeting a stranger.

Next, I thought that the name Alexis was the most beautiful name to ever exist. When my next-door neighbor and I played make-believe, that was the name I always assigned myself. We would be in her bonus room, using spare notebooks from school years past, playing college. And I was Alexis. Back then, we were ready to grow up, ready for the world. But I was not yet myself. However, myself or not, I did grow sick of the name Alexis, too. I'm not sure when, not at all. But at some point, I did grow up. And I grew away from it, away from the delicate letters that had once sounded like a perfectly tuned violin in an empty concert hall. I was not yet me, but I was growing up.

I like doing this one particular icebreaker when I first meet people. I like making people feel comfortable around me, so I always make a joke of some sort. The only one that consistently lands is telling them what name they look like. Maybe they're a Silas or a Michael or an Alice or a Rebecca or a James or an Allan or a Madeline. The name is inconsistent, but their laugh is anything but. So, I wonder. Do they know who they are? Is that why they laugh? Or do they laugh because they think it's true?

But, of course, the laughter comes to an end, and they turn to me. *"What name are you, though?"* they ask. They ask, and then they turn up blank.

I just laugh again. *"I'm Emmie,"* I say, as though I've never said it before, and it's a completely new thought. *"I look like an Emmie. But no one would ever guess that. No one really knows what an Emmie looks like, but I guess I look like it."* They always just laugh and agree.

I know what you're thinking. Didn't I *just* say my name was Emanuelle? Well, yes. But I'm also Emmie.

I always used to hate the name Emmie. I thought the letters came together to form something ugly. I thought it was blunt and short and weird and awkward and childish. And I always thought Emanuelle was too much. It was Hebrew, and I was ashamed. People always mispronounced it and called it a boy's name. It wasn't me, and I knew that. I tucked it in my jeans pocket and saved it for the future, for a sunny day. So, instead, I was Sarah. Then, I was Alexis. Now I'm Emmie.

One day, I'll be brave and elegant enough to be Emanuelle. I love the name Emmie now, though—honestly. I grew into it. It's friendly and happy. It's a good medium. It's the halfway point from a strange, unfamiliar name like Sarah and the name of someone who knows who they are, like Emanuelle. But one day, maybe soon and maybe not, I will know who I am.

That day, I will own up to my true heritage. I will have the unruly curly hair of my ancestors. It will be out and beautiful. I will be confident. I will be fluent in the beautiful Hebraic tongue. I will be completely unashamed of my views, my skills, and my heritage. I will look into the mirror and see an old friend, one whom I welcome with open arms.

Soon, I will be Emanuelle Ahava. And my ancestors will smile.

CAMRON WRIGHT

LIVES: Washington, D.C.

Camron Wright is a senior English major with a playwriting minor at Howard University in Washington, D.C.

MENTEE'S ANECDOTE:

Writing has always been a source of clarity as well as a fun way for me to express myself and be heard. I love the idea of writing pieces that others can relate to and feel seen. Although writing and I do not always get along and we do argue a lot, it will forever be part of me.

OLIVIA GOOD

LIVES: Brooklyn, New York

Olivia Good is a freelance writer and audio producer based in Brooklyn.

MENTOR'S ANECDOTE:

I am so grateful to have Camron as my mentee. We've been working together for only a few months, but I've already been so impressed by her maturity, intelligence, creativity, openness, and hard work. I'm glad that she's decided to publish one of her poems in this anthology. I hope that her confidence will continue to grow and that more of her writing will make it out into the world!

Shattered Glass

CAMRON WRIGHT

This piece is a reminder of why self-care is essential and how other people's needs are not as important as our own.

When you are walking on shattered glass
every step is painful.
It does not matter how calculated each movement is
or
how well you control each muscle.
You could try walking in socks
to protect your feet
but
the glass will always cut through.
You could put on sneakers to step over the fallen pieces
but
at the end of the day, the glass
can still cut you.
There is no treading lightly,
you got to sweep up the glass.
Sweep it up so no one can be cut.
Think about everyone else, not wanting to cause them the rush of
    blood coming from
their feet.
But as you sweep remember to
be careful
with yourself.
When
the glass pierces your skin, you should have known to put on gloves.

It's too late.
The broken glass
becomes
thousands of mirrors all reflecting back on you.
Don't look away

OLIVIA WRONSKI

LIVES: Little Neck, New York

Olivia Wronski (she/they) writes mainly poetry as a hobby. They enjoy creative writing, all kinds of dance, and art.

MENTEE'S ANECDOTE:

Working with Christine has been an eye-opening experience. I've been exposed to so many different poems that cover a vast range of styles and topics. Christine also pushed my boundaries by providing many different writing prompts that forced me to explore outside my box, something I'm thankful for. I discovered a new way to look at things and to write poetry. I am also grateful for the opportunity to learn from the works of Asian American poets and essayists like Christine. As an Asian American, it was awesome to learn through the works of people similar to me!

CHRISTINE C. HSU

LIVES: San Francisco, California

Christine C. Hsu is a poet, playwright, essayist, and short story writer based in San Francisco. This is her first year as a mentor.

MENTOR'S ANECDOTE:

I've enjoyed providing writing prompts for my mentee to get inspired by and hearing her free-writes. I shared a poem about how Oakland was gentrifying, and Olivia described the same issue happening in Flushing, Queens. Although I now live in a predominantly Asian American community in California, I grew up in a mostly white neighborhood in Texas. I feel a kinship with my mentee because we both are Asian American and share similar cultural experiences. I wish I had taken part in a program like Girls Write Now when I was younger to feel less alone.

Dreamlike Musings and Practicality

OLIVIA WRONSKI

This is a set of three poems where I explore ideas centered on the use of visual language, and in one poem I explore getting personal with my writing.

I.

A thin layer of water,
Between the earth and my toes.
At Salar de Uyuni,
The salt plains of Bolivia,
I see two skies, two suns, and thousands of clouds.

I see two of me,
Faces identical as we look at one another.
She opens her mouth to speak.
I stomp my foot and watch
As her face ripples and distorts,
And the movement of her lips are mangled by the waves.

She appears again,
As I walk the winding path along the Amazon River
She follows the way I slouch and trudge through the muddy dirt
Just as she is about to speak,
we reach Salto Ángel waterfall.

As I climb my way down alongside the waterfall,
She is not there,
And I cannot hear what she has to say about me

As the drumming melody of crashing water fills my ears.
And I gaze upon the paradise of every shade of green.

She is there once more,
Her frustrated face glaring at me from the white Yulan magnolia
    flowers,
As I grapple for ledges up Huangshan Mountain,
Taking in the scent of the native pines
growing sideways off the rock faces.

Her mouth opens wide to scream into my face,
But at the peak of the mountains,
Standing on a rocky beach before a sea of clouds,
She has faded into the rich mountain alyssum haze,
as the sun turns everything golden.

II.

Bright stars behind my eyes
Innumerably iridescent
Filling the dark space with glittering gems of stardust

I float by Aquarius as he fills his bucket with
Amethyst, garnet, opal, jasper, and moss agate.
Watering the midnight of space with twinkling sparkles.
Little buds like seeds buried into wet, black earth,
Each one to grow into a complex thought.

I hold on to the fins of Pisces, sailing through an aquamarine sea,
The shark fins of Aphrodite and Eros leading me through an ocean of
    emotions
Paving a trail through the crashing waves of anguish, passion, and
    rage.
As they escape the wrath of Typhoeus, the ancestor of all monsters.

They leave me by the garden within the cosmic space of my mind
Where Virgo herself tends to the blue sapphire, garnet, peridot, and
    citrine flora.

The Astrea of my cosmos, tending to the virtuous verdure that thirsts
    for pure water
Cultivating an extravagant creativity that lusts to grow beyond the
    confines of the garden fence.

III.

The Five of Cups.
A cataclysmic disputation
Has made loss tangible,
The liquid drained away.
I know that my wet fingers
That try to fix the fallen cups
Will eventually dry.

The Temperance.
Perhaps I should focus instead
On the cups that remain full,
Do not give up on what survives.
Fill my soul half-full
Rather than half-empty
As I regenerate and rejuvenate.

The Nine of Swords.
Do not ignore the costs that come
With victory through preponderancy:
The death of the tender umbra.
Aspire instead for the light at the end of the tunnel,
And seek contentment sans sacrifice of oneself's
Vulnerable feeling soul.

IV.

A list of things to pack when I move out of my dorm for the school
    year.
A list of things I need to do to finish this semester.
A list of things to say to my mom the next time I see her.

A list of things to text my mom just in case I never see her again: thank you, I love you, I'm sorry . . .

A list of things to chat with my sister about when she comes back from class.

A list of things I need her to bring back to the dorm before she comes back from class.

A list of things I want to do before I'm 21, my first partner, my first kiss, travel to Singapore.

A list of things I want to do after I'm 21, finish my undergrad, get a job, go to a concert.

A list of things I want to draw, saved pictures and tutorials in a folder on my desktop.

A list of things I want to eat, foodie reels and recipes sent to my sister to save.

A list of things I want to write, little snippets of prose and poetry in my notes app as I ride the subway.

A list of things I want to get into: sewing, exercising, and socializing.

A list of things I want to be better at: practicing gratitude, self love, and dancing jive.

A list of things like birthdays, because I can remember names and faces after one try, but not birthdays after years of friendship.

A list of things to say when I'm speaking to my relatives, a Cantonese basics cheat sheet so they can understand me and I can understand them.

A list of things I want to talk to my dad about, but I'm scared to be anything, but silly with him.

A list of things I want my dad to ask me about, but I'm scared to see him serious.

A list of things that I can make lists about.

Check that one off the list.

JULIA WYSOKINSKA

LIVES: Ridgewood, New York

Julia Wysokinska is a high school senior with a passion for strolling through museums with friends, often with a cup of iced coffee in tow.

MENTEE'S ANECDOTE:

My second year in a pair with Jamie has been incredible—yet again! Our virtual sessions together never feel distant, as we're able to quickly get into enthralling conversations and surprise each other with our responses to writing prompts. Her support throughout my college application process has been invaluable, and I'm looking forward to getting back to working on less structured writing and meeting in person more often! Jamie has not only been a wonderful mentor, but also a friend who I can rely on for both sage advice and moments of levity during our hour together every Tuesday evening.

JAMIE DUCHARME

LIVES: Brooklyn, New York

Jamie Ducharme is an award-winning health correspondent at *Time* magazine and the author of *Big Vape: The Incendiary Rise of Juul*.

MENTOR'S ANECDOTE:

When Julia told me this winter that she had more than forty essays to write for her college applications, I thought it sounded impossible. Then I remembered who I'm dealing with. Julia is smart, driven, and ambitious, with a skill for squeezing a superhuman number of tasks into her busy days. She is full of good ideas and has the patience and maturity to tackle anything that comes her way with grace. She (of course) finished every single one of those essays, seemingly without breaking a sweat.

getting older

JULIA WYSOKINSKA

Maybe our photos will fill the gaps my memory won't.

i'm not sure i ever liked blue raspberry
i just ate it because you didn't
your mom always hated the sight of your artificial blue tongue
so i'd let you have cherry—my favorite
time after time

i always hated horror movies
the cheap scares were bogus and frightening
but for you, i'd bear the eventual nightmares
and when i'd snuggle up to my worn, golden teddy bear
you'd poke fun at it—claiming your plush purple turtle was one of
    a kind

back when red nail polish was "for adults"
and lip balm felt so sophisticated
we'd sing karaoke into the early evening
before your parents came to pick you up
and we'd play with dolls the next day

back before prom nights and limo fights
and sickly sweet juice graduated to jittery coffee
we'd imagine our lives as grown-ups
with our dream careers and perfect pets
living side by side in the same apartment building

and as i sit in our old cafe
where we spilled our guts over pastries and tea
all i want is to watch you pull up a chair
and listen to another rant about your crazy science teacher
but i don't even know how to talk to you anymore.

ADELLE XIAO

LIVES: New York, New York

Adelle (she/her) is a current high school senior based in New York City. She loves art, volunteer work, and binging sad K-dramas.

MENTEE'S ANECDOTE:

This is Sarah's and my first year of in-person meetings, but also our third and final year as a mentor-mentee pair. From our virtual meetings on Zoom to our meetups at a Greenpoint coffee shop, getting to know Sarah and sharing moments of our lives together has been so meaningful. I can't wait for the rest of our last year in the program and to explore how we'll continue our relationship beyond Girls Write Now.

SARAH A. CUSTEN

LIVES: Brooklyn, New York

Sarah A. Custen is a Utah-raised, Brooklyn-based writer, educator, chaos demon, and musician. She loves to create, daydream, and snuggle with her cat.

MENTOR'S ANECDOTE:

This year has been about small moments, shared interests, shared stresses, and an increased sense of ease when we spend time together. For me, these brief glimmers—hours passing too quickly in the coffee shop in Greenpoint, where we always admire the pastries—are golden. We always pick up right where we left off, and in many ways it feels like we're just getting started. I'm so happy and excited for Adelle to graduate high school and go out into the world, for this next chapter of our lives.

Fishbone

ADELLE XIAO

An exploration in the aftermath of a fish's death.

My mother brought me to the Chinese supermarket for the first time when I was six years old. Aisles tinted purple and pink from reflections of fluorescent lighting, full of contents towering out of reach, labeled with characters and strokes that I couldn't recognize.

My favorite place was the fish section. I would press my nose to murky glass tanks, gaping at cloudy-eyed fish, mouths slightly parting as their sleek fins and silver bodies weaved and bumped into each other in artificially blue tanks. I watched with fascination as a gloved hand reached in and grabbed the fish with a harsh fist as the fish opened its mouth again and again in protest, no sound coming out. The man grabbed a mallet and hit the fish with a fluid motion—after flopping once with its tail sweeping through the air, stitches and seams of skin and sinew ripping apart, it was dead, the last trace of a faint pulsing heartbeat vanishing. I screamed and hid behind my mother, crying.

That day, I helped my mother carry the groceries home. The bag lurched between my fingers as I walked, and I caught glimpses of the dead fish, limp in a wrinkled bag, droplets of water scattered on its surface. On our way back, my mother told me stories of how saltwater fish can't survive after getting dumped into rivers, how their bodies bloat and harden in all the wrong places until they're unrecognizable. How freshwater fish shrivel up in saltwater, life wrinkling and collapsing into a shell of hollowed scales.

After we got home, I snuck into the kitchen while my parents were asleep, filling up the bag of its limp body and lifeless eyes with metallic tap water. I willed it to live, willed its body to pulsate and flutter with life against the filmy plastic, as if tap water held droplets of miracles. The bag filled to the brim under my fist, cascading over silver scales and overflowing in the sink with a splash. Its eyes were just as blankly glazed as before.

My mother steamed the fish for New Year's Day. She brought it to the table, haze billowing and dissipating like a prolonged exhale, rotating the platter so that the fish head faces me. For good luck, she says. I stare at its opaque eyes, delicate needle-like bones protruding as my mother digs her fork in. She picks at its stomach, sprinkling scales and slivers of skin on the plate's harsh edges.

A fish bone got stuck in my esophagus, as I shoveled waterlogged flesh and heaps of rice into my mouth, the sharp pang of a foreign skeleton skewering my spit-starved tongue and shoving into my throat. I thought that the fishbone would stay lodged there forever, piercing my own reddened flesh deeper with every contraction of a breath. I must have looked like a fish—clawing at my throat, eyes glazed over with tears, my mouth parted and gasping for air. I swallowed. A phantom sensation of bone remained.

HUDA YASEEN

LIVES: Dearborn Heights, Michigan

Huda Y. (she/her) is a high school sophomore who has a love for creative journaling, reading, and binging Asian dramas while slurping on Buldak ramen.

MENTEE'S ANECDOTE:

Alyssa has provided me more than what a mentor gives, and that is what has made working with her fun in a plethora of ways. I developed many new tricks regarding my writing with her advice, but most of all I developed a relationship that goes beyond writing. I was able to express my chaotic thought processes freely, as she was someone that would attentively listen and understand each bit of what I said. It was truly a memorable time in which I continuously found myself smiling from ear to ear and laughing during our productive Zoom meetings!

ALYSSA YUN

LIVES: New York, New York

Alyssa is a strategy consultant in New York (and currently in Tokyo!) who enjoys exploring her creative side outside of work through writing, food, and art.

MENTOR'S ANECDOTE:

Huda inspires me to be more creative, observant, and simply excited every time we chat. Her contagious enthusiasm shows in her animated writing style, which has been so fun to work with together on our pair piece, as it pushed me to think about and play with my own writing in the process. Despite the differences in our age, location, and points in our lives, I love that we keep finding topics that connect us—everything from the shared immigrant experience, to stress management, to our obsession with Korean food. We can't find enough time to chat!

Here and There

HUDA YASEEN

As an immigrant, you automatically have two homes, or maybe one home and a house. Either way, the question "Where do I find my place and comfort within these homes?" seems to never end.

Just twenty minutes from Iraq's renowned ziggurats, the grandeur of my youth thrives in a little, slightly deteriorated brick home consisting of three rooms, a small kitchen, and a lively dtarma*. It's my Jadoo's† house, which, by tradition, accommodated his children and grandchildren. I head outside, where the children's sandals are haphazardly scattered across the front door. Failing to find a pair, I let my bare feet touch the dusty, sun-baked Arabian tiles that dress the courtyard in beautiful hues of blue and red. I find myself in repose, away from the loud children, frantic chickens in the courtyard, and the backdrop of war-torn Iraq. My eyes fixate on my grandpa. As he basks in the sun, I trace his shriveled face and feeble body, wondering how he still has strength to form a scintillating smile for his grandchildren.

A metallic knocking emanates from the courtyard's rusted gates. "We're here," calls out a high-pitched voice. I open the door and see my aunt and her children. She greets me with hugs and moist kisses on the sides of my cheeks, and holds a bag of fresh fish from the Euphrates, our nation's delicacy. We walk through the narrow paths to the back entrance, into the kitchen. Though small and run-down, it embodied a cozy vibrancy that attracted many visitors. It's almost a daily routine to

---

* Traditional Iraqi secluded courtyard
† Grandpa's

have family gatherings, and nobody could complain because nothing equals the warmth that engulfs our bodies during the long hours spent conversing over steaming cups of chai alongside family and guests who traveled from all across Dikar and Basra. Enough to sprout deep-rooted love for the lively community that is present.

―――――――

"Dinner is ready," my mother announces in an Arabic accent.

After a short visit to Iraq, I'm back to the silent condo, simply living among my parents and three siblings. From the outside, it was the best house to settle in. Many envied our house, especially relatives living back home, since it is the "embodiment" of an Iraqi dream. But I never saw it that way.

I walk through the perfectly symmetrical corridor toward the dinner table. I take my usual seat and fiddle with my food when served. The dining room is pale, and so is the rest of the house. I almost pity my vision at such a sight with so few colors. Trying to drift from the prosaic moods the room is creating, my mind continuously circles back to the bliss and longing of my grand family gatherings in Iraq. Life is so different in these two places. If asked which I preferred, I wouldn't know. This is my home, but so was there.

―――――――

Cool air hits my face as I open the front door. I'm outside, but not entirely. I turn my head to the right to face the long hallway. I have to get down, but the elevator at the end scares me from stories about ghosts told at school. I dash down three flights of stairs and dip my head to bow to the security officer ahjussi as I exit the building. Several stray cats are camouflaged between tightly parked cars, or more like Tetris pieces. I turn around and see twelve floors of wide, outdoor corridors towering above—large from the exterior, but housing a cozy unit within: my first home in Seoul. I'm at ease heading to school because it's a straight path, and I know I'll see my best friend when I'm back later on the seventh floor.

Yeouido is technically an island in the middle of Seoul. To adults, better known as the finance district. I've always liked the round sound to it (*yeuh-ee-doh*) and felt comfort in the idea of being on a separate piece of land. Everywhere, clusters of twelve- to thirty-six-story apartments stand like dominoes. I imagine one leaning over to topple the rest down. Everything is systematic, labeled consistently, and erect as expected. Here, my route is clear—home, to school, to hagwon, lined up as orderly as the high-rises.

━━━━━

My home in Washington, fitting the name "Evergreen State," is adjacent to more greenery. The neighborhood itself is on hilly terrain with tall conifers shooting above, making just walking out onto the main road a trek. I could drive myself to school, but the car would be parked there all day and we have only one.

Our house is short, just like the other houses next to us, with two floors that connect from the inside. It has both carpet and wooden flooring, a backyard I don't dare step out to, and a wide, naked front driveway. I leave through the garage and stand on the edge of the sidewalk debating which way to go. As if the board of Game of Life has materialized in real life, the multiple paths form circles and loops, some straight, others winding, and at times leading to the same point that a simple walk through the neighborhood was enough to make me wonder how to re-trace my steps back home.

IRENE YIMMONGKOL

LIVES: Woodside, New York

Irene Yimmongkol is an avid photographer, reader, and professional television-watcher. She enjoys embracing creativity and exploring the world through the world of artistic writing.

MENTEE'S ANECDOTE:

When I first met my mentor, Brigid Duffy, I immediately felt comfortable being myself around her. Every meeting that I had with her truly was great, as Brigid consistently helped me improve my writing and showed me different styles of writing that gave me an improved outlet for my imagination. Brigid and I had consistent Zoom meetings each week, and since we both live in New York City, we were able to meet in person, which was wonderful. Not only did we learn to expand our writing skills, but Brigid also helped me with my college application.

BRIGID DUFFY

LIVES: Brooklyn, New York

Brigid Duffy is an award-winning writer and creative director. Her work has been published in *Reader's Digest*, *Catapult*, *Names*, and many other publications.

MENTOR'S ANECDOTE:

It's been a joy working with Irene over the past several months. Together we have written shared stories, read poetry and short stories, and tackled some college application essays. A highlight was meeting up at the Metropolitan Museum of Art and getting to talk art, literature, and life in person.

Prison Break

IRENE YIMMONGKOL

In the Amazon rainforest of South America, Larry witnesses his friends get maliciously kidnapped. After the incident, Larry is determined to rescue them and bring his friends back home.

All of Larry's friends are in jail.

Their sentences? Well, nobody really knows exactly what will happen to them or why they are in jail in the first place. Every single moment of the few months Larry's been alone, he's attempted to track down the boys and the girls who were taken from his neighborhood by the kidnappers. Those friends of his, who were there with him throughout his whole life, are the most important people Larry knows. He took a second to think—remembering all the times they spent playing together in the trees, all the funny conversations they had, and all the times they got into trouble together. If they get hurt, Larry would never be able to live with himself. He was willing to risk his safety, his sanity, and his life if it meant that he could rescue his friends and make sure they're safe.

Larry took a long twig in his sharply hooked, black beak and threw it out of his cozy nest. There was no time to waste—he'd have to be efficient if he wanted to save all the other macaws that were taken. Larry took a deep breath. After all, staying calm was the only way to get anything done. *If I remember correctly, the kidnappers had long parachute-looking things that my guys got stuck in. But why did it have holes . . . ? You know what, it's fine. Now, which direction did they go in?*

Larry spread his vibrant red wings and glided to the top of his tree. He slowly turned his head around, taking in all the information that he could from the canopy. It was pointless. All he could see was green leaves while the scorching sun hit his body. *Maybe I should ask someone.* Larry hopped down onto the branch below him and continued going down the staircase of twigs the tree provided. After a minute of searching, Larry saw someone who was a witness to the injustice. A monkey. *Hey, I remember this guy! He definitely saw where the big apes took my friends!* Larry spread his wings and glided, landing in front of the tall and lanky spider monkey.

"Hello, sir! My name's Larry and I'm looking for my friends who were kidnapped. Have you seen them . . . by any chance?"

The monkey stared at Larry, making a puzzled face. "Ooooh oooh ahhh ahhh!"

"What?" asked a confused (and scared) Larry.

"Purrrrr!" growled the monkey.

"Okay, then. What's your name, sir?" inquired Larry.

The monkey did not respond.

Larry stood still awkwardly as the wind blew on him, his feathers moving slightly to the right. This was no use. He needed to get some information. He remembered that there were other birds down in the south of the forest, so he flapped his wings, took off, and hovered in the sky, making sure he was going to the right place. As he flew, he could see nothing but green—*rubber trees, passionfruit trees, monkey brush vines . . . oh God, this isn't helpful at all*—how on earth would he be able to find anyone in this forest? Ten minutes later, he dove down into a lush palm tree, relieved that he could take a rest and get some shade from the scorching sun. He pushed through large leaves and stepped over some rough coconuts. The hairs on the fruit tickled Larry's feet, but he kept moving forward through the lush vines. Suddenly, he felt a light tap on his back.

As Larry turned around, he saw another macaw. The bird was slightly smaller than him, with bright lapis-blue feathers and mustard yellow surrounding its eyes and bordering its black beak. It was perched on the same branch as him, not moving a muscle, and both birds stayed silent and stared at each other. The blue macaw turned its head away from him, averting its eyes from the silent encounter.

"May I help you?" asked Larry. He ruffled his rainbow-colored wings, waiting for a response.

"Hi, my name is Rosa," the blue bird replied softly. "I heard that you were looking for your friends who were taken by the big apes with nets, so I followed you here."

Larry's eyes lit up, his heart pounding hard and loud. His quizzical look eased up, and he became deathly serious. "Yes. I am. Are you saying that you've seen them? Do you know where they are?"

Rosa took a deep breath. "I've seen them, but I lost track of them. I was hiding in the bushes, but the monsters took them into a cage and loaded them into a truck. They were heading south, but I don't know where. But the trucks left behind marks that we can follow. I can show them to you."

"Fine, then. I'll follow you. Lead the way, Rosa."

RAZAN ZANTOUT

LIVES: North Richland Hills, Texas

Razan is a high school student who loves reading, writing, and doing arts and crafts. She likes to express herself through writing and art.

MENTEE'S ANECDOTE:

Working with Andrea was an absolute blast. I love how we can connect our ideas so easily. Andrea is already an author, so it makes writing much easier, since she's more experienced. I had so much fun working with her on this story for the anthology; she's always listening to any ideas I come up with and cheering me on. We connect so easily and can literally talk for hours.

ANDREA BEATRIZ ARANGO

LIVES: Charlottesville, Virginia

Andrea Beatriz Arango is the Newbery Honor Award–winning author of *Iveliz Explains It All*. Born and raised in Puerto Rico, she now lives in Virginia.

MENTOR'S ANECDOTE:

I love getting together with Razan for our sessions. She is a voracious reader (across multiple genres and age categories), and it comes across in all her creative writing projects. Despite the fact that I've been writing my whole life, Razan is the first person I've ever tried pair writing with! Brainstorming together has been so fun, especially seeing how we'd approach the same idea. It's definitely something I look forward to doing again.

When You're Ready to Talk

RAZAN ZANTOUT

> **This is a story about two long-distance sisters. One struggles with anxiety, and the other desperately wants to help, but doesn't know how.**

PART I

KRISTINA (2:05PM): I'm worried about you. You haven't been answering my texts.

KRISTINA (2:07PM): I know you're mad at me, but I was looking out for you.

LIYA (7:15PM): Telling our parents my secret is NOT looking out for me.

I know my older sister thought she was helping when she blurted out that I've been having panic attacks—*at the dinner table.* She knew I'd been struggling since she saw me in the middle of one. Since then, she hasn't left me alone about it, and after that night, my parents wouldn't let it go either.

KRISTINA (7:17PM): It IS looking out for you because I was literally leaving for college the next day. If they didn't know, who was going to make sure you were ok???

LIYA (7:30PM): I was doing just fine. I don't need you all spying on me like hawks, wondering when I'm going to "get anxious" again. JUST LEAVE ME ALONE

I know Liya thinks I'm overbearing, but she refuses to get help! She should be seeing a therapist. I wasn't trying to betray her trust, but she wouldn't listen to me when I told her she needed to let an adult know.

What was I supposed to do? Just leave?? What if she got worse? Liya is my best friend.

PART II (ONE WEEK LATER)

LIYA (11:38PM): I know you're probably asleep right now, but just cause I told u to leave me alone doesn't mean stop texting me forever.

KRISTINA (11:45PM): Actually, I'm up studying.

LIYA (11:47PM): Oh sorry.

I want to go back to that connection Kristina and I used to have, but it seems impossible. I hate feeling like a burden. I hate being treated like a child. Maybe if I pretend that everything is okay, my family will believe it? Maybe so will I . . .

KRISTINA (11:48PM): It's ok. What's up?

KRISTINA (11:57PM): Liya?

KRISTINA (11:59PM): Are you ok? Did you have a panic attack? Do you need me to call mom?

LIYA (12:01AM): What?? No, I wanted to text you to tell you I've been doing so much better.

KRISTINA (12:02AM): Oh, that's great!

I wish I could just *believe* Liya, but I don't know what to think. Would she actually tell me if she were struggling? I feel like she's just pretending, but it's so hard to know what's real. I hate being so far away from her.

PART III (ONE WEEK LATER)

KRISTINA (3:30PM): Hey, I know you said you were fine last time we talked, but—why do you avoid me every time I call home? I KNOW you're not always out.

LIYA (3:50PM): I don't know what you're talking about. I've been busy with school. Everything's fine.

KRISTINA (3:52PM): Are you sure? Mom says you haven't been sleeping well.

LIYA (3:53PM): GREAT, now you guys are talking about me behind my back???

KRISTINA (3:55PM): We're only talking because we're worried. This is EXACTLY why I told them.

LIYA (3:58PM): Well, this is EXACTLY why I DIDN'T. Everyone is so pushy, it's my business not anyone else's. I don't even know why you care so much, you're not even here!!!

I went to a friend's house for the weekend to get away from all the constant nagging. I don't know what to do. No one was ever supposed to know about my stuff. Kristina found out by accident. It was supposed to be something I solved on my own, but the past few weeks have been awful. I'm so done talking to people about this. I HATE talking about my feelings, but I don't know how to make this all go away.

KRISTINA (5:15PM): Mom and Dad said you left and didn't even tell people where you were going. Liya, I'm WORRIED. I'm coming home.

KRISTINA (7:50PM): Why aren't you reading my messages? Pick up your phone!

PART IV (A FEW DAYS LATER)

"What are you doing here?" I said, shock evident on my face. The last thing I expected to see when I came back from my friend's house was my *sister* sitting on my bed.

"You said I didn't care cause I wasn't here. Well, I'm here now," Kristina calmly said. "Please, Liya. I know I messed up. I know I shouldn't have betrayed you that night at dinner, but I'm sorry. I'm here. Talk to me."

I want to dismiss what she's saying, but I'm honestly exhausted. I'm tired of lying—to my family and to myself. I *know* I need help. Why am I so scared?

"Liya, I think therapy could be good, but nobody is gonna make you do something you don't want to do. I swear. I just want to make sure you know I am here for you," says Kristina.

I try to blink back my tears, but my eyes are already getting glassy. I put my arms around Kristina, and for the first time, I believe her.

"Okay," I say, "I'm ready to talk."

ARIEL ZHANG

LIVES: San Jose, California

Ariel Zhang is a high school freshman and introvert who wants to share the joy of chamber music and writing with others.

MENTEE'S ANECDOTE:

I have learned so much from Vanida—not just what it means to be a better writer, but also what it means to be a better human. I love talking to her about aspirations and dreams and the little random bits of our lives. She has inspired me so much in the sense of not being afraid of the words I write down and learning how to just keep on writing.

VANIDA NARRAINEN

LIVES: New York, New York

Vanida Narrainen is a corporate attorney with more than a decade of experience in mergers and acquisitions, acting as principal corporate counsel at Plume Design Inc.

MENTOR'S ANECDOTE:

I had a wonderful time working with Ariel on the submission of her essay to the Scholastic Art & Writing Awards. This gave me an opportunity to witness Ariel's maturity and creativity as a writer. I am very proud of the quality of her work, her enthusiasm and passion, and, most of all, her eagerness to continually explore ways to perfect her writing skills. I am very excited to be a part of Ariel's journey as a writer and I look forward to many more writing adventures with her!

Motherhood Mural

ARIEL ZHANG

This is a story woven together with fragments of memories, notes, and bunnies. This is a medley of short-lived relics. This is a song.

My mother doesn't know love.

~ ~ ~

I never knew how to draw bunnies. I was never much of an artist.

My only art teacher was my mom, when I was little. She would hand me a paper note with instructions written in fluttering letters. How to turn on the stove. How to boil potatoes. How to cook the chewiest rice. And a little hand-drawn bunny smiling at me from the corner. We never said I love you, but that was our way of loving. And then she would leave, just like that. Her note, cold, in my hands.

———

Over the years, I've watched and observed her from a distance, and I saw the things she never said. I learned to pull words out of her mouth. I learned to understand the unspoken.

~ ~ ~

After collecting hundreds of chalk-white notes, after kindling thousands of fluttering words that lived in my mom's reflection underneath the neon kitchen lights, I still can't draw the perfect bunnies. I'm not an artist like my mom.

But these are my words, not hers. Perhaps this is only a mirage of her inside my mind. Perhaps she lives only in my own slippery shadows, flickering between letters of the words said when I was too young to remember.

~ ~ ~

The nights my mom would come home, she slept in my bed because she didn't want to be alone. I kept a warm glass of water by the bed in case she got thirsty in the middle of the night. I left her a note before I went to school. I told her where I was and when I'd be home. I never drew any bunnies because I wasn't an artist like that.

——

These words are incomplete.

~ ~ ~

My mother and I, we are a collage of notes. A photocopy of a photocopy of the words said in silence. Of the meals we cooked alone. Of warm glasses of water.

——

Not broken, just incomplete.

~ ~ ~

Years later, I always made your lunches. And I would put a note in your lunch box and draw little bunnies in the corners, even when I didn't feel like an artist. You never noticed. Was our language lost just like that?

——

I wish love would just be enough.

~ ~ ~

Please don't be angry with me on the days I leave late at night. Please don't be angry that I missed your recitals and wasn't there at your graduation.

I wish loving you would be enough.

———

This is the unfinished medley of my mom.

~ ~ ~

I don't know how to draw bunnies. But I am forever looking for bunnies, for you.

———

CAROLYN ZHENG

LIVES: Millbury, Massachusetts

Carolyn Zheng (she/her) is a high school sophomore who writes poetry and fiction and wishes her homework could disappear.

MENTEE'S ANECDOTE:

Davia is so understanding and supportive, even from all the way across the country. She encourages me to be confident and allows me to explore different inspirations for my poetry, like the Beatniks or spoken word. She is also flexible, allowing me to change when our pair sessions begin due to my naps unfortunately taking longer than expected. Whenever we write poems during our sessions, I love listening to the jazz Davia puts on, and even more, I love listening to the cascade of words and imagery she can write in a short span. It always amazes and inspires me.

DAVIA SCHENDEL

LIVES: New York, New York

Davia Schendel is a writer, musician, and filmmaker whose works revolve around existentialism, surrealism, and nostalgia and have been featured in numerous publications and radios.

MENTOR'S ANECDOTE:

Carolyn's approach to writing is like watching alchemy happen in real time. Her path to inspiration includes taking moments from the everyday, as well as other mediums of art. The results are like pearls from a beautifully cultivated source. It has been a pleasure to mentor Carolyn as she delves into the art of writing poetry as her focus this year, and I am so grateful that we get to be witness to her elucidating perspective.

Static

CAROLYN ZHENG

This is a zuihitsu that reflects how overwhelming
life is and uses the different meanings of the word
"static."

Bzzt. Bzzt.

Static. It mutes the teacher, standing in the front of the room.
Static. It covers the loud voices in the room.
Static.
Everything stops.

Analog television dominated entertainment during the twentieth
century. The film was grainy, unlike the clear, crisp video of digital
screens, but it was revolutionary at the time.

Moving pictures—truly innovation at its finest!

There are many photos of my parents from when they first came to
America. I don't remember the dates, but there's a TV in one of
them. It's one of those big, boxy kinds—a CRT TV, I think—that
took up more than half the space in the cabinet. Three people from
some Chinese program are forever frozen on the screen. The man in
the middle has his mouth wide open, but no words come out of his
mouth.

I'll never get to know what he was saying. It's fine, though. I don't
understand the language anyways.

noise

snow

storm

No signal

Too much sound in my head. All I hear is static. It makes me static.
  Static, static, static. Blocks everything out with its grainy sound.

Supposed to be moving but only paralyzed in a second of black-and-
  white film.

"Shut down in three, two, o—"

why white noise?

White is the blank paper, waiting to be filled with words—nothing.
White is the culmination of all colors of light—everything.

Everything and nothing all at once.

what should i be thinking?

A single realization of white noise is a **random shock.**

It's all too much now but I wouldn't tell.
Why would I when there's no one to trust?
Leaving me stuck here in my little shell
Inside this infinitely turning carousel

Buzz, buzz, buzz—people fly by.
We are all insects trying to get from one place to another.
Go, go, go!

Shocked!

The horde is coming!
Oh the horrors! It's too much! It's too much!

Turn the dial. Readjust the antennas.

White. Static.
So soothing.
Peace.

Reprieve does not exist for the senses that overwhelm the mind. At
   least, not in this world of modern complications. There are different
   forms of escapism one could choose to partake in. Would you like to
   read a story? Or perhaps watch a movie? Or surf the internet and
   scroll social media for hours upon hours until your alarm strikes you
   out of your daze and into the morning light, but only for you to turn
   your back and stare at your phone again?

One day, you will have to wake up.

Bzzt. Bzzt.

WRITE YOUR WAY TO THE OTHER SIDE!

When did you first know you were a writer? Maybe the answer lies not only in defining ourselves as writers, but in navigating the very experience of being human. This year, our mentees have unapologetically chronicled the precariousness of various states of being, and becoming, the stages we go through to transform into who we are—to get through to the *Other Side of Everything*.

Right now, you're on *the other side* of reading these pieces and, we hope, inspired to write your own. To guide you on your journey to the other side of your original creation, Girls Write Now Fellows have curated from this year's rich curriculum a series of wellness-oriented prompts through what we call the six stages of being a writer. Along the way, you will receive wellness tips and affirmations from Girls Write Now's Wellness Advisor Nehanda Thom and advice on writing from our Fellows. Let your emotions evolve as you progress from inspiration to creation, distortion, reflection, realization, and ultimately manifestation.

Happy writing . . . We'll see you on the other side!

—JEANINE MARIE RUSSAW, Girls Write Now Community Coordinator

The Six Stages of Being a Writer

1. Inspiration

2. Creation

3. Distortion

4. Reflection

5. Realization

6. Manifestation

STAGE 1
INSPIRATION. AN AHA MOMENT . . .
WHAT WILL IT UNLOCK FOR YOU?

WELLNESS TIP

What makes you tick? Inspiration can be found in beautiful occurrences of nature, like sunsets and the moon's pulling of the tides . . . Inspiration can even be found in the mundane, like the ticking of a clock that simply marks the passing of time. What will you choose to be inspired by today?

Affirmation: Inspiration is all around me. I am open to receiving ideas, motivation, and guidance every day in whichever form they may come.

A PLACE TO JOT DOWN YOUR THOUGHTS

WRITE YOUR WAY TO THE OTHER SIDE

If you look around, you'll find there's beauty and mystery in most everything. These prompts encourage you to look both outside and in to discover that beauty, and to unpack that mystery. It is through this discovery and unpacking that you'll find inspiration.

—ANNABEL YOUNG, GIRLS WRITE NOW FELLOW

Writing Prompt 1, from the "Photopoetry: A Synthesis of Poetry and Photography" workshop with Teaching Artist Jesse Jagtiani

What do you think are similarities and differences between a photograph and a poem or story?

Feeling stuck? Answer these questions:

- What is the purpose of a photo, a poem, and/or a story?
- What do they look like?
- How/why do we create them?

Write five values that most resonate with you and why.

Feeling stuck? Answer these questions:

- Why do I show up every day?
- What do I have to give to the world?
- What do I need?

STAGE 2

CREATION. THE FIRST ATTEMPT TO CAPTURE ALL THE MAGICAL THOUGHTS SPILLING OUT OF YOUR HEAD.

WELLNESS TIP

Have you ever made something, built something, created something with your hands? As writers, we create art with our words. What can you create today with your pen?

Affirmation: I am the embodiment of art. I am open and available to bringing what is in my mind out into the open for the creation of something beautiful.

A PLACE TO JOT DOWN YOUR THOUGHTS

WRITE YOUR WAY TO THE OTHER SIDE

Creation is a radical act. These prompts call to light all that we are capable of as writers, and all the potential that writing holds: for healing, for making meaning, for parsing through and learning what we didn't know before. Through these prompts, you too can engage in that radical act of creation.

—ANNABEL YOUNG, GIRLS WRITE NOW FELLOW

Writing Prompt 1, from the "Making It Personal: Finding Your Voice in Documentary Screenwriting" workshop with Teaching Artist Lagueria Davis

As writers, we're often told, *Write what you know.* Take a moment to jot down what that phrase means to you.

―――

Writing Prompt 2, from the "Explore Belonging through Magical Realism" Friday Night Salon with Guest Artist Alexandra Méndez

Describe a time when you felt like you were between worlds. Maybe you felt like an insider and an outsider at the same time. Maybe you felt like you were supposed to belong, but you didn't quite fit in.

Feeling stuck? Answer these questions:

- How did it make you feel to be in this in-between place?
- How did you react?
- Did something come of this experience that wouldn't have been possible otherwise?

STAGE 3
DISTORTION. THE HUMAN CONDITION INCLUDES MOMENTS OF SELF-DOUBT. BREATHE. THIS IS YOUR WAY OUT.

WELLNESS TIP

One of the most uncomfortable feelings as a writer is the "almost." The "almost" is a fun house of sorts, filled with mirrors that distort our reflection and make us question who we are, how capable we are, and how others will perceive us. This questioning, this impostor syndrome, can creep and cripple us . . . but here's the good news—the distortion stops. The smoke clears. You make it out.

> *Affirmation: I recognize and hold space for the part of me that is afraid. I counter my feelings with facts. I am prepared to share my story.*

A PLACE TO JOT DOWN YOUR THOUGHTS

WRITE YOUR WAY TO THE OTHER SIDE

Writing can often be a daunting task full of fear, uncertainty, and doubt. These prompts remind me that, at my core, my most authentic self is unabashed and undeterred, having survived so many challenges before and still finding the strength to continue.

—AZIA ARMSTEAD, GIRLS WRITE NOW FELLOW

Writing Prompt 1, from the "Journaling as Healing" workshop with Teaching Artist Meriah McCauley

Write about something that you consider a difficulty you've gone through in your life.

Feeling stuck? Answer these questions:

- What was the challenge? What were some of the feelings you had?
- Were there helpers, teachers, or other forms of support? What did you learn about yourself?
- Were there any new doors that opened, new opportunities that emerged, after that event?

Write ten chapter titles in the story of your life.

Feeling stuck? Answer these questions:

- When reflecting on the story of your life, what themes emerge?
- What past experiences helped shape the person you are today? What lessons have you learned?
- What emotions did you feel during those life-shaping events?

STAGE 4

REFLECTION. BE STILL WITH YOUR THOUGHTS. LET THEM BE THE ENCOURAGEMENT YOU NEED TO COMPLETE YOUR JOURNEY.

WELLNESS TIP

Hindsight is 20/20. It's a healthy practice to reflect on what has taken place and what we've experienced. Oftentimes, looking inward can provide us with the answers we need in the present.

Affirmation: I reflect on my past and I accept the lessons it has taught me. I celebrate the blessings it has brought me. I recognize that reflection helps me as I journey forward.

A PLACE TO JOT DOWN YOUR THOUGHTS

WRITE YOUR WAY TO THE OTHER SIDE

When done right, art engages in a fluid conversation with the deepest parts of ourselves. This conversation can bring up memories, questions, and emotions that we might not have been aware of. Use these prompts to investigate the sensations that arise.

—SALLY FAMILIA, GIRLS WRITE NOW FELLOW

Writing Prompt 1, from the "YA Fiction" workshop with Teaching Artist Amy Zhang

Have you ever cried while reading a book? Write about a novel or short story that made you feel something. Briefly describe how it made you feel and why.

Writing Prompt 2, from the "So You Want to Write a Memoir" workshop with Teaching Artist Hannah Eko

Write a thank-you note to or from a memory you are most excited or terrified to write about.

Feeling stuck? Answer this question:

- What emotions come up the most when you write about this memory?

STAGE 5
REALIZATION. SOMETIMES ACCEPTANCE IS THE ONLY WAY FORWARD. WHAT HAVE YOUR EXPERIENCES TAUGHT YOU?

WELLNESS TIP

Realization can be satisfying. Coming to the point of recognizing and realizing a truth about oneself can not only give us insight, it can give us the key information we need to move forward.

Affirmation: I realize that lightbulb moments aren't always dramatic. I am open to the realizations I will make on a daily basis and I will behave according to what life is trying to teach me.

A PLACE TO JOT DOWN YOUR THOUGHTS

WRITE YOUR WAY TO THE OTHER SIDE

Give yourself permission to live knowing that the structures of time and space are incredibly fluid. These prompts are a reminder that no matter how much we consider ourselves to be "on the other side" of something, we can access those parts of our past (or even our future) whenever we wish by looking inside ourselves. This is realization.

—JEANINE MARIE RUSSAW,
GIRLS WRITE NOW COMMUNITY COORDINATOR

Writing Prompt 1, from the "Journaling as Healing" workshop with Teaching Artist Meriah McCauley

Our life's stories, all of our experiences, live within our body. Imagine in your mind's eye a picture of yourself as a child. Notice what age you are, and how small you were in size. Then, with your dominant hand, write to your inner child. You can start by greeting them with a "hello" and introducing yourself.

Ask your inner child a question, one at a time, and listen for their response . . .

- How old are you? How old do you think I am?
- What would you like to do for fun?
- I'm very happy to be talking with you. What is something I can do for you when you feel scared? Would you like a hug? Would you like to cuddle with a blanket? Do you need a reminder that I am here to protect you?

With your non-dominant hand, let your inner child respond to your present-day adult self through their writing. It's okay if your handwriting feels awkward or appears sloppy—that is how you wrote as a child.

Take a couple of minutes to reflect on and/or answer some of these questions . . .

- What always fascinated you as a child? What did you daydream about?
- When you were a kid, how did you imagine your life would be when you were grown up?
- What does your inner child love about you as an adult today?

STAGE 6
MANIFESTATION. YOUR SUCCESS IS INEVITABLE. YOU JUST HAVE TO CREATE IT FIRST.

WELLNESS TIP

I am convinced that writers hold a special skill of writing and speaking things into existence. To be able to see what you've written down, hoped for, and thought about come to fruition is one of the most gratifying parts of what we do.

Affirmation: I can write down a plan, a goal, or a story, and see it unfold in due time. I receive the best of what life has to offer me.

A PLACE TO JOT DOWN YOUR THOUGHTS

WRITE YOUR WAY TO THE OTHER SIDE

If you can see it, you can be it. I am guided by the belief that you can manifest your soul's desire as long as you can see or visualize that desire manifested before it has come to fruition. Use these writing prompts to set those manifestations in motion.

—SALLY FAMILIA, GIRLS WRITE NOW FELLOW

Writing Prompt 1, from the "Revolutionary Storytelling: Creating Our Zine" workshop with Teaching Artist Emily Mendelson

What interesting and exciting ideas, concepts, or themes do you want to see in magazines but don't show up there enough, if at all? How would you develop your original ideas into content for your very own magazine? Think about how your magazine would look, the language it would use, the targeted audience, and the theme.

Writing Prompt 2, from the "Illustrated Industry: Creating a Graphic Novel about Publishing, Passion, and Pals" workshop with Teaching Artist Kate Gavino

You wrote a bestselling, Nobel Prize–winning book. What are your dream blurbs from your favorite writers for the back cover of your book?

CLOSING WORDS

There's so much power in our words. When we write, we often discover a version of our truth that we didn't know existed. Writing is a form of self-care because we can rediscover what we need through our written words, truths that we aren't always willing to admit out loud, but that flow from our pen to the page with ease. Remember, you will have moments when everything you're writing seems to come easily, and then there will be moments when it feels like you are completely empty of words. All of this is part of the process. Being willing to keep coming back and keep discovering is healing, too. Every time we bravely start again, we grow.

—YASMINE CHEYENNE, GIRLS WRITE NOW TEACHING ARTIST, SELF-HEALING EDUCATOR, AND AUTHOR OF *THE SUGAR JAR*

We hope that, as you wrote through the six stages, you grappled with what was happening inside of you. This is the process of becoming— and being. Lean into each moment of your writer's journey, and use it to be well. Following the advice of Yasmine Cheyenne, use the power of the written word to rediscover what you need. The process of discovery is never-ending. There is always more *on the other side of everything.*

ABOUT GIRLS WRITE NOW

We are a powerhouse of voices that have been ignored or silenced for too long. We are a pipeline into schools and industries in need of new talent and different perspectives. As a community, we follow our hearts and—through bold, authentic storytelling—inspire people to open theirs. We are Girls Write Now.

For twenty-five years, Founder and Executive Director Maya Nussbaum has grown this award-winning organization. Breaking down barriers of gender, race, age, and poverty, Girls Write Now mentors the next generation of writers and leaders who are impacting businesses, shaping culture, and creating change.

In more than thirty states across the United States, Girls Write Now matches female and gender-expansive young adults from systemically underserved communities—more than 90 percent of color, 90 percent high-need, 75 percent immigrant or first-generation, and 25 percent LGBTQIA+—with professional writers and digital media makers as their personal mentors. Mentees' multigenre, multimedia work is published in outlets including *Teen Vogue*, *LitHub*, *The New York Times*, and *The Wall Street Journal*; is performed at Lincoln Center and the United Nations; and wins hundreds of writing awards. Girls Write Now sends 100 percent of its seniors on to college, and continues to support them in school, career, and beyond through professional development, strategic networking, and lifelong community bonds.

In addition to being the first writing and mentoring organization of its kind, Girls Write Now continually ranks among the top programs nationwide for driving social-emotional growth for youth. Girls Write Now has been distinguished three times by the White House as one of the nation's top youth programs, twice by the Nonprofit Excellence Awards as one of New York's top ten nonprofits, by NBCUniversal's 21st Century Solutions for Social Innovation, by Youth INC for Youth Innovation, and as a DVF People's Voice nominee. Reaching more than 50,000 youth, Girls Write Now is a founding partner of the decade-strong STARS Citywide Girls Initiative.

STAFF

Asma Al-Masyabi, *Art Intern & Mentee*

Julia Andresakis, *Digital Media Producer & Mentee*

Azia Armstead, *Fellow*

Marian Caballo, *Editorial Intern & Mentee Alum*

Chelle Carter-Wilson, *Creative Marketing Director*

Marisa Cazanave-Steward, *Director of Community Initiatives*

Maya Cruz, *Editorial Intern & Mentee*

Kathryn Destin, *Editor-in-Residence & Mentee Alum*

Denise Domena, *Art Intern & Mentee Alum*

Morayo Faleyimu, *Editor-in-Residence & Mentor Alum*

Sally Familia, *Fellow*

Shira Feen, *Graphic Designer*

Kaya Fraser, *Video Intern & Mentee Alum*

Senjuti Gayan, *Editorial Intern & Mentee Alum*

Spencer George, *Senior Marketing Coordinator*

Irene Hao, *Editorial Intern & Mentee Alum*

Margery Hannah, *Community Manager, Writing Works*

Liliana Hopkins, *Production Intern & Mentee*

Jessica Jagtiani, *Community Manager, Writing 360*

Mi So Jeong, *Operations Manager*

Vahni Kurra, *Community Coordinator*

Kelsey LePage, *Development Manager*

Molly MacDermot, *Director of Special Initiatives*

Emily Mendelson, *Community Manager, Publishing 360*

Emily Mendez, *Editorial Intern & Mentee Alum*

Elmer Meza, *Salesforce & Systems Manager*

Sheena Daree Miller, *Diversity, Equity & Inclusion Advisor*

Maya Nussbaum, *Founder & Executive Director*

Daniella Olibrice, *Talent Director*

Lisbett Rodriguez, *Programs & Systems Senior Coordinator*

Jeanine Marie Russaw, *Community Coordinator*

Erica Silberman, *Director of Curriculum & Engagement*

Richelle Szypulski, *Senior Editorial Manager*

Karen van de Vrande, *Development Consultant*

Zuzanna Wasiluk, *Editorial Intern & Mentee Alum*

Joe Wilson, *Director of Information Technology*

Lauren Y, *Editorial Intern & Mentee*

Annabel Young, *Fellow*

Rachel Young, *Production Intern & Mentee*

BOARD OF DIRECTORS

Ellen Archer, *Board Chair*; Publishing Executive

Bruce Morrow, *Vice Chair*; Senior Development Professional

Lynda Pak, *Tech Chair*; Senior Vice President, Technology Leader for Global Brands & Corporate Functions, Estée Lauder Companies

Mustafa Topiwalla, *Treasurer*; Head of Healthcare Corporate & Investment Banking, Sumitomo Mitsui Banking Corporation

Cate Ambrose, *Finance Chair*; CEO & Board Member, EMPEA

Joy Altimare, Chief Marketing Officer, Kindbody

Judith Curr, President & Publisher, HarperOne Group

Gati Curtis, Executive Vice President, Head of Product & Services, BBDO

Lavaille Lavette, President, One Street Books & Managing Partner, Ebony Media Group

Maya Nussbaum, Founder & Executive Director, Girls Write Now

Ahu Terzi, Director of Brand Partnerships, Linqia

HONORARY BOARD

Cazzie David, Author & Screenwriter

Abbi Jacobson, Comedian, Writer, Actress & Illustrator

Tayari Jones, Novelist & Girls Write Now Board Alum

Rupi Kaur, Poet, Author, Illustrator & Performer

Emma Straub, Novelist, Books Are Magic Owner & Girls Write Now Mentor Alum

Cleo Wade, Artist, Poet, Activist & Author

PARTNERSHIP COMMITTEE

Anne Caceres-Gonzalez,
Director of People &
Culture, Mischief

Mignon Espy-Edwards,
Sales & Brand Strategist,
Greyscience

Stephanie Gordon, Director of
Corporate Banking Capital
Markets, RBC

Victoria Vo, Founder & CEO,
Haute International

TECH COMMITTEE

Raju Burnwal, Associate
Director of Sales, Virtuoso

Lisa Chai, Senior Research
Analyst, Robo Global

Felicia Dodge, Director of
Insights, Analytics, XX
Artists

Rose Else-Mitchell, President,
Education Solutions,
Scholastic

Jacob Lewis, Cofounder,
Co-CEO & President,
Authorative

Dani Slocki, CEO &
Cofounder, VSpace.live

Natalie Sorrells, Senior
Director, BetterCloud

Natalia Vargas-Caba,
Technical Writer, Google

AGENTS OF CHANGE HONOREES

Rose Else-Mitchell, President,
Education Solutions,
Scholastic

Amanda Gorman, Poet &
Activist

Jeff Gural, Chairman,
GFP Real Estate, New York

Chrissy King, Writer, Speaker,
Strength Coach & Educator

Lavaille Lavette, President,
One Street Books &
Managing Partner, Ebony
Media Group

TEACHING ARTISTS, GUEST ARTISTS & SPEAKERS

Azia Armstead

Lani Asunción

Gabrielle Bates

Linda Camacho

Marisa Cazanave-Steward

Sonali Chanchani

Yasmine Cheyenne

John Cobb

Gigi Coleman

Ami Davis

Lagueria Davis

Kathryn Destin

Hannah Shokoya Eko

Jessica Errera

Morayo Faleyimu

Sally Familia

Stacey Fayant

Alexandra Franklin

Kate Gavino
Ron Gerber
Jenissa Graham
Margery Hannah
Donna Hill
Ana Homayoun
Susanna Horng
Kat Jagai
Jessica Jagtiani
Janis F. Kearney
Vahni Kurra
Oneika Mays
Meriah McCauley
Emily Mendeslon
Alexandra Méndez
Sheena Daree Miller
Elizabeth Minkel
Andrea Morrison
Sethu Laxmi Nair

Katherine Odom-Tomchin
Katina Paron
Cynthia Pelayo
Zhenzhen Qi
Tom Rabbitt
Jeanine Marie Russaw
Mady Samsel
SassyBlack (Catherine
    Harris-White)
Melissa See
Erica Silberman
Jenny Stephens
Richelle Szypulski
Nehanda Thom
Samantha Wekstein
Jade Wong-Baxter
Annabel Young
Amy Zhang

GIRLS WRITE NOW CIRCLE

Honorary Chairs

Ellen Archer & Jeffrey Gracer
Ann & Bob Hammer
Maja Kristin
Jane Lauder

Susan & Sophie Sawyers
James M. & Margaret V. Stine
Kate Stroup & Matthew Berger

Co-Chairs

Joy Altimare
Cate Ambrose
Judith Curr & Ken Kennedy
Gati Curtis
Forsyth Harmon
Jamie Fiore Higgins
Catherine Greenman &
    Richard D'albert
Andrew Guff
Agnes Gund

Lavaille Lavette
Bruce Morrow
Maya Nussbaum &
    Todd Pulerwitz
Lynda Pak
Nicolas Rohatyn
Alina Roytberg
Ahu Terzi
Mustafa Topiwalla &
    Melissa Connor

Vice Chairs

Marci Alboher & Jay Goldberg
Rachel Bloom
Josephine Bolus
Marissa Buick

Lisa Gardner
Janice Horowitz
Sandra Matus
Hope Pordy & Bob Osmond

Patrons

Heather Allen
Nisha Aoyama
Stuart Applebaum
Maria Aspan
Claudia Ballard
Veronica Chambers
Jill Cohen
Elizabeth Frankel

Lauren Kiel
Kate Levin & Robin Shapiro
Robert Levin
Molly Meloy & Jeff Fitts
Linda Rose
Elaine Stuart-Shah
Lisa & Frank Wohl

Members

Tarang & Hirni Amin
Jillian Berman
Diane Botnick
Lisa Chai
Seth & Lynn Cohen
Donna Cornachio
Brian DeFiore
Ritik Dholakia
Renee Dugan
Rosamund Else-Mitchell
Laura Geringer Bass
Judith Harrison
Jackie Homan
Lesley Howard
Carol Hymowitz
Joyce King

Christina Kirk
Kelly & Chris Koenig
Robert Koroshetz
Meg LaBorde Kuehn
Shankar Kurra
Laurie Liss & Julie Shigekuni
Jeffrey Moskin
Molly Pulda & Gary Sernovitz
Leslie Riedel
Wendy Sherman
Amy Singer
Katy Staples
Mariko Takahashi
Joe Wilson

AGENTS OF CHANGE CORPORATE PARTNERS

Gamechanger $100–$200K

Estée Lauder Companies
News Corp

The Upswing Fund

Leadership $75–$95K

BBDO
BIC Corporate Foundation

HarperCollins

Visionary $50K

Cornelia T. Bailey
EHE Health
Genesis Inspiration
    Foundation

Macmillan
Penguin Random House

Innovator $25–$35K

Amazon Literary Partnership
Comcast NBCUniversal
GFP Real Estate
Mattel's Barbie Dream Gap
    Project

RBC Foundation
Scholastic
Warner Bros. Discovery

Champion $10–$20K

Adobe
Bloomberg
Bloomingdale's

Dotdash Meredith
Kickstarter

Supporter $2.5–$5K

Alloy Entertainment
Benchling Inc.
The Feminist Press
Nike

Princeton University Press
Strand Book Store
Tin House

FOUNDATION AND GOVERNMENT SUPPORTERS

$100K+

New York City Council
STARS Citywide Girls
Initiative

$35–$50K

Blanchette Hooker Rockefeller
Fund
Harman Family Foundation
Horace W. Goldsmith
Foundation

New York City Department of
Cultural Affairs
New York State Council on
the Arts

$15–$25K

Charles Lawrence Keith &
Clara S. Miller Foundation
Cornelia T. Bailey Foundation
The Hyde & Watson
Foundation
Literary Arts Emergency Fund

National Endowment for
the Arts
The Raymond and Gloria
Naftali Foundation
The Rona Jaffe Foundation

$5–$10K

Berger Family Foundation
The Lotos Foundation
Isabel Allende Foundation

Poetry Foundation
The Toskan Casale
Foundation

$1–$4K

Aspiring to Inspire
Damon A. Noller Community
Fund via the Idaho
Community Foundation
DuBose Family Foundation
Fondation Femme Debut

New York Women's Culinary
Alliance
Robert & Mercedes Eichholz
Foundation
The Starbucks Foundation

ANTHOLOGY SPONSORS

We are grateful to the countless institutions and individuals who have supported our work through their generous contributions. Visit our website at girlswritenow.org to view the extended list.

Girls Write Now would like to thank Dutton, including Christine Ball, Maya Ziv, Alexis Cassola, Grace Layer, and Dominique Jones, for their help producing this year's anthology, and Amazon Literary Partnership, which provided the charitable contribution that made this book possible.